ENDORSEMENTS

Steve McSwain brings a wealth of knowledge and experience to the topic of giving…an excellent job of melding biblical principles of giving with practical application.

> **– Curt C. Farmer,** Senior Vice President
> and Wealth Management Director
> Wachovia Bank

While not for the feint of heart, those who follow these practical guidelines…will be blessed beyond their imaginings. Dr. McSwain's discussion of the divinely-designed flow of the universe is brilliant and right on target…A great read and one that might just change your life.

> **– Kristine Miller,** Director of Stewardship and Planned Giving
> The Episcopal Diocese of Michigan

Steve McSwain effectively debunks the myths that pervade our materialistic culture and reveals the true joy found in generous giving. You will benefit from reading this book.

> **– Paul L. Larsen,** Senior Pastor
> Christ the King Lutheran Church,
> New Brighton, Minnesota

Dr. McSwain is a gifted leader in helping people see how material resources can make the giver's life worth living.

– **Roger Rominger,** Senior Pastor
First United Methodist Church,
Springfield, Illinois

Steve McSwain has provided a definition of life that challenges the most ostentatious aspects of our culture. This is an invitation to everyone to experience the fullness of life and faith through giving...a compelling read both critical and affirming at the same time.

– **Larry R. Hayward,** Senior Pastor
Westminster Presbyterian Church,
Alexandria, Virginia

Kudos to Dr. McSwain for having the courage to write this timely and much needed book. Every person who is serious about finding enrichment and fulfillment in their remaining years will want to read this book.

– **Dr. C. E. Jackson, III,** Senior Pastor
First Baptist Church
Lenoir City, Tennessee

A challenging, insightful and enlightening read, from an experienced leader calling others to reflect upon their giving patterns.

– **Fr. John Auer**
St. Paul Catholic Church
Colorado Springs, Colorado.

Dr. McSwain is the original "mythbuster." He understands the church. He understands finances and stewardship. The beauty of this book is Steve's ability to bring the two together in a way that's non-threatening and understandable. This book is a must read...

– **Dr. Glen S. Martin,** Senior Pastor
Journey of Faith Church
Manhattan Beach, California

One of the most difficult tasks in life is to "walk the walk and talk the talk." Steve McSwain has done both. The words that are crafted in the pages of this book reflect a journey of experiences in which McSwain offers witness to the deep joy he has found in giving. His faith and experience in giving offer rich lessons for us all.

– **Rev. Dr. Susan A. Patterson-Sumwalt,** Senior Pastor
United Methodist Church of Whitefish Bay
Milwaukee, Wisconsin

...a book I wish all of my church members would read...I loved the book. It will help people no matter how spiritually mature they are.

– **Dr. Ron Churchill,** Senior Pastor
First Baptist Church
Plant City, Florida

Dr. McSwain provides powerful and practical tools that will lead to personal and corporate financial transformation. Through wonderful insight and real stories, the reader is led to the joys experienced in true spiritual generosity. Dr. McSwain's personal transparency is especially gripping and instructive, as he models his message.

– **Rev. Greg McGarvey,** Senior Pastor
Carmel United Methodist Church
Carmel, Indiana

The connection between the will of God and the heart of people in the area of giving is vital. McSwain knows this and helps us see it exceptionally well. Lots of people tell me "you have to read this or that book." I'm glad I read this one.

– **Dr. Paul Ulring,** Senior Minister
Upper Arlington Lutheran Church
Columbus, Ohio

THE GIVING MYTHS

GIVING THEN GETTING THE LIFE YOU'VE ALWAYS WANTED

STEPHEN B.
MCSWAIN

Smyth & Helwys Publishing, Inc.
6316 Peake Road
Macon, Georgia 31210-3960
1-800-747-3016
©2007 by Smyth & Helwys Publishing
All rights reserved.
Printed in the United States of America.

The paper used in this publication meets the minimum requirements of
American National Standard for Information Sciences—
Permanence of Paper for Printed Library Materials.
ANSI Z39.48–1984. (alk. paper)

Library of Congress Cataloging-in-Publication Data

McSwain, Stephen B., 1955–
The Giving Myths : Giving, Then Getting the Life You've Always Wanted
by Stephen B. McSwain.
p. cm.
ISBN 978-1-57312-495-9 (pbk. : alk. paper)
1. Christian giving. 2. Service (Theology) I. Title.

BV772.M395 2007
241'.68—dc22
2007013653

CONTENTS

ACKNOWLEDGEMENTS 3

INTRODUCTION 7

1. WHERE IT ALL BEGAN—CULTURE AND THE BIG LIE 11

2. THE ROAD LESS TRAVELED 19

3. GIVING THEN GETTING THE LIFE YOU'VE ALWAYS
    WANTED 23

4. THE STATE OF GIVING IN THE AMERICAN CHURCH 29

5. MYTH 1—"GIVE AND YOU'LL GET RICH" 47

6. MYTH 2—"I CAN'T AFFORD TO GIVE" 75

7. MYTH 3—"EQUAL AND FAIR SHARE GIVING IS ENOUGH" 109

8. MYTH 4—"THE STANDARD FOR GIVING IS THE TITHE" 143

9. MYTH 5—"GET THEM INVOLVED AND THEY WILL GIVE" 171

10. MYTH 6—"YOUR CHARITY IS A PRIVATE MATTER" 201

11. MYTH 7—"TEST GOD THROUGH YOUR GIVING" 225

CONCLUSION A BRIEF SKETCH OF THE LIFE YOU'VE
ALWAYS WANTED 243

ACKNOWLEDGEMENTS

I would like to acknowledge a few persons. First, none of this would be possible were it not for the gift of entering a ministry of consultation to churches and church leaders that Dr. Robert Cargill of Cargill Associates, Inc. gave to me several years ago. I will always be grateful. With more than a half century of fundraising counsel in both the institutional, not-for-profit world as well as the church setting, Dr. Cargill may be the most knowledgeable individual in America when it comes to philanthropy and fundraising. Much of what I know today I've learned from him, from his son, Steve Cargill, now the CEO of Cargill Associates, the President of the Church Division, Mr. Pat Graham, and all of my colleagues at Cargill Associates, Inc., too numerous to mention. Their support and friendship through the years, however, have made my life the richer.

I must mention my editor and friend, Garrison Cox. I first met him while consulting with the church where he attends and so generously volunteers his gifts for service and ministry, St. Paul United Methodist in Louisville. He is a consummate gentleman, gifted writer himself, a remarkable wordsmith, and, quite simply, one of the smartest people I've ever known. Thanks, Garrison, for your insights, counsel, and attention to detail.

For my publisher, Smyth & Helwys, for believing in this project and being willing to place it in circulation.

And last, I want to acknowledge and express my thanks to Dr. Wayne W. Dyer. As of the publication of this book, I've never met the man. That may be the most amazing thing about this. I am acknowledging a person I do not personally know. However, I will meet him one day. That is my intention (to borrow one of his favorite words), if to only shake hands and offer my gift of thanks. His writings and insights into the human experience have been gifts for my journey. Anyone knowledgeable of his work can readily detect his influence on my life as reflected in my book. Thanks Wayne.

Steve, 2007

To my wife, Pam, God's gift to me,
I love you.
To our four children,
Allison, Jonathan, Michelle, and Phillip
God's gifts to us,
We love you.

INTRODUCTION

While waiting in an airport bookstore, I observed a bookshelf bulging with bestsellers: *The Automatic Millionaire*, *The One Minute Millionaire*, *Trump: How to Get Rich*, *Start Late, Finish Rich*, *Smart Couples Finish Rich*, *Why We Want You to Be Rich*, and *More Money than God*.

The question popped into my mind, "With all the interest in making money, who would want to read a book about giving money away?" Frankly, I don't know. But lately, I've wondered if there are others who share some of the same feelings I've been having about money, the quest for it, and all the stuff that comes with what money can buy.

Herman Melville described the "half-lived life" in Moby Dick: "For as this appalling ocean surrounds the verdant land, so in the soul of man lies one insular Tahiti, full of peace and joy, but encompassed by all the horrors of the half-lived life."

Haunting words.

Maybe you're one who has lived half your life only to discover it has been half-lived. If so, this book may help you make some life-changing decisions for the second half of the journey—decisions that will enable you to get what you really want in life and what the first half has failed to deliver.

If there are times you feel sick to your soul by the crass material-ism peddled over most religious television as Christianity, you'll find a kindred spirit in the pages that follow. Perhaps a little of my rant-ing will give expression to some of your rage. There is so much more to the Christian faith than what the world is viewing on TV.

You may be discovering that, whatever the reason for your appearance on planet earth, that reason is somehow inextricably bound up in a passionate pursuit of the divine presence in your life and a genuine concern to serve others in what little time you have left. If so, I hope to illuminate the journey for you by demonstrating how to get outside yourself and experience what I now refer to as the "blessed life"—the life we all really want.

Similarly, Jesus' paradoxical words may have resonated with you. "He who would save his life will lose it, but he that gives his life away finds it." You've been wondering how to do just that. You're already on the path toward the life that matters—the life devoted to giving yourself away. You'll discover in the real-life examples I share some encouragement for your journey.

Finally, you may have discovered that Jesus talked more about money and possessions than any other subject save the kingdom of God. You may have wondered why. I've wondered that for a long time, too. Few have enjoyed the material benefits that money can buy more than I have. But for a long time, I have awakened every morning with this gnawing feeling inside that there's something ter-ribly wrong with the fact that I have so much when so many have so little. I live in a nice, suburban home, yet the one after whom I'm attempting to pattern my life said of himself, "Foxes have dens to live in, and birds have nests, but I, the Son of Man, have no home of my own, not even a place to lay my head" (Matt 8:20). Something is wrong with that picture. I've discovered a few answers to this conun-drum. If you share a similar feeling of unease, maybe what few answers I have will help you.

You may not agree with all my views. Frankly, I don't expect you to. In fact, what I'm anticipating is a swell of reaction. Someone once said, "Where two people agree on everything, one isn't necessary." My own feeling is that there's a place for all our ideas—both yours and mine. While I make a case for my own ideas and beliefs, I encourage you to take a look at your own.

I have been honest as I can be with the teachings I find in what the majority of Americans say they believe is the Word of God. Many of the things Jesus said, as you'll see, are quite paradoxical. But I trust I have captured some of their meaning in addressing the tension those paradoxes create.

The path of giving I've chosen has brought to me a most blessed life—the life I've really always wanted. I pray that the light I shine on the path I'm following will illuminate yours and bring you a reward equally as meaningful. If so, then you will join me in saying, "I have truly found the meaning of life—the life God intended—the life I've always wanted."

—Steve McSwain

1

WHERE IT ALL BEGAN
CULTURE AND THE BIG LIE

Many persons have a wrong idea of what constitutes true happiness. It is not attained through self-gratification but through fidelity to a worthy purpose.

—Helen Keller (1880–1968)

We make a living by what we get; we make a life by what we give.

—Sir Winston Churchill (1874–1965)

I am completing this book on my tenth anniversary as a church and parish consultant. For the past decade, I've had the good fortune of assisting religious institutions in nearly every denomination in America evaluate their mission and ministries, define a vision for the future, establish goals and priorities, train leaders, resolve conflicts, navigate through long-overdue changes, conduct giving seminars and financial campaigns to broaden the annual giving ministry of the church, raise money for capital needs, and, most importantly, teach people the secret to finding the life they really want.

Without question, the happiest and most fulfilled people are those who have learned to give themselves and their resources away.

That's not only a fact but the central premise of this book. One of the paradoxical things Jesus said—and there are many—pertains to giving: "If you try to keep your life for yourself, you will lose it. But if you give up your life for me, you will find true life" (Matt 16:25).

This is just the opposite of what our culture teaches. Advertisers lure us into believing what could be described as the myth of "getting"—a cultural myth that happiness, security, and contentment are found in the sum total of your material assets and personal accomplishments.

One of the commercial airlines I frequently fly has two different classes of magazines in the seat pockets where the flight safety brochure is kept. Most of the airlines have these magazines. But this airline has two. And if you are fortunate enough to sit in the first-class section, your seat pocket cradles a magazine fit only for the fortunate. It strokes the ego of first-class passengers prone to see themselves as separate from those in the back of the plane—because, after all, they are materially and financially several links higher on the proverbial food chain. It's all a lie, but ego thrives on it. In fact, the majority of those sitting in first class are neither separate from other passengers nor more financially superior. I know because I often sit in first class—a luxury afforded to me because of the frequency of my air travel, not because of the superior size of my bank account.

One day, I thumbed through the magazine that touts itself as the luxury magazine for premium-class passengers only. Interesting, isn't it? Frankly, I was one of the fortunate this day sitting in the "premium-class" section. And, if I must admit, I did feel slightly superior.

But while looking at the fashion ads in the magazine, a dose of reality set in. Who could afford the fashions advertised there for either women or men? Not I. And I don't think most people could. There's a camelhair top coat for men priced at just under $2,000. Who spends $2,000 on an overcoat? I unbuckled my seatbelt to get up and look around in the first-class section where I was seated, and, while there were some nicely dressed people, nobody was wearing anything like what the ad pictured. Not even remotely close.

There's a shoulder bag for women priced at just under $18,000. That's more than I paid for my last car. How about an alligator tote for $15,000? I can see why they don't bother to put these magazines in the "other" section of the plane. This is the stuff for "superior" folk like me.

Isn't this all so goofy? Of course it is. And yet, your ego swings on the hinges of such fantasy. Ego loves to wear clothing so striking you imagine heads looking up when you enter the room or prepare to take your seat in the premium-class section. No wonder he's sitting in first class, your ego hopes the other passengers are thinking. He's got to be somebody famous or really important! This is the kind of illusionary dialogue the ego carries on with itself.

And this is what it's come to in our culture. Our cultural mantra, spoken or otherwise, is "Get all you can, save all you can, and spend the rest!" It's rarely expressed so crassly; nonetheless, it's the philosophy by which most live.

You hear a lot of political pundits speak of everyone deserving his or her chance at the American Dream. What is the American Dream, anyway? Rightly understood, it is the right to pursue life, liberty, and happiness. But culturally interpreted, it is a greedy obsession. It's all about accumulating wealth at any cost and achieving more and more—more than your parents achieved, more than your friends and coworkers, and most importantly, more than the guy next door has achieved or accumulated.

But isn't life more than the sum of your accomplishments and acquisitions? In spite of ego-fed delusions, the Trumps of this world do not really own it. In fact, the greatest Teacher of all time said just the opposite: "God blesses those who are gentle and lowly, for the whole earth will belong to them" (Matt 5:5). This is one of those paradoxical things Jesus said. If he's right, the people who really own this world are those whom the world cannot own and who may themselves own little. But one thing is clear: they are not owned by what they have. Not even remotely. They have learned something far more significant.

While waiting for a taxi to take me to the airport before daylight one morning, I opened my computer to surf the Web and pass a little time. An article about Forbes' twelve highest-earning twenty-five-year-olds in the U.S. was on my Internet provider's opening page. Curious, I clicked on the link. According to the tracker, I was the 2,098,034th person to hit the site that morning, and it had been up only a few hours—an obvious indication of the cultural obsession with the subject of moneymaking. The click of my mouse took me to another page that, through streaming video, not only revealed the identity of these twelve top-earning individuals, all of whom are under the age of twenty-five, but if I clicked on one additional link, I could also view thirteen top-earning celebrities distinguished by one interesting thing they shared in common—they're all dead. I refused the invitation, turned off my computer, and sat there a bit bewildered by what I had just seen.

I couldn't believe it. Not only does my culture try to engender in me feelings of jealousy over the living who earn more in one year than I would ever earn in a lifetime, but I am also encouraged to envy the dead, who apparently have mastered the art of earning more from the grave than I would ever earn even if I had the benefit of nine lives.

At every turn, our value, worth, and significance as persons is inextricably tied to what we earn, where we live, the clothes we wear, the gadgets we buy, the things we've accomplished, the neighborhoods we live in, and the sizes of the houses we build—many of which in America are large enough for several families. It is all pretty offensive. The "getting" myth is our culture's big lie. Getting money, having power, and enjoying sex have become the American Dream.

When it comes to money, it's easy to get hooked by our culture's obsession with it, especially when you begin earning enough to enjoy what money can buy. Having money does have its rewards—rewards that are obvious enough. But it is a lie that having money means you have a life. The fact that the lie is so widely believed is one of the principal reasons why the divisions between class and race may be greater today than during the era of the civil rights movement.

That's one of the reasons for this book. It is devoted to helping you discover the opposite of what our culture is obsessing over. Quite simply, this book is about giving. In that respect, my suggestions are practical. In them, you'll find a real antidote to materialism—a guide to help you discern your true priorities. It can serve as a catalyst for change and for the discovery of genuine, lasting, blissful happiness. You'll find the life that you've always wanted if you will follow the suggestions I give in the following pages.

An Amazing Journey

Muhammad Ali once said, "The man who views the world at 50 the same as he did at 20 has wasted 30 years of his life." One thing is certain for me. My world has changed in the last few years, including the way I view the world. For ten years, I have crisscrossed this country, accumulating millions of frequent flyer miles with not one but several commercial airlines. I've slept in more than 1,000 different hotel beds and driven as many rental cars. I could use a six-month cruise to the Galapagos Islands just thinking about all of this travel I've done. But I've had the time of my life, blessed not only by the journey but by the people I've met and friendships I've made. My hope is that I've been a blessing to others in a manner at least equal in degree. I never imagined when I left the pastoral ministry a decade ago that my journey would take me to so many different places, to meet so many different people in so many different religious settings. That's been a blessing beyond imagining all its own.

I decided at age fourteen to follow in both my father and grandfather's footsteps and enter the professional ministry. I made that decision at my grandfather's funeral. He had been a minister all of his adult life. My father had done the same, and at the funeral wake, I felt the desire to do so too. In those days, the "wake," as it was called, was held in the home. Granddaddy McSwain was dressed in a three-piece suit and laid in a coffin in the dining room while family and friends and neighbors from nearby dropped in, paid their respects, and had something to eat. There was always plenty of good Southern cooking at such a gathering. It was sometime during that wake that I went to my grandmother and told her I felt my "calling" was to be a minister too. I don't recall much of a reaction on her part, but I always attributed that to the grief she was experiencing at the time. In spite of her reaction, or lack of it, I was serious. Becoming a pastor would be my life purpose. So I went to college, then on to seminary, and finally started my pastoral career. As far as I was concerned, I had planned to be a pastor all my life.

How wrong I was! God broadened my life and ministry in ways that have exceeded anything I would have ever imagined. In these past ten years, I've consulted with hundreds of churches across the country. I've gone to places I would never have gone had I remained in the pastorate. I have consulted with non-Christian and Christian people alike. I have counseled churches and denominations that I would have had little if any contact with otherwise. Here's a sampling: the Assembly of God, the American Baptists, Cooperative Baptists, Independent Baptists, Southern Baptists, National Baptists, Church of Christ, Church of God, Episcopal, Evangelical Free, Lutherans, United Methodists, Presbyterians, Roman Catholics, Nazarenes, members of both the Christian Church (Disciples of Christ) and the Independent Christian Church, nondenominational churches, Pentecostal churches, and I could go on, but you get the point.

It's been an amazing journey, and it isn't over. In many respects, the journey has just begun. Since I plan to live as long as a century, I have much to do still yet. While I've learned many things, one of the most important spiritual discoveries I've made is that God has people in a variety of places. He is neither bound by one branch of the church nor dependent on any one denomination, institution, or group to fulfill his work in the world. No one has a complete understanding of God, yet I have met God in every tradition into which I have been invited. I have not always agreed with every understanding of God I've encountered. And, somewhat surprisingly, my clients haven't always agreed with me, either. But I have met many sincere and deeply religious people every place I've been. There's so much more that I understand and appreciate about the various traditions that are part of the Christian church in America, and I am a better person for it. Some people disparage the church because it has so many disparate expressions, but I have grown to appreciate the rich diversity.

In her memoirs, *Coming Home to Myself,* country music singer Wynonna Judd observes that the greatest bit of career advice ever given to her came from a most unexpected source. Recent *Time* magazine "Person of the Year" and lead singer of the rock group U2, Bono, counseled Judd, "Just show up and wait for God to walk through the room."1

While the twenty-one years I served as a minister provided me a hope chest full of memories, relationships, and religious experiences, when I became a consultant, in many respects, I came home to myself. On more than one occasion, I've watched the divine walk through the room—my own room and that of many others too.

In the last few years, the ambition or purpose of my life has become crystal clear. I know why I'm here. It is to give—to give myself away in every way possible. I have an insatiable passion to help everyone who wants to know how to discover the life that we all really want and that I'm only beginning to plumb—a life that has rewarded me with far more than I ever seem able to give back. In the pages that follow, I will encourage you to try this life for yourself. While I can only describe it to you, I wish to create within you a hunger strong enough to get you to try it for yourself. Some folks reading this will, and their lives will never be the same. Others will dismiss much of what they read as simplistic or unreasonable. What you choose to do with what you read is entirely up to you. But I can assure you of one thing: once you pursue the pathway to a life of generosity—giving yourself and what you have away—you'll experience deep peace, contentment, and happiness, and you'll never turn back.

NOTE

1 Wynonna Judd with Patsi Bale Cox, Coming Home to Myself (New York: New American Library, 2005), 80.

2

THE ROAD LESS TRAVELED

The highway to hell is broad and the gate is wide for the many who choose the easy way. But the gateway to life is small, and the road is narrow, and only a few ever find it.

—Jesus Christ (Matt 7:13-14)

The life I describe in this book will take courage to pursue and is not without its struggles. In fact, it's like a battle—and, although internal, it's a battle nonetheless. The pathway to the blessed life is neither heavily traveled nor easily traveled. Robert Frost aptly described it for me in "The Road Less Traveled":

Two roads diverged in a yellow wood
And sorry I could not travel both
And be one traveler, long I stood
And looked down one as far as I could
To where it bent in the undergrowth;

Then, took the other, as just as fair
And having perhaps the better claim,
Because it was grassy and wanted wear.
Though as for that the passing there
Had worn them really about the same;

And both that morning equally lay
On leaves no step had trodden black.
Oh, I kept the first for another day!
Yet knowing how way leads on to way,
I doubted if I should ever come back.

I shall be telling this with a sigh
Somewhere ages and ages hence:
Two roads diverged in a wood, and I—
I took the one less traveled by,
And that has made all the difference.

Made all the difference? An amazing difference, and I know it can make all the difference for you, too. But an easy pathway it isn't. Few will travel this way. Fewer still will understand why you've chosen to travel this path. Don't feel a need to defend yourself for choosing to do so. In fact, I would suggest you refrain from much talk about what you're learning and how your life is changing as you learn to give yourself away. The people closest to you will see the results soon enough and they will ask you about it. Guard against lengthy discussions about any of this, however. It is a lifestyle so foreign to our culture that your conversations can degenerate into arguments as you feel the need to defend the choices you've made. Keep most of what you're learning to yourself. If people ask and you feel compelled to explain the dramatic change in your countenance, attitude, and outlook on life, give them a copy of this book and tell them to let you know if they would like to talk further after reading it. Some will, but most won't.

That's okay. People will learn for themselves, either during this lifetime or the one to come, that the pathway you have chosen is the right one indeed. Be grateful if they return to talk to you, but don't worry if they don't. They are on their own path and you can't dictate what direction they should take. If their minds are open and they return, you will detect their openness and the two of you will have a deep connection as you share the discoveries you're making about the remarkable life you've found. Don't forget, however, what Jesus himself said, "The gateway to life is small, and the road is narrow, and only a few ever find it" (Matt 7:14).

If you decide to enter this gateway and take your first steps toward the life you really want, a remarkable thing will happen. You will begin immediately to live this life—the one devoted to giving. You'll want to see how much of yourself and your resources you can give away before your earthly journey ends. But this joy is not something you must wait to experience. To the contrary, you will begin to experience it the moment you start giving yourself away. Again, what the Master said you will discover to be true: "It is more blessed to give than to receive" (Acts 20:35). You will no longer be among those who fill pews every weekend and glibly say in a variety of religious ways that they believe these words, when actually they live as if it's more blessed to receive than to give.

You, on the other hand, will begin to know a happiness you may only have dreamed of before. You will find your life taking on real significance. You'll be at peace and experience what the mystics describe as "bliss." At times, you'll wonder why it took you so long to figure out what life is really all about.

A WORD OF CAUTION

Before going any further, however, I offer a word of caution. Throughout the first steps you take on this journey, don't be surprised when your ego rears its ugly head. Your ego is the part of your personality that will try to get you to go back and chase after our culture's myth—the "happiness-is-in-what-you-get-in-life" myth, that "big lie" that defines your worth and importance by what you have, where you live, how much you make, the titles you've earned, and so forth. This ego is what is referred to as "flesh" in the New Testament, and it is that which has driven you toward a lifestyle devoted to the accumulation of more and more, duping you all along by the illusion that what you really want will be only found in the material stuff of life.

So stay strong. Tell your ego that it no longer occupies the driver's seat in your life. Ego will have to take the back seat. You're in the driver's seat now, and you're taking a different road. You have all the infinite resources of God to help you stay the course. He will occupy the seat beside you and, like an electronic navigation system in a rental car, he'll provide your internal spirit (the real you) the guidance you need for the journey. Eventually, your ego will subside and all but disappear. The cultural myth will be silenced in your soul and the life you've always wanted will be yours forever. You will face death with peace instead of fear because you'll know that the One to whom you have given yourself completely welcomes you as you step into the journey called eternity.

3

GIVING, THEN GETTING THE LIFE YOU'VE ALWAYS WANTED

In this life we cannot do great things. We can only do small things with great love.

—Mother Teresa (1910–1997)

Generosity is not giving me that which I need more than you do, but it is giving me that which you need more than I do.

—Kahlil Gibran (1883–1931)

The life you've always wanted will be found in one way only—in giving. This book is about living to give and giving to live. It's not too complicated. While I primarily write about giving your money away, I am by no means discounting that the giving of yourself is included. In fact, I'm convinced that if people learn to give their financial resources away, they will become better at giving themselves away. I'll have much more to say about this later.

So much is written these days about one's purpose in life. It can get confusing. Yet everyone needs to discover his or her purpose in life. You and I came into this world with nothing—with no thing—and we will leave the same way—with nothing. From the moment of conception, everything we have, indeed everything we are, has been a gift to us. It's all been provided. There is nothing we must do. As infants, then as young children, we are completely on the receiving end of things. Under normal circumstances, all is provided to us, starting within the womb. As the embryo grows, it develops hands and feet, fingers and toes. A brain develops, eyes are formed, and internal organs grow. While all of it is a mystery that even the brightest are limited in explaining, one thing we know for certain is that creation is a gift to us. The air we breathe and the breast from which we draw nourishment—none of it is earned. None of it is produced by any of us. Neither is any of it a reward for achievement on our part. It is all a gift from the divine and from those who love and care for us in normal parent-child relations.

But then we grow up. As we do, we begin to develop an ego—again, what is in part meant by "flesh" in the New Testament—and, over time, our ego starts asserting its independence and celebrating the fact that we are capable of producing and providing for ourselves. Our egos tell us we need no one else. We are independent of everything and dependent on no one. We are separate and thoroughly capable of providing for ourselves and, therefore, we start to produce and provide for ourselves. In fact, the very person who came into this world dependent on everyone else for virtually everything begins to believe he has everything he needs and is in need of no one else.

This is not all bad. In fact, in many respects, it is a natural part of growing up—a normal part of the human maturation process. Without the growth in personality and body, and the development of the capacity to celebrate one's independence and self-sufficiency, we would not become fully functioning human beings. But the problem is that many never find their way back from this pathway to self-sufficiency and independence that, somewhere along the journey of maturation, turns into self-centeredness and ego absorption. That's, in part, why Wayne Dyer defines ego as "edging God out."[1] And this is what the biblical writers mean when they describe our condition as one of separation from God. As ego develops, it soon dominates us and we start thinking of ourselves as independent and separate from everyone else and in need of nothing else outside of ourselves. In fact, we don't even need God. It cultivates within us an illusion that we are, in the words of Invictus, "the master of my fate, the captain of my soul." This, then, is the swan song of the ego:

> Out of the night that covers me,
> Black as the Pit from pole to pole,
> I thank whatever gods may be
> For my unconquerable soul.
>
> In the fell clutch of circumstance
> I have not winced nor cried aloud.
> Under the bludgeonings of chance
> My head is bloody, but unbowed.
>
> Beyond this place of wrath and tears
> Looms but the horror of the shade,
> And yet the menace of the years
> Finds, and shall find, me unafraid.
>
> It matters not how strait the gate,
> How charged with punishments the scroll,
> I am the master of my fate:
> I am the captain of my soul.
>
> —William Ernest Henley, 1849–1903

The sad irony is that the man who pinned these words ended up taking his own life in despair. While that fate is rare, there's a sense in which, when ego has completed its work of "edging God out," life lived without a return to its source results in the suicide of one's significance, meaning, and purpose in life.

Add to the suicidal work of the ego a cultural belief system that encourages our self-centeredness and independence and both applauds and rewards our accomplishments with material stuff, and it becomes easy to understand how many people reach midlife with a gnawing awareness that they've yet to find the life they thought they wanted.

The life you really want is experienced only on a pathway that takes you back to that place when

- you once again celebrate life as gift;
- you discover you are not independent but both dependent and interdependent;
- you stop defining your significance by the material symbols of self-sufficiency and success;
- you know your worth has nothing to do with your wealth;
- you cease the maddening pursuit of things as if life's joy is found in material toys; and
- you gratefully start giving yourself back to God and giving yourself away as your gift to the world.

Remember, you came with nothing. You'll leave with nothing. Learning to give yourself and what you've accumulated away is the only way to start living the life you've always wanted. Leo Tolstoy said, "The sole meaning of life is to serve humanity."

Does any or all of this sound odd to you? It may. This is not the stuff you'll find in *Money* magazine. "Who wants to be a millionaire?" is an obvious rhetorical question needing no answer because it's what people in our culture are obsessing over daily. I know people who pray to win the lottery. In fact, I think I too voiced one or two such prayers myself when I succumbed to the impulse and bought a Powerball ticket shortly after the jackpot reached $250 million. If I accurately recall the prayer, I tried to make a deal with God. "Let me win and I'll give half to charity." Sounded like a pretty reasonable prayer to my ego. I pictured myself on the cover of every newspaper in America being lauded as one of the most generous philanthropists ever. Ah, what ego loves to imagine! In my own "Deal or No Deal" with God, you are correct in guessing that, when the winning numbers were published, I did not have one matching number on my ticket. Not even one.

But this is how we've come to define happiness and fulfillment in our culture. The temptation to get something for practically nothing is as old as the human race. It's the delusion that dates back to the

Garden of Eden itself—the erroneous thought that just one bite of the forbidden will reward us with all the wisdom of the world. And it's clearly why so many have entered or are entering the sunset years of life with a lot of stuff, but inside they feel insignificant, spiritually bankrupt, and eternally hopeless. I've written this to show you how I'm finding my way out of the insanity of an ego-driven life and into the life I've always wanted.

NOTE

[1] Wayne W. Dyer, *The Power of Intention: Learning to Co-create Your World Your Way* (Carlsbad CA: Hay House, Inc., 2004).

4

THE STATE OF GIVING IN THE AMERICAN CHURCH

Americans donate billions to charity, but giving to churches has declined.

—George Barna, www.barna.org (April 25, 2005)

In spite of record contributions, the state of giving in the American church is anything but healthy. In recent years, the church's interest in teaching people to give is motivated less from the desire to see the lives of people changed and enriched and more from the desire to preserve the institution. This is most unfortunate, because there's no better way to perpetuate the institution of the church than to help people give themselves to God and to give away their resources to others and worthy causes.

How is charitable giving in the church going? How well is the church doing—Catholic, Evangelical, Protestant, or otherwise?

Not too well, in fact. Here's the truth regarding the state of the church's charity. The lion's share of the resources given in and through churches last year was given by a relatively small percentage of people. And the number seems to be declining each year. In main-line denominational churches, the majority of giving is done by an even smaller percentage of members over age fifty.

I recently sat with a group of Presbyterian leaders and asked them the question, "Are you concerned that 87 percent of last year's total revenue to your church came from those over age sixty-five? If that trend continues, what does that say about the kind of financial trouble your church will face in just a few years?" I got the proverbial "deer in the headlights" response. Frankly, I find this trend is being repeated in scores of churches across America. While charitable giving may be the highest it's ever been, the percentage of people actually giving may be the lowest it's ever been.

Younger churches and newer churches aren't doing much better, either. While there may be a few exceptions, the majority of churches in America are filled with people who, for whatever the reason, give very little. The 80/20 rule no longer applies. Many of us grew up being told that 80 percent of a religious institution's resources were given by 20 percent of its constituents. Today, you would probably find that in most places a 90/10 rule would be closer to reality: 90 percent of the total resources are given by 10 percent of the members.

I'm concerned about the state of giving in the church in general and in the lives of religious people in particular. I've devoted my adult life to addressing this growing problem. But I don't believe the answer will be found in some new program of fundraising for the church—and few professional fundraisers have conducted more campaigns than I have over the years. Fundraising programs have their place, but, as valuable as they are, we do not need more financial advancement programs. Instead, I think the answer lies in helping people rediscover their real purpose in life—that is, to help people get beyond what ego is doing to them and experience the life they not only really want but the world really needs.

This life is found in one way—through giving. Unfortunately, the few who are discovering the life I'm describing in this book are normally not permitted to talk about it in their own churches— Protestant, Catholic, Evangelical, or otherwise. For much too long, people have not been told the simple truth of the biblical story: that their purpose in life is to give themselves away. What's worse, those who have discovered this purpose in life are discouraged from publicly sharing how their giving is transforming their lives and their world. The few who are given permission to talk about it usually do so in such impersonal ways that most people are unclear as to what they are really saying.

People are told to be private about their charity. For reasons I'll share later, the church has developed an entire culture of silence about giving. In fact, anonymity about giving is even taught in some places as if it were a divine requirement. If not taught outright, most people tacitly assume that the Bible condemns talk about your personal giving—that there is something boastful, even irreligious, about sharing the details of one's generosity. But silence about giving is based on a thorough misreading of the Bible. (For more on this subject, see chapter 10 below.)

Most people seldom hear about giving and its personal benefits except one or two Sundays each year during the church's annual budget or offertory promotion time. What they normally hear is more impersonal than personal. I'm convinced this is because too few religious leaders have discovered for themselves the sense of purpose and happiness that comes in giving; hence, many of them have not discovered the life they really want either. In fact, far too many of them seem more interested in climbing an ecclesiastical ladder or striving to transform their place of worship into something similar to a mega-church. If you are unfamiliar with the mega-church phenomenon, you should know that churches like these have become for many religious leaders the models of a successful church of the twenty-first century. Frankly, I do not disagree that these places, in many respects, accomplish some remarkable things for the causes they believe in, both religiously and socially. But I'm convinced that religious leaders today should be pursuing life's grander purposes themselves and modeling for their people how to do the same— namely, how to live a life devoted to giving themselves away. If the majority of the religious leaders today were experiencing the blessed life found in giving, their churches would be observing in them a thorough transformation of their own character, preaching, and lifestyle. Many would enthusiastically follow their example and the religious institutions today would be dramatically different and far more effective places of worship. Furthermore, people would be hearing about giving from their pulpits principally because the joy these leaders would experience would make it impossible for them to be silent. Their bliss would be a blessing to their own people.

But you can't give what you don't possess. If you haven't discovered this life for yourself, you will naturally be silent on the subject of giving and find a plethora of ways not only to defend your silence but to discourage others from talking about their giving—even if you have to misinterpret Jesus' teaching in order to do so. The real reason the church has developed a belief system around silence about giving is not because we believe it's morally wrong for others to know what we give. Instead, our silence is to hide from others what we're not giving.

Additionally, in the seeker-sensitive mindset many churches have embraced, the feeling is that if you talk about money in church, you'll run people off. This is nonsense.

Is it "more blessed to give," or isn't it? If it is—that is to say, if fullness in life and happiness through life are found in giving just as Jesus suggested—how can you not talk about giving? People would be drawn to this kind of church because people are looking for purpose, significance, and eternal happiness. Certainly, some would reject it but most would not.

Almost all surveys I know of indicate that one of the principal reasons people today reject the church is because the church is perceived as "always asking for money." But researchers never seem to ask the next most logical question: "When did you develop this feeling about the church?"

I have asked this question. Admittedly, I haven't conducted a scientific study, but I've been talking to people and observing people for more than a decade regarding this subject. I think what they're saying is that the church's talk about money is more for the church's need for financial support and less about the personal benefits of generous living. In other words, people feel the church talks so much about money because the church needs money more than it needs anything else.

Isn't there a ring of truth in that criticism? Doesn't the church have a collective ego problem too? Many churches and church leaders define the church's significance in terms of size, numbers, and power or, as someone put it, in terms of "buildings, budgets, and baptisms." So much so, the church today seems to need the gold of Fort Knox just to operate. The church and church leaders seem to define the church's significance in much the same way our culture defines an individual's worth—by what he has accomplished (the number of baptisms the church reports each year); by where he lives (the location of the church in the "right" neighborhood); by how big his house is (the building size and seating capacity of the church); and by how much money he has (the size of the church budget).

No one knows better than I that the church needs money to operate. I deal with this matter almost daily. I'm not finding fault with the mega-church in America. In fact, churches of that size and strength can do incredibly positive things that smaller churches can only dream of doing. This is not a call to return to those days when churches were smaller. Neither, however, am I excusing those that are small or declining. I know many small and medium-sized churches today that were much larger before, but their collective ego has been wounded by the decline they have experienced over the years. They look enviously at growing churches and spend an inordinate amount of time judging and finding fault with them. The only difference between these declining churches and some larger, growing churches is that these are frantically trying to pump life back into what truthfully is the dying of their collective ego. These churches seem more interested in preserving their institutional ego than they are in expanding the kingdom and helping people genuinely to experience the life they need and want.

I am suggesting that churches of any size and church leaders in any place may be approaching this whole matter of giving backwards. You cannot encourage people to give, no matter how scripturally persuasive you try to be, if your real motivation is to build a kingdom unto yourself or pump life back into a kingdom that's crumbling and dying around you. People will see through this motivation. In fact, people have seen through it, which is precisely why they've developed the perception that churches only want their money.

I'm convinced that there are far more important reasons why people must be taught to give. When people know your motivation is to help them become more like the Jesus of the New Testament and experience genuine fulfillment in their personal lives, they welcome talk about money and giving in church. When giving in all its aspects is understood to be the pathway to life eternal and life abundant, the church's functional needs will take care of themselves. People will listen and learn with interest and give with enthusiasm.

THE PRIORITY OF GIVING

When Jesus was at the pinnacle of his popularity, he turned to the crowds—the sheer numbers of which would make many clergy today green with envy—and laid out the conditions of genuine discipleship. You can read the conditions for yourself in the fourteenth chapter of Saint Luke's Gospel. To be frank, the conditions are so stern that most churches and church leaders find it more convenient to explain away what he says by relegating it to the status of hyperbole. I find that interesting. Jesus concluded his list of conditions by saying, "So no one can become my disciple without giving up everything for me" (Luke 14:33). I'm quite certain that single requirement emptied a few, if not most, of the front-row seats. In fact, it may have emptied most of the seats. "Give up everything? You can't be serious!"

The discipline of giving must be given a higher priority in the church than any other discipline in the Christian life. There is no debating this. Proportionately, the teachings of Jesus demand it. He talked about money and our relationship to the material possessions of life more frequently than any other subject—more than love and several times more than prayer. In fact, only one subject occupied a greater place in the daily conversations, teaching, and preaching of Jesus. That one subject was the kingdom of Heaven. Fully two-thirds of the forty or so parables attributed to Jesus concern the subject of money and possessions. All of this leads me to one of the most curious oddities of the church today. Why is it that the one subject about which Jesus spoke more than any other save the kingdom of God is the least discussed subject in the church today?

Unfortunately, the priorities of the church today are almost universally misplaced. In those churches that do talk about money, it is more often for the sake of institutional preservation than the personal enrichment of those who wish to be genuine followers of God. The church is in serious trouble if its priorities are not challenged and its mission seriously changed. I'm not sure who said it, but I concur completely: "If you help a person get his financial life right with God, every other area of his life will straighten out itself." Maybe that's why Jesus said, "Wherever your treasure is, there your hearts and thoughts will also be" (Matt 6:21).

In the decade I've been crisscrossing this country, I've met scores of religious people whose lives are in complete disarray, and if you look beneath the surface, you'll discover, as I have, that the financial life of most of these folks is disastrous. They're drowning in debt. They owe credit card companies so much that the debt would take a generation to pay off if they make only the minimum monthly payment. They drive cars they can't afford and live in houses they can't even afford to furnish.

I was in one of these houses recently while providing consultation to the largest Methodist church in a Midwestern state. The senior minister and I visited a family who lives in a beautiful half-million-dollar home. The house had a wide-open, spacious foyer and a great room with several hundred square feet of living space. Their hospitality was as large as the foyer itself with its 40-foot ceiling. But, after stepping onto the beautiful hardwood floor in the foyer, something didn't feel right; something was missing. When I looked around the room, I saw that there was plenty missing. There were no pictures on the walls except for one family portrait that hung over the marble fireplace. Furthermore, a small 21-inch television sat in the corner, and the guests were all seated in metal folding chairs except for me. Since I was speaking to the group gathered there, I qualified to sit in the one lonely recliner that I'm sure was normally used while watching the news or reading the paper.

I didn't comment because I've seen this situation more than once—the homeowners couldn't afford to furnish the house. I'm hardly finding fault or being critical. There was a time in my own life when I made financial decisions that were not in my best interest or that of my family. But the scene I'm describing is being repeated today in literally thousands and perhaps hundreds of thousands of homes across the country as people, driven by ego, are, in the words of Will Campbell, "borrowing money they don't have, to buy things they don't need, to keep up with people they don't even like."

Euphemistically, we call it the American Dream.

What's happening to people? Is this not a symptom of a deeper problem? Does not our material abundance mask a spiritually bankrupt heart? Even among people who frequent houses of worship on a weekly basis?

I believe so. It is for this and many other reasons that I am committed to helping people find freedom from bondage to ego and to discover, instead, that giving themselves away will reward them with the life they've always wanted. If the church would make this the aim of ministry, not only would the church grow, but the church would change and a changed church would help produce a changed world.

Some years ago, I found a Scripture verse that has become the mantra I recite to remind myself and others of the purpose of life. Saint Paul wrote, "Since you excel in so many ways—you have so much faith, such gifted speakers, such knowledge, such enthusiasm, and such love for us—now I want you to excel also in this gracious ministry of giving" (2 Cor 8:7). That's it, I said to myself. Excellence in giving describes my purpose and your purpose too. I desire to achieve excellence in my own giving, and I'm committed to helping any person with a similar desire achieve the same. Esther and Jerry Hicks put it this way: "The greatest gift that you could ever give another is the gift of your expectation of their success."1 Pursue excellence in giving, and I fully expect you'll succeed in finding and living a life that matters.

THE SOURCE OF THIS BOOK

God gave me this book. By that, I mean he gave me both the inspiration for it and the words to write. He also gave me a publisher. If you know anything about the publishing industry, you'd have more success these days getting through airline security armed with a gun in one pocket and a grenade in another than you would at getting an editor to look at your manuscript, much less risk publishing it. But God gave me both.

When I announced to some friends I had been awarded a contract from a publisher, one asked me, "How much will you make from this book?"

At the time, I didn't have an answer, so I dismissed the question. But I've thought about the question many times since then. I wrote a book that a different publisher released back in the early nineties and never made much money from it. Frankly, it was not why I wrote it to begin with, and certainly it is not why I'm writing this one. But this time around, my ego covertly offered the following fantasy: "Can't you picture it, Steve? It'll likely be on the *New York Times* bestseller list. You'll make millions. There will be talk shows, interviews, speaking engagements. No question about it—you'll be in demand as a keynote speaker all across America."

The flight of fantasy your ego will take is never limited by reality.

Truth is, I have no idea who will read this book. I know my mother will. At least, she says she will. Nor do I know what amount of money it might generate—if any. What I do know is that I had a vivid dream one night a few months back. I dreamt that God and I had a conversation about this very question. It went something like this:

"What do you think about the book I'm giving you?" asked God.

"I'm having the time of my life, Lord. Thanks so much for the opportunity. I really like writing, you know. But, as I'm sure you're aware, there are times when I struggle just to find the words to say. But God, I'm learning to pause, meditate, do a little praying, and then sit back down with the word processor and, not surprisingly, the words you give me just flow like water across the falls at Niagara. In fact, there are times when the words come so quickly, I can't keep up on the keyboard. So you might slow it down occasionally. Really, though, thanks for giving me the words to write."

"What do you think you'll get for the book?" he asked.

"Oh, I've been thinking a lot about that, too, God. I don't know. But it sure would be nice to make a little more than last time. Maybe enough to at least buy a new car—I mean, used, but new to me, of course. We only have one, you know. And sometimes, Pam, my wife, gets a little out of sorts having to drive me to the airport at 5:30 in the morning. Sure would be nice to have a second car. And . . . then . . . there's that addition to the house we've needed for a long time. We've about paid off the mortgage, as I suppose you know, but, if we're going to stay there and retire in a few years like we've been planning, we've got to make a few changes. I don't relish the idea of climbing stairs every night to go to bed. A first-floor master bedroom and bath would be much more convenient in our old age, don't you think?"

I went on and on like this for quite some time, and God seemed to listen patiently. Parenthetically, you should know I don't often have dreams like this, much less conversations with the divine that are this vivid. If you're going to accuse me of having lost my mind, find some other proof. I doubt you'll have to look far. And don't bother to write and ask me what God looked like either. I don't remember. What I do recall is that the dream was as real to me as the letters on this keyboard.

Sometime during the dream, it slowly dawned on me that this gift from God must be my gift to you. That may not be a significant thing to you, but the decision was profoundly significant to me. While I have no idea how far this book may go in terms of its readership or how much revenue the book may generate, I made the decision that all proceeds from the sale and distribution of this book are my gift to God and to those causes committed to making the world a better place. It will all go to kingdom causes.

This was not an earth-shaking decision. If you think about it, it was inevitable. This is a book about giving. How could I—or anyone else for that matter—think about getting anything from it? Just think of this as my gift to you. I hope, too, when you finish reading this, you'll give it as a gift to someone else. The pursuit of excellence in giving is the way to change this world for the better. It's the way to change your life forever.

THE HAPPIEST PEOPLE ARE . . .

The happiest people are those who have learned (or are learning) to give away themselves and their resources. Some of them have a significant portion of this world's material wealth to give away. They are simply learning how to subjugate their ego and are no longer bound by their wealth or tied to their titles. They are busy finding ways to give and, as a result, are experiencing an infectious kind of joy. They're finding life as they've always imagined it.

Consider following the simple advice I give in the subtitle to this book: give, then get the life you've always wanted. Risk believing that it just might be true, try it for yourself, and you will find what you've been looking for. You will find the life you've always wanted.

Jesus said, "It is more blessed to give than to receive" (Acts 20:35). That's either the truth, or it is one of the most colossal lies that ever fell from his lips. For me, it's true, but this knowledge has not come easily. In fact, when my ego slips back into control (and that is more often than I care to admit), I am prone to disbelieve his words. When I disbelieve, I experience doubt and behave in ways contrary to a life of faith. I'll find myself worrying about money and start cranking up the stockpiling routine all over again. I get protective of my possessions. I experience anxiety with every rollercoaster fluctuation of the stock market. I start saving more and counting my savings. I worry about not having enough or something happening that might bankrupt me. Does any of this sound familiar to you?

When this happens, what do I do? As soon as I'm aware (and that, I'm glad to report, is happening more frequently than in the past), I firmly rebuke my inner ego, then I ask God to give me the capacity to behave in ways that will lead me to freedom from feelings of doubt, fear, and worry. Following that prayer, I go forward as if I had never had this little setback and, within moments, I'm at peace once again.

What psychologist William James once said helps me. He observed, "It's easier to act your way into a new way of feeling than it is to feel your way into a new way of acting." Though it sounds a little like double-talk, I think what he's saying is quite simple. For example, I sometimes have to act as if I believe Jesus' words even if I don't feel like believing at that moment. I will ask God for an opportunity to give to some need or some person in need. Normally, I don't have to ask. God presents the opportunity to me and, even when I don't feel like it, I will give. When my ego shouts back, "Lame-brain! You can't afford to do this!" I do it anyway. As I act on the truthfulness of his words—"It is more blessed to give than to receive"—my feelings start to improve almost instantly. Doubt disappears. Fear and worry give way to peace and happiness, and the life I've always wanted returns. I've acted my way into a new way of feeling.

Again, the happiest, most contented people are those who are learning how to get outside of themselves and give themselves away. I've never met a giving person who was simultaneously an unhappy person. I've met a lot of unhappy people. But scratch beneath the surface, and you'll quickly discover that most unhappy people are selfish, self-centered, ego-driven people who live by the cultural myth that it is more blessed to receive than to give. Many of these are religious people. By defining their worth by their wealth and finding their significance in stuff, though, they have surrounded themselves with plenty but are spiritually impoverished.

What kind of life do you really want? Your life purpose is inextricably bound up in learning to give yourself away and your wealth away. You say, "I don't have any wealth"? Compared to whom? Of course, you do. If you could afford the purchase of this book, you've spent more money than half the world's population will earn in an entire week, maybe a month. Who do you think you're kidding? You may not have as much as Tom Cruise or Bill Gates or even your next-door neighbor. But you have more than most and you have much to give away. You might look around at others who live in more luxurious neighborhoods, make more money than you, drive more expensive cars, serve larger churches than you, or seem to get the most coveted promotions, and measure your worth by such insidious comparisons. But you have more than most in this world, and much of what God has given to you, he has done so with the intention that you will give some or all of it away. The Bible is unmistakably clear about this: "you will be enriched so that you can give even more generously" (2 Cor 9:11). When you accept this fact of life and act on it, even when your ego tells you that what I'm writing is outrageous and insane, you will then begin the discovery of the life you've always wanted. Until then, your happiness will be temporary and dependent on your circumstances. As long as things go your way, you'll feel occasionally happy. But it won't last. The party will end.

For some folks reading these words, it has. Some are unfulfilled enough to be curious to read this book. Others are just plain sick of their lives. Maybe you're grasping for something because you haven't found the life you really want. The insanity of the world has made you feel insane yourself.

TOKEN VERSUS GENEROUS GIVING

When I talk about giving being the purpose of your life, don't misunderstand me. I'm not talking about token giving—the kind most frequently practiced by people in the pew. And outside the pew, I might add. I'm talking about generous giving—even outlandish giving, giving that often defies rational thinking. Giving that may go beyond tithing (the giving of 10 percent of your income away). This kind of giving is at times spontaneous, at other times carefully calculated and planned, but always fun and fulfilling. You may be skeptical, but I dare you to try it.

Saint Paul described this kind of giving in 2 Corinthians 9:7: "You must each make up your own mind as to how much you should give. Don't give reluctantly or in response to pressure. For God loves the person who gives cheerfully."

"Cheerful" giving? A rather innocuous translation, if you ask me. It hardly captures the punch of this word, which in Greek is the word hilaron, from which we get our English word hilarious. The dictionary defines hilarity as "high spirits that may be carried to the point of boisterous conviviality or merriment." I don't know what comes to your mind when you read that slightly cumbersome definition. I get the picture of someone dancing in the streets. Or someone like Mick Jagger dancing across a stage waving his arms and jumping to the rhythm of music. That picture may come closer to capturing the real meaning of Paul's word cheerful.

Here's the response I got from a cynic who approached me after I delivered a speech on the subject of "Giving, Then Getting What You Really Want in Life": "Well, all I can say is that God may prefer cheerful givers, but my church is not nearly as particular." Maybe the church should be more particular. In fact, the church should discourage people from giving if their gifts are given out of a feeling of obligation, guilt, or manipulation instead of rapturous joy and exhilaration.

THE LAST FRONTIER TO CONQUER

Growth in giving is that last frontier to conquer within your soul. But it must become your first priority if you want to experience the abundant life. That's a fact. If you haven't already, you'll soon discover that the cultivation of a generous heart is a formidable task. A charitable heart is difficult to develop. Everything in you conspires against it. Your ego will fight you for as long as it can. Nevertheless, you can conquer this if you avail yourself of the liberating power of God's Spirit whose presence is within you to enable you. Once this last frontier—your inner world—is conquered, every other area of your life will fall into place. When you get this right, you'll understand why Jesus talked so much about it. It is that one place where the greatest need exists for life change and transformation.

If you permit God to change your heart and how you define your worth, you'll begin to experience a life filled with such incredible blessing and self-abandonment that it will defy explanation. You'll receive in return far more than you'll ever be able to give away.

I don't mean what you'll get in return is a luxury car, a beachside home, or an exotic vacation to some faraway place. That could happen, because it is true that generous people are sometimes materially prosperous people. But getting such things will not be your motivation for giving. Read that statement again. Giving in order to get is an attitude that will most certainly interfere with the flow of God's Eternal Spirit—a Spirit that is by nature selfless, generous, and abundant. Instead, your motivation to give will be the sheer joy you get from becoming free from things and free to give yourself and your material wealth away in complete self-abandonment and trust in God's promised care of your every need.

I've never met a person who has made giving of themselves and their resources a priority who was in need of anything. I will say this again, for you must not miss this statement. It's at the core of my understanding as to how this divinely designed universe works: I have never met an individual who had linked himself or herself to God's desire for generosity who was ever in need of anything. God has always provided for their needs. In fact, most are either prosperous or have chosen a simpler lifestyle, but generous people have everything they need.

Over the years, I've met many people who have had many needs. But in most instances, they are not yet at that place where they understand or live by this principle. This is one of the great mysteries of life. Indeed, it is one of many paradoxes you'll not only find in Scripture but in this book: you don't give to receive, but you do receive when you give. It's an inexplicable paradox.

Again, I've met many people in need. Some are driven by a desire to get what's "theirs" before someone else does. They are self-centered people, dominated by their ego just like I've been for much of my adult life. These people envy those who have more and live their entire lives to see how many of the material symbols of importance and success they can acquire. Ministers who seek the bigger church in the better location may be no exception.

But those who are learning or have learned the secret of giving are being liberated from the need for all the material stuff of this life even while they may enjoy some of it. They have everything they need because they are discovering that what they really want is not found in things. They may have things, but they don't need things to define their worth or significance. These people understand what Saint Paul meant when he said, "I have learned to get along happily whether I have much or little" (Phil 4:10b). They would be just as happy without the stuff they have as they are with it.

If you make the pursuit of excellence in giving the purpose of your life, you'll discover significance to a degree greater than most people around you will ever know. You'll find the life you've always wanted and most are still looking for. It won't have anything to do with the size of your house, though you may reside in the largest one in the neighborhood. It'll have nothing to do with type of car you drive or the status you've achieved in life, though you may drive a fine automobile and hold the highest position in your company. It won't have anything to do with the size of the church you serve, and you may serve in a large parish. Some of the most unfulfilled ministers I've ever known were those who finally achieved the status of senior pastor in a large church, only to be bored and eventually burn out.

The life you've always wanted will have everything to do with the internal peace and happiness you feel. You will be unattached to anything that you have acquired or any of the titles you've earned. You will be committed to and consumed with but one thing—the absolute devotion and passion to give yourself away and to share the abundance God has given you. You will no longer glibly agree that "It is more blessed to give than to receive." Instead, you will know deep inside that Jesus' words are true. Your whole life will be a testament to this generous, blessed life Jesus gives to those who give.

Isn't this the life you really want? For yourself? Your family? This world? Then what could possibly prevent you from getting it?

MYTHS AND MISCONCEPTIONS ABOUT GIVING

Myths about giving can prevent you from experiencing the life I'm describing. Ego thrives on these myths. In fact, I'm convinced that myths and misconceptions about giving are not only widely believed but also cause far too many people to miss the joy of living that comes from the practice of giving.

A myth is a belief that's grown up around something or someone. We pick up most myths about giving by osmosis—simple observation. A few are actually taught to us by sincere but misguided people. Others we have heard in sermons in the church or parachurch organizations. Every church, denomination, and religious organization I've consulted with seems to have acquired or developed its own myths about giving and perpetuates them through its philosophy and teaching from generation to generation. What you believe about giving will affect many other areas of your life. It is a worthwhile exercise, therefore, to look critically at what you believe about giving—the giving away of your life and your resources.

I have spent many of the last ten years seeking to understand my own beliefs about giving and to overcome misconceptions I've discovered in my own thinking regarding the subject. I want to expose and dispel these myths in my life and share with you what I've learned precisely because these myths will keep you from experiencing the life you want.

What you believe about giving—the giving of yourself and your resources away in the service of others—can be picked up from popular culture as well as the religious community. The myths I describe below can be found among every religious group in America. They can also be found among people who don't consider themselves "churched."

Each myth is independent. Some are interdependent. It's important to understand that all of these myths have the capacity to stand in the way of the full life God intends for you. But if you'll work at banishing them from your thinking and replacing them with the intention of becoming a generous person, the life Jesus called "abundant" and I'm calling "the life you're really always wanted" will be yours.

NOTE

1 Esther and Jerry Hicks, *The Law of Attraction* (Carlsbad CA: Hay House, Inc., 2006), 66.

MYTH 1

"GIVE AND YOU'LL GET RICH"

He that is of the opinion that money will do everything may well be suspected of doing everything for money.
— Benjamin Franklin (1706–1790)

What you get by achieving your goals is not as important as what you become by achieving your goals.
— Henry David Thoreau (1818–1862)

The myth "Give and You'll Get Rich" is the most insidious of all myths about giving. This myth is primarily promoted by a certain strain of Christian radio and television preachers. It goes something like this: If you wish to make $100,000 a year, give $10,000. If you want to make a half-million dollars, give $50,000. If you want to make a million dollars, give $100,000, and so on.

On more than one occasion, I've heard a televangelist say things just like this. When a television minister claims a divine directive to take his message to a new place in the world—precisely because he believes he's been chosen to help usher in the end of the age—he needs more money, of course. My suspicion is that either his ego thrives on the stardom a worldwide television ministry provides and the economic benefits that come with it, or he genuinely believes God has ordained him as the fulfillment of the prophecy that the gospel must be preached to the whole world before the world comes to an end (Matt 24:14). I think it must be a little of both.

Lately, I haven't heard promises like this one—"If you want to make a million, give $100,000." But it is not because these religious moguls have quit believing and preaching this nonsense. Instead, it's because I'm getting more selective about the religious television and radio I listen to. In my opinion, far too many of the airwaves are filled with these manipulative ministers, some of whom have been convicted on charges of mail fraud and money laundering and have been sent to prison. Not surprisingly, several have served their prison terms and are back on the air.

Don't misunderstand me. I'm not saying all media preachers are con artists–just many of them. I would even risk saying that the majority of these misguided preachers have suspect motives. Lately, I've been trying not to be guilty of passing judgment on others, but TV and radio preachers aren't making it easy for me.

It's not a new thing, either. These material moguls have been around for a long time. Saint Paul wrote, "You see, we are not like those hucksters—and there are many of them—who preach just to make money" (2 Cor 2:17). For at least 2,000 years, they've been here, anyway.

While not all "media ministers" are using the airwaves to make money (and in some cases lots of it), the few genuine ones have been given a glaring black eye because of the many disingenuous ones. I'm not sure what's worse, the dishonest ones who get away with their televised nonsense or the gullible people who believe in them. I'm more inclined to have empathy for gullible people. There are scores of them who are at times vulnerable, and they are so, in part, because they are experiencing some of the more difficult hardships of life.

My Own Journey

Just such a time occurred in my own life. Many years ago, I went through a separation and then a divorce. Under the most amiable of circumstances, the death of a relationship leaves wounds that are hard to heal—especially for the children involved. I was emotionally down. I left the pastoral ministry a few months before in anticipation that a divorce was on the horizon. This was the only career I had known in my entire adult life. My salary was cut in half and I had to move back home with my mother at age forty—not a move that boosts your self-esteem.

Though Mother was supportive, I was depressed, vulnerable, and certainly not thinking straight. Lying in bed one evening, I was watching late-night television. I should have known the program was suspect when it opened with a network disclaimer: "The following program is a paid advertisement." There are only two reasons these kinds of programs flourish during the late-night hours. One, airtime is cheap, and two, the majority of people who watch television at these hours are either working the third shift and have little to do or are distressed, distraught, and broken people who, under ordinary circumstances would be asleep. But they are not sleeping because they've got too much on their minds. In short, the vulnerable are gullible. I was one among the ranks of such people.

It didn't look like any commercial I had ever seen. Filled with stories from people who looked like your neighbor next door, one after another testified that their lives had been changed because of the product they had purchased. While the level of their success varied (a ploy these commercial con artists use to make it all the more believable), each had either become very wealthy overnight or, at a minimum, had notably improved their economic status in society.

That made a believer out of me. I reached for the phone, gave them my credit card number, and within seconds I was $8,000 poorer and in a deeper financial hole than I had ever been. But I had a product that guaranteed I would soon be sitting on the proverbial "mountain of cash."

"Did the product sell?" you might ask. "Did you do as well as those in the advertisement?"

Are you kidding? Not only did it not sell, although it was not for lack of effort on my part, but the product line disappeared faster than a plate of Southern fried chicken at a family reunion. Come to think of it, I don't remember seeing the product ever advertised after the day I bought it. Today, I'm convinced some wag is reclining on a yacht surrounded by bikini-clad blondes and absorbing the Yucatan sun at my expense and the host of other people as gullible as me. I'd tell you what the product was, but the whole experience is so embarrassing to me that I've already shared more than I am comfortable admitting.

THE CONTEMPORARY ELMER GANTRY

Many years ago, Sinclair Lewis wrote the book *Elmer Gantry*. It was made popular as a motion picture in the 1960s, and Burt Lancaster played the starring role as the infamous Elmer Gantry. Although a fictional character, Gantry was a charismatic, Midwestern, vacuum-cleaner salesman turned preacher in the 1920s. (Why do so many preachers seem to be associated with manipulative salespeople? Specifically vacuum-cleaner and used-car salespeople?) His eloquence and his ability to captivate the imaginations of people enabled Gantry to prey on scores of people, especially the timid, disturbed, and distraught.

Although many criticized his novel as unfairly judgmental, Lewis aptly portrayed a character we have all met at one time or another. Mr. Gantry was alive in Sinclair's day. He was alive in the days of the early church in the first century (2 Cor 2:17). And, in case you haven't noticed, he's alive and well today. You'll meet him on more than one channel where there's religious programming.

Malachi 3:1 is the passage in the Bible to which many of these televangelists turn to convince you to give to them. It is also that passage to which many sincere but misguided people turn to validate the misconception that, if you give, you'll have such an abundant return, you will have difficulty knowing what to do with all of it.

Here is one of the real dangers with this myth. It can and will mask your real love—the love of money, materialism, and the societal admiration that comes with it. Saint Paul warned his young colleague, Timothy, that the love of money is the source of all evil.

One of the most notable and notorious of these money-loving, material-minded ministers had a successful television ministry a few years ago but was charged and later convicted of wrongdoing and sent to prison. He hadn't been out of prison but a few months when he was back on television.

Was he more sincere? Had he changed? Not much, except that his hair was thinner and the lines in his face were both longer and deeper. His message, however, was the same. And his studio audience looked like some of those whom he had duped before being incarcerated. There were many times I thought he had stepped over the precipice of sanity before going to prison. He had taken the notion of "give and get rich" to a level of absurdity equal to the worst imaginable immorality. I watched in sheer disbelief as he asked his viewers to recall the story of a time when the prophet Elijah instructed the poor and destitute woman to give him her last meal. It was to be her last meal that she had planned to share with her son before the two of them would give up and die from starvation (1 Kgs 17).

What was the television preacher's point? He wanted his viewers, regardless of their circumstances, to obediently pick up the phone and make a pledge to his ministry—a ministry, if that's what you would call it, that he had the audacity to liken to that of the prophet Elijah himself.

The television preacher's promise? If his viewers would be obedient and give him their last nickel, God would give them everything they needed to pay medical bills, hold the creditors at bay, make the mortgage payment, or find a good-paying job. He might as well have promised they would miraculously pick the winning Powerball lottery numbers. That would have been no less dishonest. What he did assure is that God would open the windows of heaven and bless them a hundredfold. He offered no money-back guarantee, but he did promise the next best thing—that God would heal his donors of all their physical diseases, including their aches and pains. Again, no money-back guarantee, but a pretty good deal, nonetheless. Obey God, send the offering, and God will give you anything you need and good health to boot.

I felt sadness rush over me as I thought about all those viewers who might be duped by this diabolical scheme just as I was on that day when, gullible and needy, I had trusted not a religious huckster but one no less evil.

TELEVISION MINISTERS AND FAITH HEALERS

Many of these religious personalities on television are also faith healers. Interesting, these ministers offer the masses the two things many of them don't have—much money and good health. Often during their religiously televised circus they will receive inspiration. I think they call it a "word of knowledge." The Bible would call it "divining," which is a procedure that, while frequently practiced by God's people in the Old Testament and with what appears to be his permission, is prohibited nonetheless (Deut 18:10). Another paradox. Divining who the ill and infirm are among their viewers, they promise, if the sick will send a "faith offering," their physical condition will most certainly improve. The requirement for improvement in one's health is, of course, the "faith" gift, as they call it.

This is a slightly different version of the myth "give and you'll get rich." This is "give and you'll get well." I recently heard one of these ministers say that the persons whom he divined as being healed during his program should at a minimum send him an offering of thanksgiving. Guilt is always a great motivator to get people to give, isn't it?

These offensive theatrics in the name of Christianity take place in front of a studio audience who on cue break into a spirited applause as these actors perform on a stage of appalling hypocrisy.

I guess you can tell I don't have any regard for these monsters. And here's perhaps the primary thing I find so contradictory and most revealing: If all this faith-healing stuff on television were really true, why do we never see a radically deformed or mentally challenged person healed? Or, for that matter, a quadriplegic wheeled on stage, spinal cord miraculously repaired, and the ability to stand and walk restored? Does God only offer healing to a few favored folks whose illnesses are not too challenging even for him? Does he only heal those persons he deems worthy enough? Or those who have perfect, doubt-free faith? If faith is the requirement to receive divine healing, what are those whose mental capacities are so limited they are incapable of either exercising or verbalizing faith supposed to do?

I keep hoping someone will come forward and document one verifiable healing of Down's syndrome. Have you ever seen one? Just one verifiable case would make a believer out of me. That's not asking too much, is it? I don't wish to be unkind about this, but I want to understand what I'm missing here. Normally, what I've seen on these faith-healing programs is a person who walks with a cane, is pushed onto stage in a wheelchair, or has an unseen tumor in the breast or lung who gets healed.

Near my home is a hospital for people whose physical and mental conditions are more severe than most could imagine. I have never seen one of these individuals healed. Not one. Such people would not even be present at these divine healing services unless someone carried them. If these faith healers want to get the attention of the world, why don't they visit one of these hospitals for the radically deformed and heal one of them? That would make the nightly news, would it not? Can you imagine the impact as Katie Couric delivers the news report from the bedside of the patient whose radical mental and physical deformity has miraculously disappeared? The patient who had neither spoken nor eaten without the assistance of feeding tubes is sitting up in bed like any other normal human being but with a look of liveliness as she discovers the new world around her. Surrounding her are doctors and medical specialists from around the world verifying that the miracle of healing had most certainly taken place. It would have a phenomenal, worldwide impact. Then these materialistic, faith-healing television preachers could fulfill what they believe to be their divinely appointed purpose—namely, to preach the gospel to the whole world and, therefore, serve as the catalyst for bringing on the end of the world. To cap it all off, they could bring about the end of the age with more money in their pockets than they've ever duped out of others before.

In my opinion, it is all a hypocritical, moneymaking machine. The entire fiasco ought to make the real Christian community sick to their souls. It is a sham and mockery of the worst sort. What's worse is that the televised circus of healing has made the genuine Christian community the laughingstock of the world.

I am not implying that those who believe generosity will cause you to reap a financial reward are all followers of these Elmer Gantrys or attendees at their churches. The fact is, many sincere people believe this myth. In one respect, I, too, believe that if you give you will receive. The Bible does teach this. But I believe it has one important qualifier. If you miss the qualifier, you've missed the whole point of this chapter. Let's turn our attention first to what the Bible really teaches about wealth and then to the important qualifier. I'll discuss this qualifier in the "Suggestion" section of this chapter.

WHAT THE BIBLE REALLY SAYS

Where does it say in the Bible, "Give and you'll get rich"?

Well, in fact, it does not, although there is a philosophy that runs through the Old Testament that God materially rewards the righteous and strips the wicked of their material abundance. But is there an explicit teaching in the words of Jesus that giving will make you rich? No.

Malachi 3:10 is the Old Testament verse to which many turn for proof that giving and getting rich go hand in hand. "Isn't this a promise," I'm often asked, "that if I bring my tithes and offerings to God, God will pour out a material blessing so huge I won't be able to contain it?"

Hardly. That is not what Malachi is promising, but, unfortunately, people have been misreading Malachi for decades. I'll save the full explanation for a later chapter in the book. For now, however, understand that Malachi, who speaks for God, is mocking the people because of their faithlessness. The prophet lived hundreds of years after God first revealed himself to the people of Israel on Mount Sinai. Through Moses, God delivered them from Pharaoh's cruel hand of slavery, led them safely through the Red Sea, and established a covenant with them through the Ten Commandments. Then he journeyed with them as their God for hundreds of years and multiple generations. He cared for them and provided their every need. Yet after all that time, they still doubted his faithfulness. Their doubts of his care led them to steal tithes and offerings from God for fear they wouldn't have enough. (Things haven't changed much, for this still happens.) Infuriated, the prophet Malachi told them to put God to the test, and the words he used to make this challenge are drenched with sarcasm. We must read his words with that kind of intonation. He's hardly giving the people permission to test God. He's sarcastically scolding them for failing to trust in God's provision.

But why would the Israelites distrust God after he had cared for them and supplied their every need for centuries?

They were afraid. Fear caused them to steal from God and behave in ways drenched with doubt. Even serious followers today can doubt God and act in ways contrary to faith. Fear has led many devout people who have more reason than even the saints of old to trust in divine provision to sidestep giving or to steal from God. Why? They, too, are afraid that there won't be enough to go around or that something unexpected might happen and they won't be financially prepared for it. I'll have more to say about this in the next chapter. Though there is the promise "My God shall supply all your need according to his riches in glory by Christ Jesus" (Phil 4:19), when fear and feelings of insecurity and uncertainty dominate your heart, those are words easy to forget.

The Israelites were stealing the tithes and offerings from God. Like them, instead of giving, many people today are taking what should be given away and investing it in stocks, bonds, certificates of deposit, and high-yield investments in what is really a self-serving, self-saving act of distrust. That's plainly the reason why Malachi spoke these words long ago—words all the more applicable to people of faith today: "Test me now . . . if I will not open you the windows of heaven . . ." (Mal 3:10) They should not have had to test God for anything. Besides, Jesus condemned testing (Matt 4:7).

We have no need to test God. In fact, we have a far greater reason to trust in God's abundant care and provision. That reason hung from a cross and was laid in a tomb to prove God's provision and care could be trusted. For a person of faith today to distrust God is a like saying to one's spouse at the seventy-fifth wedding anniversary, "If you really love me, then prove it!"

After seventy-five years, what's there to prove?

It's clearly a misreading of Malachi to say his words prove that if we give, we will reap a financial windfall.

WEALTH AS A SIGN OF GOD'S BLESSING

As I indicated earlier, there was among the Old Testament saints a strong belief that wealth was a sign of God's special favor. Incidentally, there are people today who believe this. In fact, it's what motivates some of them to give. Materially, they've got it made and have come to believe that all they enjoy is a reward for being faithful, hard-working, and, of course, sincere persons of faith.

The classic New Testament story that demonstrates this philosophical view is found in the Gospel of Luke. One day, his followers asked Jesus, "Then who can be saved?" (Luke 18:26). A little background may reveal the reason they would even ask this question.

It grew out of a conversation they overhead Jesus having with the rich young ruler (Luke 18:18-25). If anyone deserved eternal life by the standards of divine acceptance held by the religious community of Jesus' day, it was the rich young ruler. He was a ruler because he had earned the professional credentials that afforded him a superior social status. He was also rich, having not only plenty of material treasure but also an unrivaled religious heritage and tradition. Hence, in the eyes of his peers, the rich young ruler was religiously and materially impressive and of all people, therefore, the most acceptable to God.

But Jesus was impressed by neither his trophy case full of religious credentials nor his hefty bank account. In fact, he admonished the young man to go sell everything, give it to the poor, and follow him. The rich young ruler was saddened by Jesus' words and walked away. As far as we know, he never came back.

The disciples were bewildered by all of this, for their traditions had taught them that no one was more deserving of salvation than someone of the rich young ruler's moral and social stature. That left them scratching their heads and asking, "Then who can be saved?" They held to the notion that if one had wealth, heaven was smiling on that person, opening its windows, and allowing the showers of material blessings to freely fall upon him or her.

But Jesus shattered that notion when he said, "How hard it is for the rich to enter the Kingdom of God! Indeed, it is easier for a Cadillac to go through a revolving door than for a rich man to enter the Kingdom of God" (Luke 18:25, Cotton Patch Version). (I can see Clarence Jordan's image a little better than a camel through a needle's eye.)

THE POVERTY OF JESUS

Just as certainly as Jesus shattered the myth that wealth is a sign of God's blessings, his own lifestyle should make any person of wealth uncomfortable. Think about it: By his own admission, he had nowhere to lay his head and apparently was not always certain of the source for his next meal (Matt 8:20). Yet if anyone ever deserved to stay at the Jerusalem Ritz-Carlton, dine on grilled Pandora with dried tomato pesto, or be chauffeured around on a luxury model of Hertz Rent-a-Donkey, Jesus certainly did. How can anyone be so shallow as to think that their giving should produce for them opulence and wealth when Jesus himself had absolutely nothing?

Furthermore, we don't see Jesus' followers in the New Testament reclining in luxury's lap. Saint Peter once said to Jesus, "We have left all we had to follow you!" (Luke 18:28). As a matter of fact, we see just the opposite. The New Testament is filled with stories of people who, upon following Jesus, become almost absurdly generous toward others while expecting nothing in return from either God or anyone else.

How about Zacchaeus, who said, "If I have cheated anybody out of anything, I will pay back four times the amount" (Luke 19:8)? Or the early Christians in the Acts of the Apostles? Of them, Luke writes, "No one claimed that any of his possessions was his own, but they shared everything they had . . . . there were no needy persons among them. For from time to time those who owned lands or houses sold them, brought the money from the sales, and put it at the apostles' feet, and it was distributed to those who had need" (Acts 4:32-34). Why not suggest something similar at the next council meeting where you attend church? If you do, don't be surprised if you're ignored or dismissed.

Here are two additional verses of Scripture often used by those who wish to believe giving will make people rich: "You know how full of love and kindness our Lord Jesus Christ was. Though he was very rich, yet for your sakes he became poor, so that by his poverty he could make you rich" (2 Cor 8:9) and "Remember this—a farmer who plants only a few seeds will get a small crop. But the one who plants generously will get a generous crop" (2 Cor 9:6).

One of my seminary professors used to say that there are people who have perfected the art of what he called a "kangaroo" exegesis. Many people leap from Scripture text to Scripture text in an effort to craft a belief system that defends some indefensible religious view. If you knew the context for Paul's words and the economic conditions facing early believers, you would know he was hardly promising his readers that their faithfulness in giving would make them the material envy of Caesar himself.

The "give and you'll get rich" myth is just that—a myth. To try and shroud a love of money and materialism behind misread and misapplied Scripture may be the ultimate hypocrisy. Some of the most sincere people I've ever known have generously given all of their adult lives, and they have little to show for it materially. To be sure, they always seem to have enough and perhaps are simply content with their chosen economic state in life. While they may not be materially rich, there's no question that they are spiritually rich toward God.

Giving to get rich is an act of the ego—that part of you that defines your value by the material stuff you accumulate. It is thoroughly misguided and in the end will only succeed in frustrating you and causing you to miss the life you've always wanted.

Giving as a means of testing God to see if he's going to do something favorable on your behalf, bail you out of the financial mess you've made of your life, or deliver a family member from a horrible disease simply won't work. Check your motive before you give any gift. Or, for that matter, before you pray any prayer. This is the important qualifier referred to earlier in the chapter. Your motive matters.

THE DIVINE HUMAN PARADOX
—THE LAW OF GIVING AND RECEIVING

"Then," you ask, "how do you explain the words of Jesus, 'If you give, you will receive'" (Luke 6:38)? Here's where it gets interesting. While I have just spent the bulk of this chapter debunking the myth that, if you give, it must not be to get anything in return, I am now going to offer an idea that you may reject as not only paradoxical but thoroughly contradictory. But I hope that you are the kind of person F. Scott Fitzgerald once described when he said, "The test of first-rate intelligence is the ability to hold two opposing ideas in mind at the same time and still retain the ability to function."

Any serious student of Scripture knows it is loaded with paradoxes. The subject of giving and receiving is just another example. That's what makes a recent article in *Time* magazine so interesting to me. The cover story asked, "Does God want you to be rich?" Although the article was well written, the authors were asking the wrong question for the simple reason that the question, as they asked it, cannot be definitively answered. Consider what I'm saying. You have, on one side, best-selling author and TV preacher Joyce Meyer defending prosperity by asking, "Who would want something where you're miserable, broke, and ugly and you have to muddle through until you get to heaven?" On the other side, you have Rick Warren, author and megapastor, saying this idea that God wants everybody to be wealthy is a lot of "baloney." He's quoted as saying, "It's creating a false idol. You don't measure your self-worth by your net worth."[2]

So who's right? They both are. Both sides can find plenty of biblical support to defend their positions. For example, on one side of the debate, the writer of Deuteronomy says, "Always remember that it is the Lord your God who gives you the power to become rich, and he does it to fulfill the covenant he made with your ancestors" (Deut. 8:18). Even Jesus said, "If you give, you will receive. Your gift will return to you in full measure, pressed down, shaken together, to make room for more, and running over" (Luke 6:38).

On the other side of the debate, you find both the Old and New Testaments giving stern warnings to guard against the pursuit of riches. The most striking are the words of Jesus himself: "Don't store up treasures here on earth . . ." (Matt 6:19); and "It is easier for a camel to go through the eye of a needle than for a rich person to enter the kingdom of God" (Mark 10:24).

There are two conclusions. One, Scripture will not answer this question for you. You'll have to draw your own conclusion between you and God. No one can do this for you because, as Jesus said, "Wherever your treasure is, there your heart . . . will also be" (Matt 6:21). That is to say, this is a personal matter—indeed, it goes all the way to the core of what's important to you and what you value in life.

Second, it seems to me that a more important question is, "What does God want you to do with your life and the wealth you do have, whether much or little?" What you do with what you have is a much more poignant question than that of what you have. The former gets at the heart of your life's purpose.

All of this debate about whether having wealth is right or wrong is a smokescreen. If you want to discuss what's important, why not discuss what determines the "worth" of a person's life, not the wealth she or he may possess?

In the end, all of us will leave this life the same way we entered it—with absolutely nothing. Admittedly, you may leave this life having been at the top of the food chain, or you may leave this life having been at the bottom most of your life. But the fact is, eternity knows no distinctions. W. C. Fields used to say, "A rich man is nothing but a poor man with money." We're all the same. The only thing that will matter at the end of your life is what you've done with your life. Nothing more, nothing less.

THE LAW OF ABUNDANCE
—GIVING AND RECEIVING

While I have tried to explode the myth that giving will automatically make you rich, there is a sense in which the Bible affirms that giving sets in motion a divinely designed cycle of operation and that those who give find it coming back to them. It is hard to understand and harder still to explain. But there is a direct correlation between generosity and material abundance. When people give, God returns it to them. They give again and more returns to them. These people give not because they have to or because they're trying to use their giving to get something in return. Instead, they give because they want to give. No minister has promised either a material windfall or a healed body. Instead, these givers believe it's their purpose to do so and they do it for the sheer joy they get from it. They give neither to test nor to coerce God to act favorably on their behalf or on behalf of someone else. Instead, they give because they have found incredible meaning in it. They've found that giving themselves away rewards them with the life they've always wanted.

These people do not wait till they get before they give. To the contrary, they are giving before they receive anything in return. In other words, it would never occur to these people to say, "One day when I'm in a better position financially, I'm going to be generous and start giving stuff away." Instead, these people start developing a generous lifestyle even when they may have little to give. The only difference for these people is that now that they are richer, they simply have much more to give away.

Olympic Gold Medalist Joey Cheek is a prime example. As a speed skater who was known as the "fastest cheeks on ice" in the 2006 Winter Olympics in Torino, Cheek was quoted during the Olympics as saying that he would not be keeping the $25,000 that the U.S. Olympic Committee awarded gold medalists. Instead, he would donate the winnings to a program to help the thousands of Sudanese children who have been turned into refugees by warlords in that conflicted region of the world. Cheek said, "For me, the Olympics have been the greatest blessing. I've always felt that if I ever did something big like this I wanted to be prepared to give something back."

Cheek was "prepared" long before he was prosperous. That's the spirit I'm describing. This is the same spirit Saint Paul was referring to when he said each person must make up his or her own mind as to how much to give (2 Cor 9:7). Generosity is a decision of the heart—deep within your soul. You resolve to reverse what ego has done to you, so you start practicing being generous. Ego makes you greedy and self-serving. The decision to give sets in motion a process that changes you over time. With practice, you get perfect.

The generous person does not get rich and then morph into being generous. Generosity is seldom the result of your circumstances. Instead, generosity is choice forged in the crucible of your convictions. I suppose there are some people of privilege who on occasion give generously to various charities either to silence the voice of guilt within or because their financial advisor or press agent encourages them to do so. But this kind of generosity, for all the good it may do, is sporadic and at best rewards the giver with a temporary joy.

I'm talking about a lifestyle of generosity produced by an act of your will—a choice you make to give. I can guess where the will to make this choice comes from—from generous parents or a significant and demonstrative benefactor who models for you what it means to be generous. Or God simply gives you the will to be generous without asking or because you have asked him to do so. In any case, even the will to give is itself a gift.

I cannot explain the paradox of giving and receiving. Yet I know it is true because I have seen it work consistently. It has worked in my own life, and few people are by nature more skeptical than I. But by almost any standard, I am a rich person, and I have discovered there is an inescapable connection between my giving and receiving. The more I give away, the more of what I give away keeps coming back to me. I give because I love it. I give because I am the happiest when I do. And I give because it's when I give that I get the life I've always wanted.

There is a principle at work in the universe that what you give away will come back to you. While I can neither prove this phenomenon nor persuade you to believe it, what I can say is that I have never met a person whose generosity resulted in deprivation, except perhaps for the person whose giving was for the purpose of getting something in return or to force God to deliver some special blessing. For those who give for no other reason than because they're learning this is the purpose of life, the return is automatic.

This is the law of giving and receiving. The most widely quoted words of the New Testament are those found in John 3:16: "For God so loved the world that he gave . . . ." It's God's nature to give. Just as surely as Newton's law of gravity applies to the physical world, nature's law of generosity applies to the spiritual world. The fact that you can't see it does not negate its reality. Gravity is unseen, yet it works and you see its results. Generosity may be seen or unseen, known or unknown, but its impact is far-reaching. What you give away comes back to you.

When you give, you are never in want. Instead, you have everything you need and even your "wants." That's right. Even your wants. Today, I enjoy material abundance. But I enjoy much more the happiness, security, inner peace, and significance that giving affords me. As I give myself away, I am discovering my "wants" are being edited too. They change and are refined. I actually find myself wanting less precisely because what I get from giving is not only far more important but certainly more lasting than the temporary thrill I get from anything material. Remember, it's your ego that defines your worth by what you have, what you earn, where you live, and the recognition others give you. By giving yourself and your resources away, you diminish the power of your ego, and those things you once pursued with such passion are no longer so important. When that happens, your wants and desires undergo a conversion of their own. That doesn't mean you cease to enjoy the material abundance that may come to you, but it's no longer important. You are not controlled by it. You neither live for it nor really even need it. Your neighbor can park his new Lexus in full view of your kitchen window, and while you're happy for him and may even elect to drive such an automobile yourself, you are as content in a much more modestly priced automobile. No longer do you need such toys to bring joy or to trumpet your importance to the world. Instead, you are finding your happiness in simplicity and generosity. You know a peace that "is far more wonderful than the human mind can understand" (Phil 4:7). In fact, you are able to echo the words of Saint Paul: "I have learned how to get along happily whether I have much or little. I know how to live on almost nothing or with everything. I have learned the secret of living in every situation, whether it is with a full stomach or empty, with plenty or little" (Phil 4:11-12). You have learned that Jesus' promise is true: "Your Heavenly Father already knows all your needs, and he will give you all you need from day to day if you live for him and make the kingdom of God your primary concern" (Matt 6:32-33).

Giving and getting, getting and giving—this is the rhythm of the world as God has created it. It's fascinating and fun to observe. In fact, there are two waves of happiness that swell over you when you spontaneously and generously give and do both with no strings attached. One is the peace you feel inside at giving to someone or something when there is no expectation you will do so. Then there's joy you feel at watching how God takes your gift and multiplies the return to you. This practice frees you of worry and anxiety. You know God will continue to supply you with everything you need, and such knowledge frees you of materialism even as you enjoy some material items. You also become less bound by the need for the security you once thought your wealth could provide. This is precisely because you have found the real Source of security. You have found the life you've always wanted.

Why is the return multiplied to you when you give? Again, Saint Paul provides the explanation: "God will generously provide all you need. Then you will always have everything you need and plenty left over to share with others" (2 Cor 9:8). Notice that the "plenty left over" is to "share with others." God does not give to you so you can stockpile it. Stockpiling is not the way to find life. To be sure, you should plan for your retirement. I'm not discouraging prudent saving. In fact, I'm saving for my future. But stockpiling is hoarding;

it's seeing how much you can save. It's driven by your fears—fear of the unknown, fear of sickness, or fear of a financial setback. Henri Nouwen once observed, "The two greatest obstacles to faith are anger and greed, and both are motivated by fear."

Stockpiling is an act of an ego that's under the illusion of providing security for you and your family. Wealth can't provide security. Admittedly, it can buy good health care and help you avoid some of the struggles others might experience with downturns in the economy. But wealth can't give you health. It can't shield you from the normal process of aging or protect you from the ominous prospect of dying. What wealth can become, however, is an idol as you trust in it to provide security against the universal issues of life and death that all must face.

I frequently meet people who not only believe their wealth is a reward for their hard work but also have the mistaken notion that they are supposed to see how much they can store away in order that they might have happiness when they retire or plenty to pass on to their children and grandchildren when they die. Scores of these people take exotic cruises around the world, spend winter months in beachside homes, drive luxurious automobiles, and dine in all the finest restaurants, and they are at best aging and dying and doing both as miserable and unhappy people.

The word "miserable" comes from the same root word for miser. There is an obvious connection. Stingy, grasping, miserly people are not only miserable inside but are most often those who inflict misery on others. Many have yet to figure it out. God gives to them so they can give it away. When these decide they want permanent rather than passing happiness, they will choose the pathway of generosity.

There is something else you must know. Transferring to your heirs a fortune they have neither earned nor will likely appreciate or guard with appropriate devotion is not the way of the universe either. While I don't recall the source, I recently read that 85 percent of inherited wealth is squandered within the first five years—that there are more divorces, more family squabbles, and more personal tragedy in people's lives after inheriting money than before.

I'm not telling you not to leave anything to your children and grandchildren. But the question you need to ask of yourself is, "How much should I leave them?"

Self-made millionaire Warren Buffett has the best advice I've ever heard. He recently donated the lion's share of his vast fortune to the Gates Foundation. He suggested you should leave your children "enough money so that they would feel they could do anything, but not so much that they could do nothing."

Why not set up a trust for your children or grandchildren, share with them what they can and should expect from it, and explain that your ambition is to give away the rest of what God has given and will give you before you die? You'll spare them the expense of hiring attorneys and be much more likely to leave the family intact and out of the courts after you're gone. Furthermore, you'll be a much better example to them. They will more likely grow up as generous people themselves.

Ever noticed how frequently the news reports on the Kennedy family? I know they are hardly the only ones, but their family seems to experience more than its share of human tragedy. Or maybe it's simply that they get more press. What I do know is that their family makes the news not only for their tragedy but for their charity. Just last night, my wife Pam and I were watching as Larry King interviewed Bono and Bobby Shriver. Bono is a famous rock star who is himself a model of humility and generosity; Bobby Shriver is the nephew of President Kennedy, brother of the First Lady of California, and son of the Peace Corps founder who also founded the Special Olympics. It's amazing when you think of the heritage of charitable work out of which he has emerged. The two have teamed up to launch a line of products, all in red, from T-shirts to cell phones, called Product Red. By buying these products, consumers help the cause to raise money and bring help, hope, and medicine to the AIDS fight in Africa, where it is estimated that more than 6,500 die every day from complications associated with AIDS. Pam looked at me and asked, "What is it about the Kennedys? You always see them giving of themselves to help other people." I can't help but believe it has something to do with the example of generosity that family has passed down from generation to generation. Before long, it takes on a life of its own.

As you start giving your wealth away, however great or small, don't be surprised to find it coming back to you. It is likely you'll discover just how difficult it is to give it all away before you die. But more importantly, you'll find the life you've always wanted. Filled with intoxicating and infectious joy, you will be happier and healthier than ever. You will give and God will give back to you, and by continuing to give, you keep the cycle going. You will also be a great role model for your children and grandchildren, who then have a better idea of what to do with the windfall that you've left them.

In all the years I've been encouraging people to try living this sort of life, no one has ever returned to me and said, "You know, I took your advice, started giving, and it has bankrupted my life and made me miserable and depressed." To the contrary, the opposite has occurred. Here are the kinds of comments I often receive:

- "This life has liberated me from material things."
- "I have more joy and happiness than ever."
- "The irony is that I have as much or more today than I've ever had in all my life."
- "I get a kick out of giving stuff away and it doesn't matter to me if anybody knows where it's coming from."
- "I have found the purpose of living."
- "I'm free."

When you give up the need for material things and the illusory security it brings, you will, paradoxically, have more of both. It's an inner recognition you know and an inner security you feel.

A few months ago, I met a wealthy man and his wife. In fact, they rank among some of the wealthiest people I've ever known. They're also some of the most generous. When I met them they had already given to their parish approximately 100 acres of land on which their new church was being built. Had they given nothing else, the land alone would have been generous. Land in that part of the country had escalated in value to absurd levels. Developers were paying a premium dollar for any acre of land they could find. This couple could have made several million dollars with the sale of the land. Instead, they gave it to help their church with no strings attached and no expectation of special recognition.

As we talked and discussed their desire to do still more for their faith and their church, I was deeply moved by their boundless generosity and selfless words: "We have been very blessed in life, both materially and spiritually. While we thank God for all we have, we are smart enough to know that we are no more significant or important in the eyes of God than anyone else. We've just been very blessed, and because of that we want nothing more than to be a blessing to God, to others, and to our parish. So we made the decision some time ago to set aside just enough to enable us to live comfortably for the rest of our lives. We also decided to leave to our children and grandchildren just enough to help them on their own paths. With the rest, we want to see how much of it we can give away before we die."

Amazing! What a life they are living and what a role model they are for others! Can you imagine the bliss and happiness that fills their lives every day? The two of them proceeded to tell me that they wanted to give an additional $2,000,000 to help their parish build the new church their growing community desperately needed.

They've found the life few will ever find. Why?

Many people simply will not believe that what God gives is for the purpose of giving it away. As you give it away, God enjoys giving it back to you just so that you can continue to give it away. This is the flow of God's economy.

If you want to find the life you've always wanted, start with changing your mind about yourself, your purpose, your wealth, your work, and your earnings. Jesus said, "It is more blessed to give than to receive." You either know that deeply, live by it, and experience the blessedness that comes with it, or you continue to believe that what you earn is yours to keep and to stockpile for the future. If you choose the latter, in the end, you never figure out what life is all about and never find the life you've always wanted.

So which will it be? Give to get rich? Never, I hope. Give and it will be given to you? It's a paradox to be certain, but true nonetheless. And it's the life you've been looking for.

SUGGESTIONS FOR GIVING, THEN GETTING THE LIFE YOU'VE ALWAYS WANTED

• Gandhi once said, "I believe in equality for everyone except reporters and photographers." I would add to his list most "media ministers." While I come down hard on these television preachers, you must decide for yourself what their motives are. More importantly, start with yourself. What are your motives for giving? Here are some questions you might ask yourself: Why do I give? What really motivates me? A tax deduction? Public recognition? Protection of my reputation? Am I trying to use my gifts to purchase God's favor either for me or someone I love? Discerning your motives is one of the most difficult things to do. But it is the place to begin if you wish to find the life you've always wanted. Giving for any other reason than the joy of giving in response to a need interrupts the divinely designed flow of the universe—receiving and giving . . . giving and receiving.

• Learn to live with paradox. You'll not figure all of life out. You'll enjoy it a whole lot more if you stop trying and start flowing with the world as it is, appreciating its diversity and contradiction. Even your own life and faith is filled with polarity. A. W. Tozer once described the polarities between which a Christian lives:

> *A real Christian is an odd number. He feels supreme love for One whom he has never seen; talks familiarly every day to Someone he cannot see; expects to go to heaven on the virtue of Another; empties himself in order to be filled; admits he is wrong so he can be declared right; goes down in order to get up; is strongest when he is weakest; richest when he is poorest and happiest when he feels the worst. He dies so he can live; forsakes in order to have; gives away so he can keep.*

That is the place where we must live. Don't feel the need to explain everything that appears inexplicable. Appreciate the complexities you find in life, in nature, even in the Bible. Mark Twain used to say, "It ain't those parts of the Bible I can't understand that bother me; it's the parts that I do understand."

The best definition I've ever heard of the Bible was expressed in an acrostic. B. I. B. L. E.—Basic Instructions before Leaving Earth. Whatever platitudes you wish to make about the Bible, the bottom line is that the Bible is simply basic instruction for your short journey on earth. All the accolades you or others may feel compelled to make about it won't do you a thimble's worth of good if you don't read it as a manual for making meaning out of life—your life. Some folks are so afraid that the Bible might appear to contradict itself that their egos drive them to act as if they've been sent to save the Scriptures. So what if the Bible seemingly contradicts itself? Does that mean it's not dependable? Uninspired? Incapable of providing guidance? Not at all. Don't forget that the Bible has been around longer than you have and will be here long after you're forgotten. The Scriptures need no savior. You and I need a savior. Feeling the need to save the Bible says more about our lack of faith in the Savior revealed in the Bible than it does anything else.

Maturity is the capacity to live with these polarities, even to relish in the contradictory. What is expressed in an old English proverb may be life's most wonderful paradox: "The hand that gives gathers." If you act on this law of abundance, you'll order your life by it while standing in awe of its operation in the world. It works.

• Consider how frequently the church dismisses or discounts the stringent demands of discipleship by explaining away Jesus' demands as hyperbole. He said, "So no one can become my disciple without giving up everything for me" (Luke 14:33). Jesus was not merely exaggerating to make a point. Have you given up everything? He does not appear to be mincing his words here. To the contrary, he is clear that being a disciple requires giving up everything. What does "everything" leave out? Feel the tension? The paradox? Don't diminish his demands by using religious rhetoric. He wishes to leave us within the tension. On one hand, he calls us to leave everything and follow him. Then he turns around and tells us to ask for anything and it is ours for the asking (Matt 7:7-11). What does asking for "anything" leave out? This divine tension is intentional and unquestionably paradoxical.

God is infinitely abundant, and in him we are both infinite and abundant. Yet, you and I know there are many people who have no place to sleep at night and little or nothing to eat by day. How, then, can any Christian live in wealth when so many in the world have nothing on which to live? You will have to decide the answer to that question on your own. But I know one thing: as you learn to give more and more of yourself and your resources away, you will become increasingly uninterested in all the material stuff of this life. You'll start finding more joy in giving it away and less satisfaction in seeing how much you can get. You'll experience real contentment through giving, not gathering. Ego will be relegated to the proper place in your life and it will no longer matter to you whether you drive the latest model car or wear the finest clothes. You'll live free of that nonsense. Once you know the freedom generosity brings, you will never go back into slavery to things. André Gide said, "All that you are unable to give possesses you."

• Are you willing to risk believing that it is more blessed to give than to receive? Giving is the secret to finding your purpose in life and the life you've always wanted. As I noted earlier, so much is written these days about finding one's purpose in life. These books and tapes have their place, but there's one truth that, if you get it, will propel you toward a clear understanding of your purpose whether you drive a cab or are the CEO of a *Fortune* 500 company. "You must love the Lord your God with all your heart, all your soul, all your strength, and all your mind. And love your neighbor as yourself" (Luke 10:27). Love God. Love your neighbor. Love yourself. The upward, outward, and inward dimensions of the human experience. In any direction, it boils down to this: give yourself to God, give yourself to others, and give yourself to yourself. This is life's purpose. Your life will be balanced when you live it in this order. Your divine purpose is experienced when you love God, love others, and love yourself. Get it backwards and your life is out of balance and your priorities get mixed and misplaced. No place is that more obvious than when you look at how you spend your money. Your spending patterns reveal the real priorities of your life. If you're not giving much of yourself or your resources away, then it's not rocket science to figure out that the focus of your life is you. It's not surprising, therefore, that you are discontent, feel as if your life has no purpose, and are unhappy. You may have moments of happiness. And as long as you can exercise some control over the happenings of your life, you can arrange those happenings to provide fleeting moments of pleasure and happiness. There's one problem with this: it won't last.

I once heard someone say that "there are those who believe their happiness depends on their happenings happening the way they happen to want their happenings to happen; so they go through life organizing their happenings, believing their happiness depends on their happenings happening the way they happen to want their happenings to happen." Try saying all of that without a slip of the tongue. No one is capable of controlling all of the "happenings" or circumstances of life. Happiness is always fleeting and capable of being interrupted.

Lasting joy does not depend on your outward circumstances—what's going on around you. Joy is an inner contentment found only in the proper ordering of life's priorities. The world's greatest teacher gave us the plan for the proper ordering of priorities and the inner joy that naturally results. It begins with love directed upward toward God, followed by love directed outward toward others, and then love directed inward toward yourself. While it is all simple, it requires a lifetime of discipline to make a reality. But it is a discipline worth exercising—a journey worth making. Should you decide to take this pathway, one day you'll look back and with Robert Frost, you'll say,

> *Two roads diverged in a wood, and I—*
> *I took the one less traveled by,*
> *And that has made all the difference.*

Og Mandino put it like this:

> *Realize that true happiness lies within you. Waste no time*
> *and effort searching for peace and contentment and joy in*
> *the world outside. Remember that there is no happiness in*
> *having or in getting, but only in giving. Reach out. Share.*
> *Smile. Hug. Happiness is a perfume you cannot pour on*
> *others without getting a few drops on yourself.* [3]

• Make a decision today to travel the pathway toward a lifestyle of generosity. Oscar Wilde said, "As the purse is emptied, the heart is filled." Vow to give more of yourself away beginning today. That's all it takes. Little steps at first are all that's necessary. You don't have to become a philanthropist like Bono or Buffet overnight. You can start where you are and with what you have. Someone once said, "If you don't start, you won't arrive." If you're married, begin with your spouse. Can't afford a dozen roses? Buy one and give it to her. It's not the number that matters, but the message. Put the newspaper, magazine, or remote down and invite your spouse to take a walk at sunset. The next time you feel an impulse to give to someone or something important, do it. Don't critique or judge either the recipient's worthiness of your gift or the amount you give. Follow your heart. Don't be concerned if you're thanked or recognized for your benevolence. Do your charity for the sheer joy of doing it. Then pay close attention to how it makes you feel. Relish that feeling, for it's just the beginning of what's to come. With the continual practice of this discipline, it will become the common, inner feeling—while always joyful, it'll manifest itself as a deep sense of peace and contentment. The joy is in the journey, not the destination.

George Eliot said, "It's never too late to be what you might have been." I saw a recent news report that a 100-year-old woman in Florida died and left her vast $35 million fortune to the University of Miami's Diabetes and Research Institute and to the university's Sylvester Comprehensive Cancer Center. Though she had donated her fortune before her death, she refused the request to disclose her generosity publicly until after she had died. While she could have afforded a lavish lifestyle, she chose instead to live frugally in a small condo in south Florida. Later, I'll devote a whole chapter to the question of whether one's charity should be kept private. The point here is that giving with no thought of personal reward or recognition is where the real fun in giving is found.

• Henry David Thoreau once said, "Heaven is under our feet as well as over our heads." If you wish to make the world under your feet a little more like heaven above, remember that you are the one who's in control of your responses to what's happening around you. If someone pulls in front of you today and you have to swerve to avoid a crash, instead of giving the person the finger or yelling profanities, whether demonstratively, to yourself, or in your mind, why not give them a silent blessing? Why not offer a friendly and grateful wave to them that this close encounter didn't get any closer? Or just smile? I know that this may sound goofy, and you may be inclined to dismiss such a suggestion as absurd. So be it. But don't forget that you get what you give. If you give away anger, don't be surprised to find it coming back to you. This is a fundamental law of our universe: "What goes around, comes around." While you may not be able to control what happens to you, you are certainly in control of how you respond to what happens to you. Someone correctly said, "There are no accidents, only interpretations." You choose your responses and you choose the life you wish to live. By choosing to give kindness instead of what you think someone deserves, you'll be making this world a little better and your own life much richer. Just remember, "No act of kindness, no matter how small, is ever wasted" (Aesop).

NOTES

[1] "Bring all the tithes into the storehouse so there will be enough food in my Temple. If you do," says the Lord of Heaven's Armies, "I will open the windows of heaven for you. I will pour out a blessing so great you won't have enough room to take it in! Try it! Put me to the test!"

[2] David Van Biema and Jeff Chu, "Does God Want You to Be Rich?" *Time* (18 September 2006): 48-56.

[3] *A Better Way to Live: Og Mandino's Own Personal Story of Success Featuring 17 Rules to Live By* (Bantam Books, 1990.)

6

MYTH 2

"I CAN'T AFFORD TO GIVE"

The greater danger for most of us is not that our aim is too high and we miss it, but that it is too low and we reach it.

—Michelangelo Buonarroti (1475–1564)

When you argue from your limitations, the only thing you get are your limitations.

—Wayne W. Dyer (1940–)

If there are those who give in order to get rich, there are those at the other extreme who will not give because they feel that if they give, they won't have enough. I frequently hear people say, "I can't afford to give."

Personally, most people I meet have this opinion. They find every possible reason, and many of them good ones, not to give. It takes little to discern why they are afraid. They fear that, if they were to give, there might not be enough left over to meet their own needs or those of their family.

If you listen to their explanations, you'll frequently hear them use the words "what if" to explain the low level of their generosity. The words "what if" mask the fear that gives rise to such questions.

Fear may be the "the greatest obstacle to faith" as Henri Nouwen once observed, but it's also the biggest hurdle when it comes to generosity.

Again, I'm talking about significant giving. There are many people who are token givers—people whose giving is similar to tipping. Tippers are those who give little more thought to what they give than one might give to calculating the tip for a restaurant server. There's low personal involvement. In fact, it's more a culturally conditioned response. Just as a company or union might withhold a few dollars from an employee's paycheck as a payroll deduction donation to charity without the employee's emotional involvement, some people give with little personal involvement or meaning.

A Determined Religious Education Teacher

I once had a religious-education teacher who believed it was her divinely appointed responsibility to teach the children in her class to give. Every Sunday at the close of the instruction period she would say, "Okay, children, it's time to give an offering." With that, she would pass an offering plate. It was a well-worn plate, as I recall. The brass veneer had been rubbed from the surface, and it had more than its share of dinks and scrapes, as though somebody had used it as a Frisbee before putting it to a more sacred use on Sunday.

I came to the class twice before I figured out that, if I did not want to be the only kid who showed up empty-handed, I'd better ask my parents for money. By the third Sunday, I came prepared with loose change in my pocket. This became a regular practice until I was promoted one grade up. My next teacher was not nearly as interested in teaching us to give. In fact, I don't think she ever mentioned it. I have always suspected it was because she was not giving herself.

The discipline of giving was good for my classmates and me. Though it was only loose change and the amounts given were insufficient to relieve any serious suffering, the practice was good and affected me deeply enough that I still remember it today. But the reality is that many children who might have had teachers as I did are now adults, and when an offering plate is passed to them today, they still think of the offering as the loose change in their pocket.

Giving is not something they do with much intentionality or forethought. It may be an impulse when they are emotionally moved, a habit they've developed, or a reputation they are trying to protect. If you were to suggest to these people that they not only plan their giving but plan to give something significantly substantial, they would look at you perplexed, as though you had just asked them to leap from the edge of the Grand Canyon.

Why?

FEAR AND THE RICH FOOL

Fear. Fear assassinates generosity. If you let fear keep you from giving, the life you really want will elude you. No story more aptly demonstrates this than a conversation between Jesus and an unnamed man in the Gospel of Luke. While discussing weighty subjects with his students, Jesus was interrupted (Luke 12:13ff). When I first read the story, I wondered what could have been so important that someone would interrupt Jesus in the middle of a teaching moment. Maybe the intruder was facing a crisis in his life or an emergency that demanded immediate attention. Or perhaps he simply felt an urgency to enlist as one of Jesus' followers.

Apparently, none of this was on his mind.

MONEY

The fact is, he was concerned about how much money he was going to get from his father's estate. I think I've met this guy on more than one occasion. Our society is filled with people jockeying for the coveted position of the favored heir to the estate of a rich relative. When money is your preoccupation, you are ego-driven and you can be quite rude—usually without being aware of it. When you define your worth by your wealth, you are a fearful soul when it is threatened. You are, in fact, the kind of person who is looking for life in all the wrong places.

In Luke 12:13, the man pleads, "Teacher, please tell my brother to divide our father's estate with me." This was neither the first nor the last time family members have stood before a judge to debate the equitable distribution of a deceased relative's estate. For months, the news has been occupied with Anna Nicole Smith and the legal battles she faced over her claim to half the $1.6 billion estate left by her late husband, Texas tycoon Howard Marshall. The two of them met at an adult club where she was a dancer, and they married in 1994, when she was twenty-six and he was eighty-nine. They were together about one year before Marshall died of cancer, leaving no mention of Anna Nicole in his will. For months she battled Marshall's son, Pierce, who had been trying to keep her from inheriting half the estate. Just when it appeared the news reporters would find something or someone else to obsess over, Anna Nicole's son died and, suprisingly, soon thereafter, she did too. Now, it appears the saga will never end as legal battles get more complicated and involve more people fighting over custody of her youngest child and the estate she leaves.

Sadly, many families have a similar story to tell—stories that may not involve such vast fortunes or make the nightly news but are no less significant to those involved. Presumably, Jesus refused to act as an arbitrator. Instead, he told the intruder and everyone standing nearby the story of a rich fool.

I once picked up a contemporary twist on the parable Jesus told. It reads like a story you might find in the financial news section of the New York Times:

> The stocks of a certain rich man did very well. So well, in fact, he thought to himself: "What shall I do? I bought these stocks in an IPO and in just five years they've split more than twice, earning me a vault full of dividends." So he met with his CPA and asked, "What should I do?" Whereupon he was advised, "I recommend you buy more stocks. Besides, if you cash in now you'll get eaten alive with capital gains taxes. Wait a few years until you get closer to retirement and are in a lower tax bracket. Meanwhile, why don't you diversify and invest in real estate? Then you'll be set for

*retirement. You'll be able to eat at exotic restaurants, drink
piña coladas, and take luxury cruises in the Bahamas."*

Sounds familiar, doesn't it?

The story from Luke closes with a scorching indictment: "Fool," said Jesus, "this night your soul will be required of you" (v. 20).

The protagonist in the parable had prepared for everything except the inevitable. Two fears consumed him. He feared the same thing that keeps many from exploring a life of generosity—the fear there might not be enough. It seemed to occupy his every waking moment. And then there was his fear of death.

"Death?" you say. "But he doesn't seem remotely aware that his ultimate demise is but a sunset away."

To the contrary, he was so afraid of dying that he dismissed all thoughts of death, and in that respect he's like most of us. He refused to face the inevitable. Any time the thought of death invaded his consciousness, he immediately drove it out. Like many folks today, he developed the capacity to deny death by delving into his work, career, and immediate concerns about having enough to live out his retirement years comfortably. Fear of deprivation and death led him to pursue greater and greater returns on his investments to the point of obsession.

I was recently browsing a magazine stand in an airport when I picked up a copy of Oprah Winfrey's *O* magazine. In it, Suze Orman, the TV financial coach, was quoted as saying, "Fear is the biggest obstacle to wealth." While I normally agree with much of what Orman says, here she missed it. Rather than being the greatest obstacle to wealth, fear is the biggest motivator to get wealthy. I don't mean the kind of fear you might feel while flying on a commercial airline during an electrical storm and nervously watching as the wings of the plane bounce up and down. This fear is more psychological in nature, and it unconsciously drives much of the wealth-building in our culture.

Fear is the mistress of your ego. Surviving and thriving, producing and accumulating are all the work of your ego. A famous actor once confessed, "The fear of death infused me with the desire to live, and to live harder." Ego is the part of you that will drive you to live harder and work harder because ego is totally into you—with all of your accomplishments and material embellishments that signal to the envious eyes of those around you that you have arrived and they have not, at least not to the level that you have. It is the work of your ego to get you to be preoccupied with possessions because death signals the end of both. Your ego will drive you to strive for such significance and social status in society that you can easily imagine yourself as the subject of the tabloids.

Celebrities may hear the whisper of their ego say something like, "Why, just look at you! You've become so prominent the paparazzi will not leave you alone." While celebrities may resent them on one hand, every time the camera flashes in their face, their ego, on the other hand, smiles at the affirmation of their own self-importance.

But it is not only celebrities who can be ruled by ego and robbed of the life they really want. Ego will motivate a minister to secretly to envy the success of another minister or church and try to copy that success in his or her own church. Ego is the part of you that silently resents those who are successful, gloats over the failures of others, and judges most everyone else as inferior to you. Furthermore, ego believes being a genuine person of faith depends on one's personal performance. Ego cannot accept salvation by grace through faith. The mere idea makes no sense to the ego.

In this respect, not much has changed since the days Saint Paul wrote to the Galatians, "Oh foolish Galatians! What magician has cast an evil spell on you? After starting your Christian lives in the Spirit, why are you now trying to become perfect by your own human effort?" (Gal 2:1-3).

The answer to that one is easy. Ego does not want you to experience the freedom that comes from knowing your acceptance to God is not based on you but on Christ. As long as ego succeeds in controlling your beliefs about this, your ego controls you. Your life, under ego's control, is a constant struggle to win God's approval. Until ego is dethroned, you will not experience the life you've always wanted.

That's not all.

Ego is thoroughly consumed with form: how you look, what you wear, the roles you play, and the titles you hold. Ego will have you spare no expense to be one step ahead of your competition and to look the part. When anything threatens your ego and the worth, wealth, and personal significance it feeds on, your fear will raise its ugly head. Fear will then propel you to grasp at and cling to as much material stuff as possible. This is because your ego has depended on all this stuff for its defining worth even as it perpetuates the illusion that this stuff you're gathering is providing security for your future, protecting you against uncertainties in life, and keeping you safe from the inevitable—death itself.

THE RICH FOOL AND THE WISE RICH

The rich fool was not just an ego-driven, self-centered, or materialistic maniac. Admittedly, he was all of that. But he was not called a fool because he had riches. To the contrary, some of the richest people who have ever lived were anything but fools. We're told, for example, that Solomon was rich, and much of the great wisdom of the Old Testament is attributed to his authorship. Barnabas in the Acts of the Apostles was rich and generous, and the early church called him the Son of Encouragement.

There are many people in our world whom I would describe as the "wise rich." They are both wise and rich because they've discovered the secret God has woven into the fabric of his creation.

Take Ally and Jim. I met them at a quaint seafood restaurant near the beach in south Florida. While much younger than I, the two of them have earned more money in the few years they've been together than most people would earn in a lifetime. He's a successful infectious disease doctor with a clinic the size of a small hospital employing an army of doctors, nurses, and support staff. The two of them are also entrepreneurs with business adventures that include owning several hotels and restaurants across Florida. Their material wealth isn't so obvious when you meet them. They are unpretentious. They live comfortably but modestly, drive new but not luxurious automobiles, and dress nicely but not ostentatiously. In fact, if you met this couple for the first time, you would not guess them to be anything but ordinary people.

Yet they are anything but ordinary. They are not only wealthy; they are generous. They sponsor semiannual mission trips to South America, taking equipment, medicines, and scores of medical personnel with them. Once there, they set up and operate medical clinics that offer free assistance to hundreds of impoverished people. All at their own expense.

They are as equally generous to the people of south Florida. When Hurricane Charlie slammed the coastline in mid-2004, killing many people, injuring many more, and leaving a wake of economic wreckage, this couple was the first to set up and operate a free medical clinic. It became so successful that it drew both the praise of Florida's governor, Jeb Bush, and recognition from his brother, President George W. Bush.

I was meeting this couple for dinner because they wanted to discuss how they might make a large, anonymous gift to their parish, which was entering a badly needed renovation and expansion campaign.

This selfless couple is rich, but they were not made fools by their riches. They are among the few who are both wise and rich. They have learned the divine secret that most people will live and die without learning: God gives to those he knows will just as quickly give it away.

Want proof of this? Then recall Jesus' parable of the talents in Matthew 25 and what the reward was for those who managed well the talents that were given to them. They were given more talents. This is a universal principle at work in the world.

Take time as an example. Those who manage time well find they have more time. It's not that their day becomes longer than anyone else's. That won't happen for anybody. But these people always seem to get more accomplished during twenty-four hours than almost anyone else does.

Think of your talents—and, yes, even your money—as gifts and opportunities. If you invest your talents and gifts, God gives additional talents and gifts. If you seize the opportunities to give yourself away, God gives you more of the same—more talents, more opportunities, more gifts. This secret applies to money as well. God returns it to those who give it away. Those who've learned this are those you'll often hear say, "I can't seem to out-give God."

If you interrupt this divinely designed system as the rich fool did and you're interested only in seeing how much you can accumulate for yourself, you miss the secret and its reward. You might be successful in getting rich monetarily, but the life you've always wanted will keep disappearing over the horizon. Certainly, you'll have moments of pleasure, but that momentary pleasure will have no enduring power. You'll succeed in becoming a contemporary rich fool.

But for those who invest what they are given in worthwhile kingdom causes and in those who have need, God will find a way give it back to them. As they keep giving it away, God will keep giving it back. This is the secret to abundant and meaningful living. You will always have what you need as you generously respond to needs God brings to you. If you're wise enough to figure this out and practice it as a lifestyle, you'll soon discover there is no greater happiness than the joy you feel when you flow with the divine principle regarding the time, talents, and treasures of your life.

While most of the rich are fools, having riches doesn't make you a fool. If you are rich, you'll find it isn't easy to keep from becoming a fool. The good new is that it's possible. The rich fool was called a fool only because he never figured out life's secret. If you'll read again the story, you'll notice the number of times the first-person personal pronouns "I" and "my" are used. This will clearly reveal to you his problem. His "I's" were too close together. His ego saw himself as separate from everything and everyone else. This illusion of separateness contributed to his foolishness.

In truth, we all come from the same source. As long as you see yourself as separate from others, you'll feel like you're in competition with everyone around you and that you must scramble to get what you think is rightfully yours before someone else gets it. This is why giving anything away is the last thing on most minds today. It is especially true for those who are rich and those who desire to be rich for the sake of riches. Such folks are preoccupied with profits, possessions, and the power that comes with them.

The strata of society provide abundant examples of how the drive for riches separates people. For example, I see almost daily the distinction made on commercial airlines between first-class passengers and those seated in coach. Most passengers who fly in first class with any regularity are doing so only because of the frequent-flyer programs airlines started several years ago to reward customer loyalty. Few are there because they have purchased a first-class fare. As I noted in a previous chapter, I know because I'm one of those whose frequent-flyer status often awards me the opportunity to sit up front where the seats are wider and the leg space greater. But observe the attitudes and behaviors of many first-class flyers, and you'll quickly get the impression these passengers are in first class because they think they are superior to ordinary flyers who must sit in coach. Indeed, they are even separate from each other as they compete to see who among them can board first. It's as if they entertain some illusion that to board first makes them superior to other first-class flyers. I know this is true because I, too, have felt smug and superior at times as I've taken my seat in the forward section of the plane.

If ego is "edging God out," it reflects itself most clearly by "edging giving out." That is, ego is rarely benevolent. Give up your first-class seat to some older passenger who can barely make it down the narrow aisle to his or her middle seat near the rear of the plane? Why, it would never occur to ego to do such a thing.

The rich fool is an average guy, much like some of the people you know. In fact, you and I can be like him if we are not cautious. Ego thrives on your fear, too—your fear that you don't have enough or won't have enough or that you are not being recognized for the exceptionally worthy and superior person you are.

"I'm one of your elite flyers," I heard a passenger say to a gate agent. "What do you mean I didn't get an upgrade to first class?"

"Sir, I don't know why you didn't," the agent replied. "I do know you are one of our most loyal customers and we certainly appreciate your business. But I'm sorry, first class has checked in full."

"I don't give a #$%$# how sorry you are. I demand to speak with your superior. I want my seat in first class."

If you've flown much, you've witnessed a similar conversation between a passenger whose ego has been offended and an airline check-in agent who probably couldn't care less about frequent flier status.

Yet it was fear that set off the complaining passenger. Fear edges out any benevolence, whether that's a benevolent personality or a generous pocketbook. Fear edges God out, and when you lose faith in God, you are anything but generous. In fact, when you are driven by your worries and fears, the only thing that makes sense to you is to do what you must do to protect yourself and your stuff and to accumulate more stuff while you've got half a chance.

The first thing I did after the hijackers crashed planes into the World Trade Center on September 11, 2001, was to go out and buy a hand gun. I look back on that with amusement and a little embarrassment. I was too oblivious at the time to see that my actions were driven by fear—the feelings of insecurity, vulnerability, and the need for self-protection my ego had created in me.

Our materialism and pursuit of wealth is often subconsciously masked by our fears. In fact, we tell ourselves that those who pursue wealth are wise. We admire and enviously applaud them as if they are the only ones acting with reason and common sense in our society. The opposite is more likely the truth.

On a recent newspaper front page, for example, was a picture of *Forbes* Top 10 Richest People in the World. Their combined wealth is higher than the Gross National Product in many countries of the world. I read with amazement as I wondered how long it had been since I saw any newspaper print an article featuring the ten most generous people in the world. I doubt they ever have, and I suppose I shouldn't expect them to—because that's not what sells papers. Our culture lauds and applauds the rich. They alone have managed to get to that enviable place in life where they are free of dependence on anything and anyone—including God for many of them. At least they think so. And that is the real danger of being or becoming rich.

God likes it when we need him. He enjoys when we recognize our dependence on him. But the rich fool trusted in himself—his own creativity and ingenuity. He depended on himself and his wealth to provide security in his life. So Jesus concluded, "a person is a fool to store up earthly wealth but not have a rich relationship with God" (v. 21).

What is a rich relationship with God? It's one into which you invest your time, your trust, and, yes, even your treasure. That's why the happiest people in the world are those who live in total trust and dependence on God. You'll never find the life you've really wanted when your trust or confidence is in anything other than God. This is precisely because you'll never have enough to feel safe and secure. Before long, nothing will hold at bay the feelings of fear that rob you of inner peace and happiness. Neither a handgun nor a bulging bank account will suffice.

In fact, the irony is that the more you have, the more insecure you are likely to feel. Take as an example our society's propensity to wage war. We have the richest and largest arsenal of weaponry in human history. But one little bearded and elusive Osama somewhere in the Middle East can strike fear in the bravest. The pursuit of weaponry to protect our interests (which are mostly our wealth and our lifestyles) is silly, self-serving, and counterproductive. How many weapons must we stockpile to quell our fears? The irony is that the greater our arsenal, the greater our fear. The more guns we bear, the more ghosts we fear. Or, as the old proverb puts it, "If you choose to wage war, better dig two graves."

It is the same irony with the money we stockpile in savings accounts and investments. You may enjoy a temporary feeling of security as you "eat, drink, and be merry," thinking you have enough for every situation you might face. But, eventually, some unantici-pated reality will hit you. You will meet someone who appears to be a little more secure than you are or who has earned and saved more than you have. Your ego will make you feel tinges of envy, but, dis-guised as need, ego will drive you to pursue what's missing in your life and get you back to that place where you are at least on equal footing and, preferably, a step or two ahead. It is an endless and vicious spiral that robs you of the peace, the contentment, and the real security you seek.

If it isn't your own health that breaks, someone close to you may unexpectedly suffer a massive coronary. And, unlike you, he exercised daily and ate all the right foods, which leaves you feeling all the more vulnerable and insecure. Suddenly, something else is missing. So you resolve to take better care of yourself. The cycle of fear and madness starts all over again. You decide you must get in shape. You invest in the latest diet craze, buy the most advanced athletic equipment, and, of course, charge your financial advisor to improve on your investment returns, too. After all, you just never know what might happen.

"One must always be prepared for the unexpected," you tell yourself. It all sounds rational and sane. But the reality is, you're living insanely. What you really want in life eludes you. You're afraid and don't even know it. Fear masked as ambition and the desire to get ahead has fooled you. In fact, you have become the rich fool yourself. "Do I have enough health insurance . . . life insurance . . . fire and casualty?" "Have I saved enough for my retirement?" "What if I got cancer or a protracted illness resulted in medical expenses beyond my ability to pay?" "What if there is another hurricane next season and we lose our home?" Behind these questions stands one reality as tall as the Twin Towers once stood—fear.

What are you afraid of?

Following his encounter with the intruder and the subsequent story of the rich fool, Jesus turned to his followers and introduced them to the twin sister of fear—worry.

WORRY— FEAR'S TWIN SISTER

Worry is fear's twin sister. But don't picture worry as some neurotic person pacing the floor of a psychiatric ward anxiously wringing his hands over some imagined monster lurking in the darkness. Instead, picture a normal man going about his life in a natural fashion. Picture the guy who for all practical purposes could be your next-door neighbor. Or, better yet, picture yourself.

The Greek word for worry is merimna. In its root form, it is simply the picture of a person whose mind is distracted and divided. It is the picture of today's successful person.

When I was a child, I remember my parents taking me to the Ringling Bros. and Barnum & Bailey Circus. Next to the flying trapeze artists, my favorite part of the circus occurred when the lions and the lion tamer entered the ring. Armed with a six-shooter at his side, a whip in one hand, and a four-legged chair in the other, the lion tamer would prance around with reckless confidence snapping the whip and barking out commands as the lions roared in defiance but obeyed nonetheless.

On occasion, a lion would challenge the tamer as if he were preparing to attack him. Immediately, the lion tamer would hoist his four-legged stool squarely into the face of the lion and, almost like magic, the lion would freeze and become paralyzed. I learned later that the lion was attempting to focus on each of the four legs of the stool at once, causing the great beast to become disoriented, distracted, and divided.

Sound like anyone you know? When you try to make too many priorities the priority, you are paralyzed. If your mind is divided and distracted by so many demands, concerns, and worries, you should hardly expect to find the life you really want. You will not even be sure what kind of life you'd like to have.

Here's a sobering thought someone once shared with me: "If you knew who he was who walks with you on your daily journey, worry would be impossible." This means our worries not only divide our minds but reveal the bankruptcy of our hearts.

What worries distract you?

FOOD AND FASHION

As if opening a curtain on a stage, Jesus demonstrated the many roles worry plays. One by one, he removed the masks that conceal the faces of worry. "So I tell you, don't worry about everyday life—whether you have enough food to eat or clothes to wear" (v. 25).

There are the first two: food to eat and clothes to wear. Granted, most of us don't worry about the origin of our next plate of food.

But we do worry about the food on our plates. Am I eating too much? The wrong kind of food? Is it organic or not? Healthy or unhealthy? High in calories? Too many carbs? Laced with preservatives? We are distracted by food, are we not?

Then there is fashion. Our clothes—how we look and what we wear. What others will think about what we're wearing. Have you ever thought about how long you stand in front of the mirror every morning and evaluate your appearance? We are worried about what we wear. But usually, we are completely unaware that our obsession with fashion is often motivated by worry and fear of rejection.

FITNESS

It isn't just food and fashion. It is also our lives we worry about. In Matthew's account, Jesus said, "Do not worry about your life" (Matt 6:25), and later he says, "Do not worry about tomorrow" (Matt 6:34). But we do. We worry about life—about whether we're physically fit, how we look, whether we're physically in shape or out of shape, whether we are attractive or unattractive, and whether we look our age or younger than our age.

What is behind the billion-dollar cosmetic industry and the growing interest in cosmetic surgery? Isn't much of the growth of those industries propelled by worry over our aging bodies? Of course. Many facelifts, tummy tucks, breast augmentations, and dental and hair implants are nothing more than expressions of our worry gone haywire.

But what's interesting is how our culture shrouds these preoccupations with food, fashion, and fitness. American culture and the food, fitness, and fashion industries that market their products have made our obsessions over these things seem normal. This masks the reality that our preoccupations with these areas of life stem from worry and anxiety. The other thing our society does not tell you is that worry is the flip side of fear. Fear is the opposite of faith. And the two make fools of us all.

This whole enterprise is a sign of our culture's spiritual condition. Just as our bank accounts are getting fatter, our spirits are getting leaner. All of this is symptomatic of a spiritually sick society.

Your spiritual health is always in jeopardy when worry and fear dominate your heart. Worse still, you cannot find the life you want when the focus of life is your obsession over food, fitness, fashion, and the future.

FUTURE

The future is yet another of the more common worries Jesus pointed out. As if you don't have enough to worry about already, try the future on for size. There's plenty to fill the few gaps in your daily thoughts and give you nightmares while you sleep.

How about worry over aging . . . getting sick . . . going to war . . . being attacked by terrorists? How about worry over the rumors that the company may merge and you'll be without a job, or, God forbid, how about worry over something horrible happening to one of your children?

FINANCES

Oh, and don't forget your pocketbook. Or the stock market. Talk about an uncertain future. "What if inflation outperforms my stocks?" "What if I don't have enough for my retirement?" Worry over finances brings you right back to that place where you started. Since you worry about the future, your finances will have to figure into the equation somewhere.

"Will I have enough?" "What if I have to care for my aging and penniless parents?" "What if the stock market crashes again?" "What if I become disabled and can't make the mortgage payment?" "What if I have too much debt, can't pay my bills, and creditors swarm around me like vultures?"

Questions that begin with the words "What if . . ." unleash your imagination to explore all of the uncertainties of the future and distract and disorient you all the more. Is it any wonder there are so many unhappy, unfulfilled people who never seem to find life? But real life will always escape you when you're distracted and driven by worry and fear. One sage of old observed, "Having lost hope of ever returning to the source of everything, the average man seeks solace in his selfishness." Greed can be fear and anxiety masked as the American Dream.

ANTIDOTE TO FEAR AND WORRY

What's the answer? How can you find peace and happiness—the life you've always wanted—when so much seems to be conspiring against you?

On the heels of Jesus' catalogue of worries, it is noteworthy that he turned once again to his followers and said the following:

> *So don't be afraid, little flock. For it gives your Father great happiness to give you the kingdom. Sell what you have and give to those in need. This will store up treasure for you in heaven. And the purses of heaven have no holes in them. Your treasure will be safe—no thief can steal it and no moth can destroy it. Wherever your treasure is, there your heart and thoughts will also be. (Luke 12:32-34)*

You're not surprised by his counsel, are you? The antidote to fear and its twin sister worry is to give. "So don't be afraid . . . give to those in need."

Your ego will question everything about this simple solution to the spiritual problem of your life. It seems so unlikely that the antidote to fear and worry is giving. But that is plainly what Jesus said.

As noted earlier in this chapter, our culture has programmed us to believe the antidote to worry and fear is more money, the stuff money can buy, and the illusion of security both might provide. But not according to the greatest teacher who ever lived. He said the antidote to fear and worry is the inner peace that is your reward for the generous practice of giving.

This you must learn if you wish to get to that place of knowing—if you wish to find the life you've always wanted. Our infinitely abundant God has an infinitely abundant supply of all things to bring fulfillment and abundance to your life. Furthermore, he is more than willing to give you whatever is good, wholesome, and enriching, and he is willing to give it to you in abundant quantities.

In fact, Jesus insisted it gives God great joy to give to you and me. The one condition is that you give it away. If you don't, you stop the flow. And when you interrupt his way of doing things, you might get the stuff you want, but it will be at your own doing, and nothing is more exhausting and unfulfilling.

If you wish to experience real life, you must come to a place of inner knowing—that place where you know this abundant Spirit is at work to give you everything you need. You must know that. Believe it. Or at least act like you believe it even if you don't at first.

It starts with believing. Then, as you practice believing, you'll begin to know it internally. It's in the knowing that the living takes place.

Believing and knowing are two different things. To believe something is to behave as if it is true. I believe in electricity. I can't see it or touch it, but I believe in it because, when I flip the switch, light comes on in my room. I have believed it long enough that I don't have to think about it anymore. I behave in ways that demonstrate my knowing. When I walk into the dark house, I don't think about it. Instead, I instinctively reach for the light switch and turn on the lights. I know there is electricity somewhere in the lines connected to that switch. In fact, I am so certain of this that if the switch for the light does not produce instant light when turned on, I am more prone to think the bulb has burned out—not that electricity is an illusion and really does not exist.

In my own life, I'm somewhere between believing that God is infinitely abundant and more than willing to give me everything I need and actually knowing that. I'm not to the point yet that I never doubt it. But it is so liberating to be moving toward that place in my life where I just know, without ever questioning or doubting again, that God is here to provide everything I need and that whatever I need will show up when it needs to show up to provide for me.

Trusting in God's provision goes hand in hand with giving that provision away. You must believe not only that this infinitely abundant God is more than willing to provide everything you need but also that God anticipates you will take what he supplies and give it away. Of course I do not mean all of it. You must live, too. But I do mean far more than you are currently giving.

God gives you the capacity to know and love him and to know what you should give away. This is the miracle of grace and faith, both of which come from him. In return, God wants your love. He wants you to give yourself to him and he wants you to give yourself to others. This is the way to peace—to the life you've always wanted.

You might be wondering, "How will I know to whom or to what I should give?" Start with your family. Give to that place where you receive your spiritual instruction and to those who need you. In addition to your love and time, give yourself and your resources away at every opportunity when God prompts you.

Follow your heart. Act on the Spirit's prompting and trust your intuitions. If you feel at peace as you begin to act on the prompting of the Holy Spirit, then you will know that you are living in concert with the spirit of generosity.

Most surprisingly, you'll discover that you are never without what you need. You will have all the abundance you want but you will not be possessed by that abundance. Nor will you worry about it anymore. You will use things and love people, not the other way around.

At that place of knowing, you'll experience happiness and free-dom from worry and fear. You'll get glimpses of this joy in your early days of believing, but not complete freedom. This is because, just as quickly as you have believed and felt freedom from anxiety and worry, something will likely happen that will cause you to doubt again. When that happens, those feelings of peace will be subjugated by worry.

Don't judge yourself. Instead, as soon as you are aware, gratefully acknowledge that you are still learning to live in complete faith in our incredibly generous God and that, while you may make two steps forward, sometimes you will invariably take a step or two back. It's all part of your spiritual maturation. This, too, can be fulfilling, however, if you'll give up the self-recrimination.

In time, it will become increasingly easy to believe and to be free of doubt and the worry that follows. As you get more proficient at believing and trusting, what you believe will gradually become what you know. And once you know deep within your soul that God gets what he wants by giving you what you need and want, all worry and anxiety will gradually disappear. You will experience contentment, pleasure, peace. You will have freedom from worry and fear as your inner knowing grows with the exercise of a believing heart. You will become a complete person. You will find life that few ever find.

Janice L. was recently speaking to a group where I was present. She described the greatest gift her parents ever gave her. Janice's father was a minister with a remarkable gift for starting new churches. That was his life and ministry until the day of his death. Because he served only small churches, he never earned much money. Yet they made it a practice every year to try to step up their giving at least one percentage point. By the time Janice went off to college, her parents were giving away 33 percent of their yearly income.

Janice said, "When I would tell people that, they would say, 'That's absurd!'"

From the perspective of our culture, it is. But Janice's parents enjoyed giving. While they never had a lot of material stuff in this life, it is likely because they chose to give it away and to live simply and modestly. Janice explained that they had a profound sense of joy, contentment, and freedom. They never once worried about where and how they would make ends meet. In fact, she explained, "They always had more than enough for every need and all the material stuff of this life they ever wanted."

Janice then made this probing observation: "My parents taught me that, when it comes to giving, you don't have to be cautious with God." Faith in God's provision will overcome any fear of deprivation. You would never have heard Janice's parents say, "If I give, there may not be enough."

Fear enslaves you to stuff. Faith frees you to share. And as you do, you become both happier and more content. You become one of the few who finds the life you've always wanted.

SUGGESTIONS FOR GIVING, THEN GETTING THE LIFE YOU'VE ALWAYS WANTED

• Where did you learn to give? Generosity is not automatic. No one is born generous. Instead, generosity is learned and cultivated. There may be people who have a personality prone to generosity. But the kind of giving I am describing in this book goes far beyond a charitable disposition or an occasional act of benevolence. I am describing a radical lifestyle. Aristotle said, "We are what we repeatedly do." Giving, then, is not an occasional activity but a habit you develop.

• The kind of giving I am writing about is both planned and spontaneous. Planned charity requires you to look at your income, lifestyle, and priorities and ask hard questions: What should I give? How much should I give? Where should I give?

Spontaneous charity is more random and impulsive. For example, I was recently filling my car at a gasoline station when a rough-looking fellow approached me.

"Could you spare a dollar?" he asked. "I'm hungry."

I don't know how you react in similar circumstances, but I find myself often slipping into old patterns of judgment clothed with criticism. "Go get a job!" "Leave me alone!" "Quit being a victim, for God's sake, and take charge of your life!" Ever had thoughts like this toward those who have approached you with an outstretched hand?

I paused a moment to give myself time to divorce those thoughts. Then I said, "Sure." Reaching for my wallet, I impulsively passed the ones, fives, and tens, and took the only twenty-dollar bill I had and handed it to him. He was surprised. And so was I. I had not intended to do that. After all, he only asked for a dollar. But the twenty just felt like the right thing to do.

As he turned to walk toward the service station, he said in a tone of voice that clearly unmasked his surprise, "God bless you!"

You may disagree with this kind of charity. There was a time in my life when I would have, too. I don't anymore. After all, he seemed to need the money and I needed to follow my heart. Besides this, I believe it's the seemingly little and insignificant things we do that make the greatest difference in the world, even if we never know it in this life. It was Gandhi who said that most of what you'll do in life will seem insignificant, but it's important to do it anyway.

"Wait a minute," you say. "How do you know he didn't take that twenty and buy a drink or, worse, illegal drugs?"

I don't. He may have. But I'm trying to quit judging others and second-guessing the motives of people. Trying to determine whether someone deserves my benevolence is exhausting and takes all joy out of living and giving.

Besides, think about this for a moment. Who among us deserves God's benevolence and grace? Of all the material and nonmaterial blessings he gives us, who among us has always used those gifts in ways proper and wholesome? Yet he gives it to us, anyway. If I'm going to err, I wish to err on the side of generosity. It's a whole lot more fun and certainly more fulfilling.

• How would you describe your giving? Impulsive? Planned? Spontaneous? Guarded? Like tipping a waiter or waitress after a meal? Are you one of those who cannot bring yourself to give because you're fearful there might not be enough for your needs and those of your family? Or are you actually one of the few who is asking God to give you faith to believe him when he says, "Give and it will be given unto you"? Are you learning to focus less on accumulation and self-preservation? To be less ego-driven, self-absorbed, and primarily interested in making and saving money and, instead, more interested in giving your money away? These are probing questions that will help you get at the heart of your own values and priorities as reflected in your earning and spending patterns and your gifts to charity.

You may find that none of what I'm saying in this book makes much sense because your financial life is in shambles. You may be on the verge of bankruptcy or seeking legal counsel to find solace from the creditors who are knocking at your door.

"I'm drowning in debt," one desperate man said to me after a speech I gave. "How can I possibly think about giving when I need to be on the receiving end?"

There's a financial crisis faced by scores of people in this country to be sure—greater by far than most even realize. A recent statistic in a finance magazine suggested that many Americans now owe at least $9,000 to credit card companies alone. That's bad enough, but I know a young woman who owes more than $90,000 to six different credit card companies. If you were to make minimum monthly payments on just $9,000, it would take more than forty years to pay it off. Doug Larson said, "What some people mistake for the high cost of living is really the cost of living high."

If this in any way describes you, what should you do?

1. Accept the fact that you need some help. You are not alone. It's been a problem many have had for a long time. Remember the story Jesus told of the son who took his inheritance, frivolously spent it, and found himself in a financial condition from which he could not recover? The story is found in Luke 15. Before he could get help from his father, he had to swallow his pride, decide he wasn't going to live that way any longer, and seek help. If you are willing to do something similar, God will help you find a way to recover.

2. Get into a program like Dave Ramsey's *Total Money Makeover*. There are many such programs around, although this one may be the most popular today. You can find the program at his website, www.daveramsey.com. He is its creator. At one time, Dave was himself in a financial mess. But he took charge of his life and got the help he needed. Today, Dave Ramsey is a successful counselor offering practical, no-nonsense help in his popular, sold-out seminars held all over America. A money makeover is likely what you need more than anything else. This kind of program will give you practical guidance in dealing with the principal culprit in your financial crisis—you. With few exceptions, most people get into financial difficulty not because of things that have happened beyond their control (loss of a job, a costly medical condition) but because they mismanage the things that are within their control (frivolous, uncontrolled spending, living beyond their means, the abuse of credit cards). How you spend your money is a spiritual barometer. If you

are willing, what your financial condition may reveal to you is the spiritual emptiness in your life. You can change, but the road to recovery will not be easy. You must be disciplined and determined to get your financial house in order.

3. It might be best to seek the professional help of a financial advisor. But be cautious here. Just as there are unscrupulous lending institutions that will offer credit and make loans to virtually anyone in an effort to earn the highest interest allowed by law, there are financial advisors who do not have your best interests at heart or simply do not know how to help you. Avoid debt consolidation companies or debt and credit repair companies. Most of them will be of little help and may even make your financial situation worse. Run from any person or company that offers you a quick fix. Getting out of your financial condition will take a lot longer and a lot more effort than it's taken to get into it. It will take self-discipline, hard work, and a significant amount of time, depending upon its severity. But remember what I heard someone once say, "Infinite patience will produce immediate results." Be patient. Be smart. Pick yourself up and stop putting yourself down. (At Dave Ramsey's website, click on "Financial Counseling." There you can enter your state of residence and find a listing of reputable financial counselors to whom you may wish to turn.)

4. Don't dismiss the principles in this book as untrue simply because your financial mess makes it impossible for you to see the forest for the trees. The principles in this book work. Even in your current adverse financial state, you could start making small changes in your lifestyle by giving yourself to God and to others. As God may prompt you, give small gifts of financial charity to something or someone in greater need than you. First and foremost, those changes will help you change the way you feel about yourself. That is a significant part of your recovery from financial woes. Also, the small steps you take will lead you to make greater strides toward financial freedom and a life of generous living—the life you really want. Your current financial condition was precipitated because you, like scores

of others, bought the big lie that our culture promotes and about which I wrote in the first chapter. You now know what you believed is not so. It's important that you believe and know that you can experience financial freedom. You can become a generous giver. It may take you a little longer than someone whose financial condition is not as enslaving as yours, but you can make it if you plan your work toward financial freedom and work your plan.

• The pathway to the life you've always wanted is paved with generosity. That is the plain truth. You can choose to live as I did and most people do, absorbed in getting all the material stuff of this life and pursuing all the symbols of status. But in the end, you'll feel empty and lost. Like me, you'll find yourself buying the latest self-help books on how to find purpose and happiness precisely because you have neither. You'll absorb audios of popular authors and self-help gurus who promise to give you the latest formula for cultivating what's missing in your life.

This is not a judgment but an honest observation. I've written this book to remind you that, for all the insights you will find on the self-help shelves in bookstores, you will find purpose, peace, and contentment when you start doing one thing—giving yourself away, first to God and then to others. That giving is not exclusively monetary, but will involve your money and possessions as well as your time, your conversations, and your life. In fact, I'm suggesting you start with your money. Give your money to the causes in which you believe. Share your possessions with any needy person whom God might bring across the path of your life and prompt you to help.

You are reading me correctly. Let the giving of your money be the place you start. Everything else about your life will start falling into its proper place. Jesus said, "Wherever your treasure is, there your heart and thoughts will also be" (Matt 6:21). Do you want your heart and thoughts to be more on God? Then start giving your treasures away. Want to be a better spouse and parent and give more of yourself and your time to those you love? Then give your treasures to those whom God brings to you who have needs. It's not complicated. Your life will change for the better in every other aspect if you start with your checkbook and your pocketbook.

I often remind people when I speak across the country, "Giving money to the religious organization or charity you believe in is like putting money into a bank. The more you put in it, the more your interest grows." The pun is intended.

The life I'm describing will be discovered when you get on this path of giving. When Jesus said, "It is more blessed to give," he was either right or wrong. I know he was right. What I know may seem unbelievable to you, but I hope you'll risk believing it. It takes but a little trust on your part to get you started. It will take but one or two experiences of giving to convince you that this is the path you want to follow.

Are you willing to trust that Jesus is telling you an eternal truth? Even if you have doubts about what he said?

This morning, I returned a rental car to the Dallas-Fort Worth Airport. It was a short drive to the rental lot, and I thought for sure I knew the shortest route. I reached for the Never-Lost system, nevertheless, and pressed the computer selection for directions to the rental car location. Within seconds a voice instructed me to "proceed to the highlighted route." But the directions seemed unfamiliar and bizarre, since I've returned cars to this rental car lot dozens of times. The suggested route seemed it would take me way out of the way even though I had selected the "shortest travel time" option. I doubted the directions' accuracy, even questioning out loud as if the voice of instruction would engage me in a debate.

"Where are you taking me? This can't be the right way!" I almost dismissed the instructions as unreliable and followed the route that was familiar to me. After all, my flight was leaving soon. I had little time to spare traveling in the wrong direction.

On an impulse, however, I chose to risk that the directions might be right. In the end, they were. As a matter of fact, I saved a good ten minutes in travel time by trusting and traveling a route that defied my logic.

I realize many of you have doubts about some or all of the suggestions I have been making. Will you risk believing, however, that they might be right? The pathway to the life you've always wanted begins at the moment you start giving—generously and spontaneously. It's your decision.

• Charles Schulz once quipped, "Don't worry about the world coming to an end today. It's already tomorrow in Australia. The Buddhists have a saying made popular by Shantideva: "If you can solve your problem, why worry? If you cannot solve it, what's the use of worrying?" Good logic. Either way, worry is counterproductive.

Again, worry and fear are two sides of the same coin. Jesus identified the preoccupations of our lives that give rise to our worries—the foods we eat or refuse to eat, the fashions we wear, the fitness of our bodies, the future, and, of course, our finances. Any of these preoccupations has the capacity to draw your focus away from that which could free you from worry and anxiety—namely, the giving of yourself to the kingdom of God. Jesus promised, "And he will give you all you need from day to day if you live for him and make the kingdom of God your primary concern" (Matt 6:33).

Tell me what "he will give you all you need" leaves out. Can you think of anything? But the promise is conditional. Living for him is giving yourself to him and making the kingdom of God the central focus of your life. Until you do that, you will not find the life you've always wanted.

Maybe you're asking, "What's the kingdom of God?" Admittedly, it's difficult to comprehend, harder still to explain. I'm not sure the most brilliant theologians have the capacity to plumb the depths of its meaning. What I do know is that Jesus was not referring to the church. You can be in the church but far from his kingdom.

I believe the kingdom is within you. It is that place we all aspire to attain—the place of perfect peace, joy, happiness, and complete surrender to God's presence and his will in life. When the kingdom of God, often referred to as the kingdom of heaven, is the primary focus of your life, you are living the life you've always wanted. The stressors people obsess over every day will no longer cause you inner turmoil. You will be free and at peace.

The irony is that when you have ceased stressing over food, you are enjoying it more and in moderation. Weight issues can be overcome because you're no longer using food to comfort yourself or to calm a nervous and ill-at-ease mind.

Your appearance will be far less important to you than your purpose, which is to pursue God's kingdom. You will find yourself taking better care of yourself. Exercising will not be something you stress over for doing too infrequently. Instead, you'll do it as often and as regularly as you can. The aging process will no longer be something you obsess over even though it's one of the ways nature reminds you that you're dying. When you get to this place of living the life you've always wanted, you are much more capable of accepting life as it is with all of its wonder and amazement. Sure, you might seek a facelift, a tummy tuck, or buy the latest hair-growth formula, but you no longer seek these things to help you hide yourself from the fact that part of what it means to be living is that you are both aging and dying.

I once heard Paul Harvey tell of a man he knew who had his dentist put braces on his already straight teeth so he would look younger. Stress-reducing formulas and pharmaceuticals that stimulate sexual prowess may have their place. But their popularity is driven by our culture's preoccupations with the external form—the physical body—and a greed that wants to exploit the fear of aging and dying for profit.

Within the person who has found the meaning of life, however, lies a quiet acceptance of what is. You become a worry-free person who can appreciate every stage of life. You find that the miracle of living and aging stirs awe instead of striking anxiety. When you are living the life you've always wanted, all of your life is beautiful, for you are learning that all of life, its ups and downs, hills and valleys, successes and setbacks are all part of the divine plan for your life.

You view the future with hope and optimism. You are no longer worried about what tomorrow holds because you are absorbed in living today. You have no time to be concerned about stuff that may or may not happen tomorrow. Though the philosopher Montaigne said, "My life has been filled with terrible misfortune, most of which has never happened," you don't waste your time worrying about the imaginary and fictitious.

I have on my desk a stuffed piranha fish that a friend once brought me after visiting South America and the region around the Amazon. She found it in a souvenir shop. Although it has been many years since she gave it to me, I've never forgotten what she said as I stared at the stuffed flesh-eating fish with sharp, protruding teeth. "Piranhas are threatening only when they attack you in schools. Anybody can handle one piranha at a time," she observed.

One day at a time is how you handle life when you are living the life you've always wanted. You live in this moment—what Eckhart Tolle calls "the power of now."1 You know that worry over tomorrow only robs you of today's joy. You meet each day as a welcomed challenge and an opportunity to fulfill your primary concern—kingdom living. Death begins to lose its grip over your mind and life. In fact, for you, death has died. You know the kingdom of God has no end and that the heaven you are experiencing here on earth is but a prelude of the eternal kingdom you will one day enjoy. People who go through life without ever discovering the secrets in this book suffer death every day.

When you discover the life you've always wanted, there's no more fretting over finances, either. You have committed your financial life to God and your lifestyle is now devoted to giving your resources away. Your giving is both planned and spontaneous. You think through and pray about your giving and about those causes into which you should invest kingdom resources. Your giving is generous. You always have plenty to give because you are discovering more and more each day that you really cannot out-give God. As you give, he gives to you and the cycle keeps repeating itself. Someone has correctly called this the miracle of miracles: What you give away comes back to you.

Your giving will also be spontaneous. You will find that God brings people to you just so you can give something to them—your love and acceptance, a word of encouragement, a gesture of kindness, or the $20 bill in your wallet. No judgment. No lectures. You'll just give yourself, your time, your conversation, your presence, and, yes, sometimes your money. You'll know what to do. God will inspire you. Others may look at you perplexed. But you'll just be living your purpose and what they may think will be of no concern to you. You will be having fun, living your own life, and enjoying the life you've always wanted.

• One final observation: Over and over again, God affirms to me why he has inspired me to write this book. I no longer simply believe that he has given me a message to share and the stories to demonstrate the message. It is more than that. I'm convinced there are really no accidents in life—only what someone has called "interpretations." Everything that may come into your life and every person who crosses the path of your life does so for a reason. The experience is God's gift to you.

Saint Paul said something similar to this: "And we know that God causes everything to work together for the good . . ." (Rom 8:28). It's noteworthy that the apostle did not say God causes everything to happen to you. Instead, he causes everything that happens to you to "work together for the good." That's a huge difference in interpretation.

The task in everything is to figure out what the "good" is that God makes available in everything that happens. When you figure out what it is, then you are once again on the receiving end of God's generosity, and that is the joy, enrichment, and mystery of life.

Here is an example of how it might work: Rather than missing the message in all the good that happens, getting bothered by all the bad that happens, or being annoyed by the people you meet whose personalities could easily disrupt your peace of mind, why not develop the discipline of asking yourself, "Why did this happen in my life?" "What might I learn from this?" "Why did this person or event come into my life?" This kind of self-discipline brings the experience and encounter into the spiritual realm of living and makes all of life a discovery waiting to happen. It squelches ill feelings and negative reactions before they rise in you. It is part of what you must learn if you are to live the life you've always wanted. You must start seeing everything that comes into your life and every person you meet as gifts given to you to enrich your life and enable you to have something more to give to others—in terms of your own personality, presence, and possessions.

The day I wrote this page, I sat down in the waiting area at Chicago's O'Hare Airport excited about going home. There were scores of empty seats. I could have chosen any one of them. This was Saturday, and O'Hare, normally crowded and bustling with noisy, hurried travelers, was unusually quiet. Nearby, a woman I guessed to be in her late seventies, maybe early eighties, was sitting in a wheel-chair, although she hardly looked as though she needed to be.

She spoke first. "You traveling to Memphis like me?"

"No," I said. "Louisville is my home. I guess I should have sat down over there where other travelers to Louisville appear to be sit-ting. For some reason, I just sat down here."

"That's so we could talk," she responded as if she knew that is the way life works—as though there are no accidents in life but opportunities, divine-cidents, I've started calling them, coincidences that simply await our recognition of God's presence.

"Looks like you're eating a tuna salad sandwich," she observed.

"Yep, I left so early this morning to fly to Chicago, I've had nei-ther breakfast nor lunch."

"You came up here from Louisville just this morning and are already heading home?" she questioned.

"Yep," I responded. "I had a meeting to attend and now I'm going home."

I imagined she was wondering what kind of work I do that would have such odd hours on a weekend. We exchanged more casual conversation for what I would guess was about twenty-five minutes before they called for my flight. Just a simple conversation; nothing profound was exchanged. No earth-shattering revelation.

Or so I thought. This encounter would turn out to be God's gift to me.

As I am learning to do in every experience of life, I started won-dering why I sat down beside her when I could have sat anywhere. There was something about her that I found charming and interest-ing. Perhaps it was because her face defied her age and spoke of an inner peace with herself and with the world around her. Though an older woman, the lines on her face were soft and gentle and seemed to smile rather than droop and frown like so many I see. She started the conversation with me just as normally as she might have with someone she had known all her life.

What you do not know about this is that I was experiencing, on this very day, what some writers refer to as writer's block. Since I do an enormous amount of flying, I do much of my writing on airplanes. I had been wondering how I might bring this chapter to a close and demonstrate the lessons I'd been sharing. As yet, nothing had appeared on the mental radar screen. But I wasn't too concerned. I have learned that God gives me everything I need in his own time and way. This work has been and continues to be no exception.

Little did I realize at the time, however, that the gift from God was about to appear in this brief but blessed conversation with the old stranger whom I had met in the O'Hare Airport.

"So what brought you to Chicago?" I asked between bites of the tuna sandwich.

"Oh, I came to see my daughter, grandchildren and great-great-grandchildren."

"Great-great-grandchildren?" I asked, incredulously.

"That's right."

"Wonderful," I said, while thinking that surely anyone her age would hardly mind me asking her age. So I braved just that.

"How old are you, anyway?"

"If I live till next month, I'll be ninety years old!" she replied with a tone of deserved pride.

"You hardly look it," I followed. I wasn't simply saying that to be kind. She really didn't look her age. I was also amused by the fact that nobody but little children and old people calculate their age in terms of months and days. Ask a four-year-old how old she is and you'll likely hear, "I'm four-and-one-half . . . almost five!"

She went right on.

"I got a younger sister, too, but she looks lots older than me."

"Why's that?" I asked.

"My sister . . . well . . . she just don't enjoy life, it seems," she continued as if she didn't hear my question. "As for me, I believe in having fun and getting out and doing things for people." She paused as the two of us turned to catch a message from the airport intercom, and then she went on. "But not my sister. She pretty much stays locked up in her house and just seems pretty sad toward life."

There was a brief lull in the conversation. I took another bite while I watched and wondered, Why am I in conversation with her? What is she here to teach me? These thoughts are like prayers and they often help me focus—to closely look for what I am to learn from any encounter.

Since she told me her age and hardly looked it, I decided to ask her to venture a guess at my own. That was a mistake.

"How old do you think I am?"

Without hesitating she said, "I'd guess . . . uh . . . uh, sixty-five?"

"Sixty-five?" I reacted in a half-offended fashion. I'm only fifty. I couldn't believe it. I'm accustomed to people guessing my age much lower than it actually is. I won't be asking that question of anyone ever again. I thought to myself, Is that what I'm to learn from this encounter—to give up my vanity? My ego does get worked up at times when I look at my form in a mirror.

I quickly turned the conversation back to her. "I'm curious. What keeps you young at heart and so obviously full of happiness and peace?"

"Well . . . I don't know . . . I guess it's because I just get a kick out of doing things for others!"

"How so?" I asked. "What do you do for others?"

"Well, for one thing, I plant this garden every summer. And I love to can and put fresh vegetables away, and I got three freezers full of frozen vegetables. I enjoy giving this stuff away in winter months to people who don't have much to eat or don't know what home-grown vegetables taste like."

She stared off for a moment, caught another airport message, and continued, "Funny thing, I can't give it all away . . . seems like every time I open a freezer to get some frozen vegetables for somebody, or just for myself, and I think, 'Supplies have got to be getting low,' the freezers' seem just as full as ever! I tell people this, but they just can't believe it."

I smiled. I can believe it.

Are you beginning to get the picture? Is the message of this encounter dawning on you as it began dawning on me? Here is a ninety-year-old woman, traveling a long way from home and all alone, who plants and harvests a garden each summer large enough to fill three full-sized freezers with fresh vegetables, and all for what? Because she must? Not hardly. Because she's bored with life and needs something to do? I doubt it. Because she can't afford to buy vegetables at the supermarket? She seemed materially comfortable to me. I cannot believe this was her motivation.

No! There's only one explanation. It's love that motivates her. It is giving that fills her with passion and desire. She does it for the sheer joy she gets out of giving garden-grown vegetables to people who don't have much to eat or don't have the luxury of eating and enjoying homegrown tomatoes, peas, okra, beans, and corn during the cold winter months. She has found a life she's always wanted—and she has found it in giving.

There you have it. God could not have given me a better story to give to you at the close of this chapter. Again, what Saint Paul said is correct: "But the one who plants generously will get a generous crop . . . . Then you will always have everything you need and plenty left over to share with others" (2 Cor 9:6, 8).

Want to find the life that'll give you the same sort of joy and peace? Then you must give up the myth, "If I give, there won't be enough." Stop acting as if you'll never have what you or your family needs if you're generous.

Take some risks.

Have some fun.

Start emptying your freezer.

NOTE

[1] Eckhart Tolle, *The Power of Now* (Novato CA: New World Library, 2001).

7

MYTH 3
"EQUAL AND FAIR SHARE GIVING IS ENOUGH"

The only gift is a portion of thyself.
—Ralph Waldo Emerson (1803–1882)

Be thankful for the least gift, so shalt thou be meant to receive greater.
—Thomas à Kempis (1380–1471)

If some give to get something in return (God's blessing, more money, recognition from others, their name or that of someone they love inscribed in granite or on a plaque, etc.), and others don't give for fear there won't be enough for their own needs and that of those they love, where does that leave those who share the desire to give to charity? They're asking, "What should I give?" In my work, I often hear this kind of question, and I also often hear the same response from some who have it all figured out. "Just give your fair share. That's good enough, no more, no less."

NOT-FOR-PROFIT SECTOR

Equal, "fair share" giving is commonly perpetuated in two places. One is outside the church among the many charities and not-for-profits that blanket the landscape of American society. Incidentally, this isn't a judgment, just an observation. But in the last twenty-five years, the not-for-profit world has grown at a disproportionately faster rate when compared to almost any other financial segment of our society—from approximately 350,000 nonprofit organizations to, by some estimates, more than 2,000,000 today. These nonprofits compete for what is now more than $250 billion dollars given each year to charity. It is staggering when you try to imagine that much money given every year to charities and that the lion's share of that total, more than 75 percent, is given by individuals, not foundations and corporations. That makes fundraising at least the third largest financial sector in the American economy every year.

Want to know something else that's mind-boggling? Over the next few years, my generation, known as the boomers—born between 1943 and 1964—stands to inherit, according to some conservative estimates, as much as $50 to $80 trillion. I know what you're thinking: "I'd like to meet some of these people, because it isn't me!" You might not be one of the fortunate ones. I know I'm not. I don't expect to inherit anything. My mother enjoys reminding my two brothers and me that she's spending what little inheritance we might expect. A trillion dollars, however, let alone $50 trillion, means nothing to most of us because it is completely beyond comprehension. Somewhere I found an explanation of the power of a trillion dollars, and, after doing a little calculation of my own, I developed a way that may help you comprehend $50 trillion.

If you stacked $1,000 bills on top of each other, 50 trillion would rise 400 miles high, which is approximately how high the space shuttle flies in outer space.

The Queen Mary 2 has nearly 3,000 rooms. Fifty trillion dollars could buy you not 1,000, not 10,000, not even 25,000 of these ships. Instead, you could afford 50,000 of them. Furthermore, you could afford to staff the 50,000 ships and pay the annual salary of the 1,250 crew members it takes for each one.

If you are a generous person, with $50 trillion you could give away to every man, woman, and child in this nation of 300 million people more than $150,000 each.

There are 86,400 seconds in 1 day. One million seconds in 11.5 days. One billion seconds in 31.5 years. One trillion seconds in 31,500 years. The next time you think about $50 trillion, consider that number represents $1 per second for 1,575,000 years.

You might not include yourself, but someone is inheriting this staggering amount of money. And the question becomes, "What are these boomers going to do with all that inheritance?" Pay off the mortgage? Many will. Buy vacation homes? You bet. Take expensive trips and cruises to faraway places? Of course. Acquire expensive hobbies and drive pricey cars? You bet.

But what moral and ethical responsibility does my generation have to address the poverty, education, and healthcare issues faced by American families? And what of the genocide and vast human suffering that's taking place in Darfur? Or the AIDS and hunger crisis that still claims the lives of thousands of people every day in places like Africa and Asia? These are hard questions, but they must be asked nonetheless.

FAIR AND EQUAL SHARE GIVING TO NONPROFITS

Those in the fundraising profession should carefully scrutinize their fundraising protocol when approaching my generation, and indeed any generation, for contributions. Just this evening, for example, I was sharing conversation with a high-powered prosecutor in Colorado who said he had told a representative from United Way earlier that he wouldn't be making a donation this year. When I asked why, the prosecutor said, "I didn't like the way he approached me."

"What do you mean?" I asked.

"Well, unlike past years, I was going to make the biggest gift ever this year. But when I got his letter, it said, 'Your colleagues in this area with a giving capacity similar to you are giving in the range of $15,000 and $20,000, and we want you to do the fair and equitable thing and make a similar kind of gift.' I said to myself, 'To hell I will.' So, when he showed up today, "I looked at him and said, 'Listen, fella, tax and guilt techniques don't cut it with me . . . you'll not get a dime from me this year!'"

"Tax and guilt" is just another way of saying "equal and fair share." It's a common method used by many charities to solicit donations. With this lawyer, it didn't work. And, ultimately, it won't with many folks.

EQUAL AND FAIR SHARE GIVING IN CHURCH

The other place I see this misconception about giving is in the church and particularly among people raised in the Roman Catholic tradition. Whether the not-for-profit venue or the local church, this myth will work temporarily in that it's practical and appeals to a person's sense of logic. It is pragmatic and a popular technique in the fundraising world. But it's hardly a sustaining motivator for giving, as you will see.

Let's say, for example, your parish needs a $1 million annual budget to fund its ministries and your church has 1,200 households. When you divide the cost of those ministries funded by the annual offering by the number of households, you arrive at what is referred to by many as the "equal and fair share" each household should be asked to give. When you do the math, the example I've just given amounts to a little more than $800 per year per household. Experts say this is close to the national average currently given to churches by the households attending those churches. This per annum amount puts little burden on any single household, and the ministry needs are more than met through the weekly offertory. This is what I mean about this myth working. It's also what is known as "average" giving. Each household gives an "average" gift, the amount of which is reasonable. The church's budget needs are met. Everyone is happy. Right? Not so fast.

Several things are wrong with this approach to giving.

For one, it's too calculated and prescribed. It relies on guilt and competition as motivators, and can even border on being legalistic. Furthermore, it isn't taught anywhere in Scripture, which for many people of faith would be reason enough to reject it. Yet if you're in a religious tradition that assigns as much credence to church tradition as it does to Scripture, it isn't enough to say that "equal and fair share" giving or giving your "average" gift is a concept foreign to the Bible. Besides, you may be in a church where this method of motivating people to give is commonly used. Here, then, are some reasons why this misconception about giving is a myth that, like the others, will steal the joy of giving from you.

Though it sounds reasonable and there are scores of churches that promote this kind of giving, the fact is that there isn't a church in America where the members practice this methodology consistently. Those who promote this method of giving try to motive others to do so in two ways. First, they appeal to the logic or "reasonableness" of this way of calculating one's giving. Using the example above of an annual offertory need of 1 million dollars and 1,200 families in the church, these advocates will reason, "Who among us can't afford to give $800 a year? After all, that amounts to little more than the price of a cup of Starbucks coffee per day."

Second, advocates of this method of giving try to motivate people by tapping their guilt. While grace is a much better generosity motivator, guilt may be the most widely used method of generating charitable giving. Just think of the televised charities that parade images across our television screens of poor children with extended stomachs who suffer from impoverished conditions and malnutrition, and it isn't hard to figure out the motivational method to get you to give is guilt. This is a common fundraising technique.

But "shoulds" and "oughts" about giving are not sustaining motivators. People will tire of them sooner rather than later. Giving out of a sense of guilt will only make you a resentful or competitive giver, one who gives just enough to silence the guilt within or, worse, one who gives nothing at all. Giving motivated by guilt will rob you of joy in giving.

There's something else. To give simply your "fair and equal share" reduces giving to the lowest common denominator. Think about it. Charity that amounts to little more than the cost of a cup of coffee per day is neither inspiring nor exemplary in an affluent society like ours. Most everyone reading this could do better—a whole lot better.

PARABLE OF THE TALENTS AND THE WAYS OF GOD

Consider the parable of the talents in the twenty-fifth chapter of Matthew. There are approximately forty parables attributed to Jesus by Matthew, Mark, Luke, and John. In this one, Jesus tells of a wealthy man who represents God. As the owner of all things, he distributes talents to three different individuals. To one, he gives five talents, to another two, and to still another one talent. To all three, he says, "Go and trade with them." Today, he might say, "Go and invest them."

When I first read this story, I was bothered because it appeared to suggest that in God's economics we are not all treated equally. The more I thought about it, the more bothered I became. Then one day it dawned on me that God cannot treat us equally. Furthermore, contrary to how I might feel about it, that's exactly how it should be.

It would be a mistake to think I'm saying that God bestows his love with partiality. To the contrary, he loves us equally. He fairly and justly distributes mercy to all. It is in the distribution of gifts, talents, opportunities, and even money that he deals with us differently. He gives these gifts only as we demonstrate our ability to handle them.

Now, you might go through much of your life, as I did, resentful over the way things are. Why do some people get all the breaks? Make more money than you? Score higher on the MCAT and get the one opening to med school? Get the promotion for which you are clearly more qualified? Live in a better house, in a better neighborhood? Serve a larger church than you and, to add insult to injury, in a community that, unlike yours, is actually growing?

While it took me almost half my adult life to get to the place where I am, I finally figured it out. God knows me better than I know myself. Because he knows me so well, he gives me his gifts in direct proportion to my demonstrated capacity to handle them. As I wisely manage those gifts, he gives more gifts. The issue, then, is not how equal your opportunity is, but how responsible your management is.

If you've got problems with this, then I suspect you'll disagree with both my interpretation and my analysis. There was a time when I would have, too. But today, I know that God not only distributes his gifts as we responsibly manage them, but, as we do, he entrusts us with greater gifts and larger responsibilities. This is the way he has designed creation. This is not so hard to understand, especially if you're a parent. You don't give your thirteen-year-old the same degree of responsibility that you give his sixteen-year-old brother—unless, of course, the thirteen-year-old demonstrates more maturity. You give responsibility as you feel your child is capable of handling it.

God deals with his children in much the same way. He gives and we receive. He entrusts us with greater responsibility as we demonstrate our ability to manage his trust. He gives. We invest. He gives more and we invest more. It is in cooperation with this divinely designed flow of creation that you and I experience life as God intended it. In other words, the secret of living life to the fullest is found in the grateful acceptance of the way things are and in the creative participation in the way life works. It is getting to that place where you no longer resent but respect God and surrender to his ways of dealing with the world and with you—ways that are sometimes inexplicable.

WAR IN MY OWN WORLD

For a good portion of my adult life, I carried on an internal war with God over all of this. I simply could not accept the ambiguities I found either in him, the Bible, the world, or my own life. I tried to package neatly everything I believed about God and the world— including my understanding of his ways in the world and his ways with me. It was a frustrating and unfulfilling experience to say the least. Instead of bringing me closer to God, my attempts to fashion God into my own understanding drove me further from him. Eventually, I got to the place where I had little relationship with him at all. Though I weekly exhorted others to know God, my appeals rang hollow in my own soul. I always felt that my spiritual life, though somewhat part of me, was also separate from me—that is, the real me. I'd wake up on Sunday morning and be an anxious bundle of nerves, knowing I was preparing to tell others about things I wasn't sure I even believed myself. That is not to say I never sensed God's presence in my life or had an occasional moment of divine inspiration. To the contrary, I knew a few such times—enough to keep me in the game, anyway. But they never lasted, and I rarely had any lasting inner peace.

One Sunday afternoon, however, everything changed. I experienced a complete transformation—what Princeton theologian James Loder might call a "transforming moment," an evangelical might call a "conversion," or an Eastern mystic might describe as "satori." It was indeed an awakening for me, an inner enlightenment that has changed my life forever.

I saw no flashing lights. The earth beneath me did not shake. I had no visions or dreams, although I've had plenty of those since then. What did happen, though, was transformative and started me on a journey that has brought me to the central premise of this book: that life, all of life, is a divine gift. We come into this world with nothing. We will leave with nothing. Someone said, "Who we are and what we have is a divine gift to us. What we know, become, and do is our gift to God and his world." The irony is, as we begin to grow up and accumulate things, our ego dupes us into thinking we deserve the recognition we've earned and that we own all the stuff we have collected. But we own nothing, and there are few things that more clearly reveal this truth than when death ends life—we leave just as empty-handed as we came into it. In this little "parenthesis in time" as someone has described it, what we earn and accumulate, everything we accomplish, including the titles we receive, the wealth we attain, indeed every breath we take, is a divine gift from an incredibly prodigal God.

Getting the picture? Or are you still intoxicated by your ego, believing that you have had anything to do with your accomplishments and the material stuff with which you have surrounded yourself?

The dramatic change in my life took place while watching, of all things, a PBS television broadcast and listening to Wayne Dyer, a psychologist in the field of spiritual development, talk about life in ways I had never thought about before. He was lecturing on the subject of his latest book, *10 Secrets for Success and Inner Peace or The Power of Intention: Learning to Co-Create Your World Your Way*,[1] and the more I listened, the more drawn to his words I felt. In fact, it was as if he were speaking to me alone. By the end of the broadcast, I was propelled on a journey that has changed my life forever. I felt peaceful and more connected to God than ever before. While that experience was quite some time ago, the peace and knowledge of God's immediate presence has never diminished. Not even slightly.

My internal war with myself and with God ended. It was as if I signed a peace accord. I found the life I had always wanted. Today, the journey on which that experience catapulted me has gotten only richer and more meaningful.

Am I suggesting that everything has been "perfect" since then? Of course not. But almost. I have joy, genuine joy. I can laugh at life and, more importantly, at myself. When I'm not laughing, I am almost always smiling on the inside. I am experiencing what Jesus called "the abundant life."

One wise person once described his life with these words: "In my world, nothing ever goes wrong." There was a time when such a statement would have thoroughly angered me. I would have vehemently argued that that there is plenty wrong with this world, not to speak of my own life. Today, however, I share that worldview. While the depths of its meaning I'm only beginning to plumb, I now know there is nothing wrong with the world while I know there's plenty wrong in the world. And we're here to give ourselves to making it better for all. Isn't that what Jesus meant when he said we are "salt" and "light" in the world?

My life and this world is what it is and as it should be. Am I what I will be tomorrow? Next week? Next year? Not yet. But the future will take care of itself, and the Father above will take care of me. If nothing in my world ever seems to go wrong, it is only because I now know that God is never absent from my world. He is at work in me and in—and through—everything in my life. To fret or rage over what's happening to me or in me is to blind myself to his presence. While I am not what I will be, the remarkable thing is, I am not what I was. I am who I am. I exist in this moment and for this moment only. It's the ego that wants me to fret over what might be, to find fault with what is, and to regret what was. But not anymore. I'm done with that stuff.

I'm more myself today than I've ever been. That Sunday afternoon, I committed myself to the pursuit of life's grandest purpose. I made it my lifelong intention to give away myself and the resources that God has given to me. That intention has transformed how I think, how I live, and how I feel about life in profoundly significant ways. I know it will do the same for you once you know that the purpose of your life is to give. There's no need to struggle to figure out why you're here. You are here for one reason, and that is to give yourself back to God and to give away your life and what he entrusts to you before the end parenthesis closes on your life.

As I often do, I write, edit, and rewrite while I crisscross the country fulfilling the purpose God gave me that Sunday afternoon. God gives me everything I have and need, and today is no less an example of that truth. I was seated in front of two people, neither of whom I know but both of whom were on their way to the same destination in Colorado—a beautiful area nestled more than 8,000 feet up in the Rocky Mountains called Buena Vista. I don't always eavesdrop on conversations between people I don't know, but I did this day. The gentleman's rich, baritone voice may have had something to do with it. Though the volume was the initial draw, it was the richness of his soothing voice that held me. I found it hard not to listen.

I now know the real reason why. Their story belonged right here. She and her husband were going to spend a few days in what was the newest of several houses they had been building around the country in the last several years for the pleasure of their retirement years. They own a beachside property, a house on some lake in Texas, their principal residence in Arlington, and now this, their trophy house in the Rocky Mountains. The gentleman she was speaking with was also going to the Rockies, but he was planning to spend a few days with a friend and do some elk hunting in the mountains. Like the woman he was conversing with, he owned several houses and was contemplating adding another one to his collection of residences. He was trying to decide whether to build a house in the Buena Vista region.

Before you conclude that I'm finding fault, please understand I'm not suggesting that there's something wrong with owning a first or second house in the Rocky Mountains, or the coast of Puerto Vallarta, for that matter. There's nothing wrong with having your name on more than one title deed. There was a time when I owned a second home—a vacation home where my family and I would spend time each year. I share their conversation only because the woman herself made an interesting observation.

"I'm not sure why we have all of these houses in so many different places," she observed. "In a way, it all seems so silly."

"What do you mean?" her seatmate asked.

"Well, it's like this: we have this yard man who takes care of the lawn at our Arlington house and, frankly, all that does is free us up to go to the lake house on weekends to take care of the grounds out there. How goofy is that?" she asked. "We never get to enjoy the lake. We spend what little time we have just keeping the place up. Now we have this beautiful house in the Rockies and we've been there twice in two years. Lately, I've been wondering why we have so much to enjoy but so little enjoyment in our lives."

I'm not sure to what conclusion she may have eventually come regarding her vast real estate holdings, but I am certain it had not yet occurred to her that the joy she was missing in what they had bought, built, and believed would bring them enjoyment could be found with one simple decision—the decision to simplify and give away at least some of it. The reward for stockpiling a lot of stuff is not joy. God gives us lots of stuff for one reason, and that's so we have lots of stuff to give away. It's in the giving that the joy is found. And until you get it, you will go through your life looking for life but missing it at every turn.

I'm aware that the critics of this book will want to protect themselves from the life I'm describing by saying that while I say on one hand that giving is the supreme purpose of everyone's life, I talk more on the other hand about giving money away and the stuff money can buy than I do about other important ways of giving—like the giving of your life, time, conversation, presence, or love.

If you're one of these, you've missed the point altogether. I talk so much about giving money away for three simple reasons. One, it's what I know so well. Second, I know that what you spend your money on is a reflection of the real you—your ego. And, third, I know that if you will learn to give your money away, you'll get much better at giving your life away—your time, abilities, conversation, presence, and your love all follow naturally. I am a much better husband and father since the intention of my life became the giving of myself and my resources away.

Now, on a daily basis, I meditate and pray and attempt to question everything I have been taught to believe. No longer do I feel obligated to please others or "fit in" with those around me. Neither do I feel it necessary to accept blindly everything I'm told to believe. I am free from that nonsense. I know liberation from the opinions of others, both good and bad. I no longer desire to attain a position that will make me the envy of those my ego would like to regard as inferior to me. I am free of the empty pursuit of the things that are really so vastly unimportant. Who cares whether I wear an Hermes tie or you carry a Burberry purse? I don't care—not anymore, that is. Oh, I like to dress nicely and wear fine clothing. But what I thought at one time I possessed, I discovered possessed me. That is no longer the case. I am truly free.

Do you know this kind of freedom? If you do, then the life you've always wanted is the life you are experiencing and you're probably nodding in agreement with virtually everything I'm writing. But if not, it's the life you can have if you choose to focus your attention on life's higher purpose, then become intentional about pursuing such a life.

You may be asking, "What does any of this have to do with the myth of giving your equal and fair share?"

It is of primary importance. Those who go through life calculating their "equal and fair share" of anything must be among some of the most miserable of persons. I cannot imagine they know much lasting joy, and it must have something to do with the fact that their significance in life is measured on the basis of what they and others deserve. "Work hard and you'll get your just rewards" must surely be one of their mantras for living. For these people, life is anything but a gift. Rather, life is earned. It is reward for hard work. To these people, the only thing that makes sense is Benjamin Franklin's words, "God helps those who help themselves," which is, from my own perspective today, a lot of nonsense. While at one time I would have concurred with such a notion, I know today that God helps those who don't help themselves and, perhaps more accurately, can't help themselves. For all he was right about, here Franklin was wrong.

"Equal and fair share" people understand his words, however. Their soul resonates with them. That's why they are inclined to look at a disadvantaged person and think, "Why don't you get a job and work like normal people?" The status these people have achieved and the stuff they've accumulated conspires to validate their significance and the belief that they deserve what they've earned.

Their charity is no different. They might give, but they do so with little spontaneity and less joy. Their generosity is calculated and measured by how it compares to the generosity of others. Their giving is predicated on the proof that the recipient is a legitimate case of need. Furthermore, they enjoy it more when their charity is recognized and applauded. In fact, just as they derive their significance by the symbols of status that hang on their office walls, they are seldom motivated to give unless their name is inscribed on some Wall of Gratitude. And, frankly, they would prefer that their inscribed name be in a class all its own. Seeing themselves as separate from the ordinary, they would prefer their name on a larger plaque more in keeping with the size and significance of their own public persona. I can't help but believe these people enjoy a temporary happiness with their perfunctory charity and may occasionally relax and feel at peace. But I suspect that, when the significance of their charity wears off or is forgotten, the peace is gone and the routine starts all over.

I am learning to relax, however. Truly relax. Anytime, anywhere, and under any circumstances, I am learning to enter a place of peace because I have learned that all of life is a gift to me. Conversely, all I am and all I have is my gift to the world. I look for ways to give, not because of the recognition it will bring me, but because I want to give. I'm compelled to give. I am most fulfilled when I am giving. I came into this world receiving. I will leave this world once again receiving—receiving the gift of eternal life from the One who said his departure was to prepare a place for me (John 14:1ff). In between these two receiving points, my life purpose is to give. When you get this, you are propelled as it were toward the life you've always wanted.

Here's an example of how this new life works for me.

While the announcement by a gate agent that the flight is delayed would have at one time sent me into an emotional frenzy or, worse, offended me, today I am seldom bothered by such inconveniences. I am much more capable of relaxing and accepting all things, however annoying, contradictory, or inexplicable, as God's gift to me at that moment. I now look for what he wishes to say to me or to teach me through each of life's daily experiences and annoyances. This view of everyday life has transformed everything I see. Little things seldom bother me anymore.

I am not suggesting that I have no concerns whatsoever or that I no longer care about such inequities in the world like the growing disparity between the rich and the poor or the conflict in Iraq or the escalation of international conflicts. To the contrary, I am deeply concerned and I am more involved in making a positive difference in my own world and in the world around me than ever before. Why? Because I now look for the God I know in everyone I meet and in every encounter I have.

When I see God's face in the drug addict on the streets of New York, the vastly overweight woman who supersizes her order at the local fast food restaurant, the emaciated child who roams Calcutta's streets pleading for a morsel of bread, or the radical Islamic who threatens to kill anyone who will not conform to his narrow world-view, more than anything else, I now feel compassion. How may I feel anything but compassion and understanding when I see the face of God in him or her?

It was because his heart was filled with love that Jesus looked upon every person—even his enemies—with love. Your ego might dismiss what I'm saying by telling you that Jesus could look upon his enemies with love because he was God and you're not. But didn't Jesus tell us to "Love your enemies" (Matt 5:44)? Of course, and he also promised that you and I would have the capacity to be and do greater things than even he did. Although Christians in every denomination attempt to do so, there's no dismissing these words of Jesus. Because every person is part of the human family, then even my enemy is a human being for whom Christ died. That makes him or her a potential brother or sister, and while at one time in my life I would have felt differently about such persons I have just described, this is how I now view the human family. I did not set out on that Sunday afternoon to feel this way or to start to view the world in this fashion. Nevertheless, since that day, I see everyone and everything through a different perspective. This was one of God's gifts to me that day and I must share it. To be sure, remnants of those old feelings and prejudices occasionally slip back into my consciousness. The difference is that I now witness that happening inside me and, almost instinctively, relegate my ego, the source of such judgments and prejudices, to its rightful place in my life.

This goes for all that happens in my life, too. I now know what Saint Paul meant when he said that God is at work in everything for my good (Rom 8:28). Think about the scope and magnitude of his words. In everything, God works for my good and yours, too. Can you tell me of anything that everything does not include? Why, then, should anything ever bother you or me? It shouldn't. And it won't when you experience a transformation similar to that which I have experienced. The events of my life, both good and bad, I now view differently. This is what Wayne Dyer meant when he suggested that if you "change the way you look at things, the things you look at change."

As strange as all this may sound, the fact is, if God is at work for your good in all things, why should anything that's going on around you disturb your inner peace? It shouldn't. And it won't. Instead, what you'll find yourself doing is looking for God. You'll start asking, "Why has this occurred in my life?" "What does God want me to learn through this?" Questions like these will quickly change your feelings about what's happening in your life. This is not to make God the culprit in all that happens, whether good or bad. Life is filled with both good and evil, no matter where it comes from. It's what we do with what happens that makes the difference.

On those occasions when I start to feel disturbed by something or someone, it's as if God reminds me that there is nothing happening to me that surprises him. All of life is a gift. When that thought reenters my mind, guess what I do? I open my eyes a little wider. I want to make sure I do not miss his presence at work for my good in the daily transactions of my life.

Today, I live in peace with the paradoxes that at one time perplexed and even annoyed me. In fact, I even enjoy them. They add such a rich dimension to life. I've quit debating with myself, with others, or with God about things I can't logically explain, and I've stopped demanding that God resolve the inconsistencies I see in the world. Instead, I celebrate God's presence everywhere and all of his gifts to this world and to me—gifts that are more abundant than I deserve. This approach has brought to me a permanent peace and a plentiful supply of everything I need. In other words, when I gave up being resentful over those who had more, started giving thanks for all I do have, and committed to live out my purpose of giving myself and my resources away, not calculating what my equal and fair share of giving should be or judging what would be an equal and fair share for others to give, I began to experience greater peace and more abundance than I have ever imagined.

NOT EQUAL GIVING, BUT EQUAL SACRIFICE

There's an old proverb that goes, "He who gives, gathers." It is the way of the universe. I had always thought I was at best a two-talent person. I now realize I am as most of you reading this book—a five-talent person.

Some would say that our society has a few five-talent persons, many who have two talents, and a majority who are persons with just one talent. But compared to a large percentage of the rest of the world, most of the people in our society are five-talent people. This is true in terms of personal abilities and financial capabilities. You'll have to decide which you are. But don't be too fast to dismiss yourself as a five-talent person just because you didn't qualify as a contestant on *American Idol* or don't have the financial resources of Bill Gates.

God has never asked a one-talent person to produce a fivefold return any more than he asks a five-talent person to be content with a onefold return. Rather, each of us is to invest what we've been given. This is known as the principle of "equal giving, not equal sacrifice," a principle I often share with people in my work. If you want to find the life you've always wanted, just start giving based on your capability. Be responsible with what you've already been given, and God will give you greater opportunities and gifts. This is the way to find life. The world will be blessed, and both you and the world will be the better.

The focal point in Jesus' parable is that the one-talent person, rather than investing what little he had, went out and buried his talent in the ground. That means he did nothing with it, which is precisely why the owner was angry. Upon returning from the far country, this one-talent person had nothing to give back to the owner except the gift he was given.

Can you imagine inheriting a significant sum of money from the estate of a generous but deceased relative? You in turn give the money to your financial counselor with instructions to invest it in some high-yield stocks. Just as your relative trusted you to handle wisely the estate she left you, you trust your advisor to take what you have given him and earn some nice returns with it—returns that will not only benefit you but him as well. But several years pass, and you visit your advisor to see how your investment is going. You are outraged to discover that, rather than investing your inheritance, your advisor simply put it in a safe deposit box where it earned nothing—neither for you nor for the advisor. In other words, it benefited no one.

Someone might argue, "Shouldn't you, the benefactor, bear some responsibility in checking to make sure your investment has been wisely handled by those in whom you have placed such a large investment as a trust?" Perhaps. But, in the story as Jesus told it, the owner is far away and presumably not in a position to do anything more than trust those into whose hands he had placed his gifts.

I believe this is what God has done in his world. He is the creator of all things. He distributes his gifts to human beings as he wills. These gifts to us, however simple or complex, equal or unequal, express his hope in us. Everything we have—indeed everything we are—is an expression of his reckless hope that you and I will respectfully respond to his gracious trust and take responsible care of this world, treat all people as potential members of our own family, and share our abundance with everyone.

THE MEASURE OF "GIVE-ABILITY"

What does all this mean? God expects you to take the gifts he gives and do your best with them. In the same vein, God measures what you do give by the degree of "give-ability" he has given you.

Recently, a newspaper with a nationwide circulation featured a cover story about celebrities such as Bono and Angelina Jolie, who have been donating much of their time and hefty financial resources to worthwhile causes around the world.

Nothing is wrong with any of that. In fact, what amazes me is that their actions draw so much press. They are five-talent people in the sense that they have been richly rewarded for their music and movie careers. They should be giving something back. In fact, they should be giving much of their wealth back to the world. They and scores of other people could follow the example of Warren Buffett. Buffett has donated the lion's share of his multi-billion dollar fortune to the Gates Foundation—$37 billion to be exact. His gift makes the Gates Foundation by far the largest private foundation in the world. Buffett did this at about the same time the story of Brad Pitt and Angelina Jolie appeared in the press. In my opinion, Buffett's generosity was a newsworthy story. I have my doubts about the other. It's the public fascination with Pitt and Jolie and other such movie stars that draws such press. As a result, the paparazzi pursue these celebrities armed with high-tech cameras and snapping pictures like a rapid-fire machine gun in hopes of securing profits for themselves as they sell these pictures to magazines willing to pay to satisfy the public's sordid fascination.

"For stars' resumes, charity work could become as important as the Oscars." That was a recent headline I saw in a nationally syndicated newspaper. Press writers are understandably suspicious of the motives for the charitable giving of Hollywood stars. I share their suspicion. The fact is, however, whatever their motives may be, of those to whom much is given, much is required. I find their acts of generosity, while admittedly helpful to worthy causes, are hardly worthy of praise from the press. They are simply doing what they should be doing.

The same is true for you and me, too. While we'll not likely ever be offered millions of dollars for pictures of our babies, as People magazine recently did for Jolie and Pitt, you and I have been given nonetheless an abundant life and vast resources—all from the hand of God himself. God's expectation is that we will view both of them as gifts to invest in worthy causes rather than as rewards to hoard for the pleasures of our ego. When you understand this and begin to live accordingly, you will find the life you've always wanted.

THE MYTH OF AVERAGE GIVING

In almost every church where I have provided consultation, I meet at least one member who is convinced that the myth of "average" giving—that we should give an equal and fair share and that's enough—is what the church should preach and teach. With pen and paper in hand, this person will have the entire financial need of the parish figured out and ready to package as an appeal to the members at large. As demonstrated earlier in the chapter, by dividing the financial need of the church by the number of member households, he will have arrived at the precise amount that each household should be asked to give.

While it makes good sense on paper, it doesn't work in practice. In principle, it's not the way to motivate giving. Furthermore, it will not lead people to experience from their giving the life that God desires for them. Their giving will likely become calculated and meaningless. The spontaneity will disappear. Giving will quickly degenerate into insidious comparisons as people measure the worthiness of their gift by comparing it to the gifts of others. Instead of giving based on the prompting of God's Spirit and in grateful response to God's grace and gifts, giving becomes a competition to see who can give the largest gift and get the most recognition and praise.

There are two practical reasons why this method of motivating generosity won't work. First, there are those in every church who couldn't give their "fair and equal share" even if they were so inclined. They simply do not have the financial resources to make the gift. They might be one-talent people. Or, more likely, they are multi-talented people who are facing challenges that require a greater investment of their time and resources somewhere other than the church or other viable cause. They might be able to give something, but if the church's message is "Give your equal and fair share," these folks are made to feel as if what they could give is not significant enough. That's hardly the message the church wants to convey.

The second reason it won't work is that there are in every parish those persons who could give far beyond their "equal and fair share" precisely because they are materially blessed. They are, without debate, five-talent people. But you know what you are likely to get from a five-talent person when all you ask for is an "average" gift? You usually get only what you ask for. Didn't Jesus say, "Ask and it [that is, what you ask for] is given?" That should not be surprising.

These five-talent people, unfortunately, miss the opportunity of giving based on their potential. By not asking these people to give based on their capability, the church puts them at risk of interrupting the divinely designed flow. Remember, God gives his gifts to each of us, and as we wisely manage and invest them, God gives more gifts.

If you're a five-talent person, it may be a relief to you that your church expects nothing but an average contribution of your time and resources. But think about it. There are reasons why God has blessed you materially as he has, and it probably has much to do with the demonstration of your wise management of those blessings—at least so far. This much I know for certain. What you have accomplished and earned isn't because you are more loved by God or because you're half as smart as your ego might like you to think you are. But it's likely you've been making some good and responsible decisions and God is entrusting you with more of his gifts. Guard against ego's subtle deception. God's gifts are not meant as trophies to your ego.

There's something else, too. You are blessed for only one purpose—so that you might be a blessing to others. God has given you all that you are and have in the hope that you will prove to be like the five-talent person in the story Jesus told. You ask, "Doesn't God know what I'll do with what he's given to me?" Frankly, I'm not sure he does. But that's a question you'll have to direct to the theologians. What I am sure about is that every talent, gift, and resource you and I have is a divine trust—a blessing given so that you might in turn be a blessing to this world. The interesting thing is that you will instinctively know what I'm saying is the truth so long as your ego hasn't slipped back into the driver's seat of your life. If that's the case, your ego, on the one hand, will make you feel as if what I'm saying is a lot of bunk because what you have and what you've accomplished is something you have done yourself. You've lifted yourself up by your own bootstraps.

If, on the other hand, you are holding your ego at bay, you will feel what you have and what you've accomplished is truly a gift. All of it. In fact, you'll find yourself looking at all this stuff you've accumulated with genuine humility and amazement. You'll feel blessed and want nothing more than for your life to be a blessing. As you seize every divine opportunity to be a blessing, that's when you will begin to experience and enjoy the life you've always wanted.

Abraham of old did. Why God chose him and materially blessed him over someone else is a mystery. But what God chose him to be and do is no mystery. God said, "I will cause you to become the father of a great nation. I will bless you and make you famous, and I will make you a blessing to others" (Gen 12:2).

His purpose was clear and not so different from anyone else's purpose in life. It was to recognize with gratitude that all of his life was a blessing and to respond by offering his life as a blessing to the world.

BLESSED TO BE A BLESSING

Not long ago, I was consulting with church leaders in a financial campaign to raise money to build a new church. In efforts like these, I often challenge the members to make a gift over and above what they regularly give of themselves and their resources to support the ministries of their church or parish. I often encourage them to be sacrificial in their gifts of talent and treasure with the understanding that a sacrificial gift is one that grows out of a change in lifestyle or the temporary or permanent rearrangement of priorities.

This was a large church that was, by necessity, meeting in two different locations and offering eight different worship opportunities every weekend. They asked me to speak in every service. I agreed to do so and, as you might imagine, by Sunday night I was ready for a week on the coast.

A sophisticated, educated, and relatively wealthy audience of several thousand people filled both sanctuaries those eight times as I delivered my remarks based on this story of the parable of talents. At the close of one service, a man introduced himself as the founder and principal stockholder in one of the largest retail chains in America. While you might not personally know the gentleman any more than I did, you would know the chain of retail stores if I revealed its name. He was bothered by my interpretation of the story and the application of this principle "Not equal giving, but equal sacrifice."

As in the parable, I had likened the talents to money and material blessings. In my speech, I said that it's normally not too difficult for one-talent people, or those of ordinary means, to figure out what might be an equal sacrifice for them. But the people who will have the hardest time determining what for them is an equal sacrifice are those who have many blessings or much wealth.

"You know who I am?" he asked rather arrogantly, as if he might be offended if I admitted I didn't.

"No sir, I'm afraid I do not," I explained. "But I have a feeling you're getting ready to tell me."

He did. And then he proceeded to tell me, "I don't like these words 'Not giving equally, but equal sacrifice giving' or something like that."

"That's close enough," I said with a smile. "What about it bothers you?"

"Well," he explained, "if that's the expectation in our church's financial campaign, what's a person in my position supposed to do?"

"I'm not sure I follow."

"What kind of gift is expected from someone like me?" he asked in a clear tone of defensiveness and disbelief. To be sure, he wasn't looking for spiritual guidance in determining the level of his gift. He was looking for a way to dumb down the expectation. "Give a gift of equal sacrifice? You've got to be kidding!" is something of the nature of the internal conversation I'm sure he was having with his ego while I spoke. I could not have asked for a better example of a person with the "equal and fair share" mentality. Giving was hardly something this man did with self-abandon and sheer joy and pleasure. His giving, at least to his parish, was hardly expressive of his gratitude toward God for all of his obvious blessings and accomplishments. He was one of those I described earlier who calculates all of life on the basis of the bottom line.

I'm not normally one of those persons who can think of just the right response at the right time. I usually think of profound things I wish I had said as I later replay the conversation in my mind. So I think my immediate and matter-of-fact response was nothing short of a divine gift. I looked straight at him and said, "Sir, I truly cannot say what a sacrificial gift would be for you, but this much I'm sure about: it's probably a whole lot more than you're currently thinking!"

He was stunned. When I think back on it now, I'm surprised he took it as graciously as he did. I later learned he gave the largest single gift ever received in the history of that church. In light of our exchange, this was a welcome surprise.

I don't know how he arrived at the financial gift he chose to give, but I hope he did so not out of guilt or obligation, but because he began understanding that generous giving brings a joy unspeakable and a life indescribable. If so, he has joined the ranks of those who understand what I'm saying about generous giving. If he hasn't already, he will move beyond believing that all that he has accomplished made him separate and more special than those who may have preceded him or will follow him. Instead, he'll interpret his material blessings as a divine test to determine whether he's going to respond appropriately by investing less in the stuff that strokes his ego and more in circumstances and causes that build the kingdom. In fact, he'll know that everything he is and has is a divine gift to him for one purpose and one purpose only—so that his life and resources might be a gift to the world. When that understanding begins to dawn, then he will find himself enjoying the life he's always wanted. As the writer of Deuteronomy put it, "All must give as they are able, according to the blessings given to them by the Lord your God" (Deut 16:17).

SUGGESTIONS FOR GIVING, THEN GETTING THE LIFE YOU'VE ALWAYS WANTED

• Think about your own background. Have you grown up in a religious tradition that taught you to limit your charity to what is your "equal and fair share"? If so, your giving could be doing far more, making a greater impact on the world around you if you decided to give for reasons other than what's your "fair and equal" share. In some cases, maybe way beyond what's your fair share. This much is certain: the joy you may currently experience in giving will take on a whole new dimension when it moves beyond what's expected or your average and fair share. But don't take my word for it. Why not give it a try? What have you got to lose? It's just money. Or time. If you're like me, you've wasted both on far lesser things. What you must remember is that what you give away will come back to you. Do you really have anything to lose?

This truth bears repeating: what you give away will return to you. If you're like me, it'll take you some time to wrap your mind around this principle. Again, it's a fundamental law of the universe that some call the "law of abundance" or the "law of the harvest," and Jesus was referring to it when he said, "If you give, you will receive. Your gift will return to you in full measure, pressed down, shaken together to make room for more, and running over. Whatever measure you use in giving—large or small—it will be used to measure what is given back to you" (Luke 6:38).

By any measure, those are remarkable, even disturbing, words. But Jesus is plainly saying that what you give away returns to you. I have decided to accept that what he said is what he meant, and I've stopped trying to explain it or discount the gravity of it.

This is largely because my own experience has validated it. When I went through my divorce, I went from making almost a six-figure income before the divorce to less than half that amount afterward— a huge hit. I had family responsibilities that continued regardless of my failure and a mortgage to pay as well as a car payment. I had to have a car because my former spouse kept the family car. Fortunately for me, my mother had decided to sell her own car about the same time as my divorce. Thank God for mothers. Not only did she graciously take me in for a while, but she was benevolent enough to discount the price of her car in an effort to help me.

Unless you've been through something like this, you probably can't imagine the degree of emotional stress associated with such an experience, not to speak of how shattered your self-esteem becomes. As for me, I felt like a complete failure as a person and as a father for many months after that experience. Everywhere I went, I imagined people were talking about me and judging me. To say the least, I was depressed.

I may have been a failure when it comes to my first marriage, but there was one thing I was not going to fail at fulfilling: the financial support due my children and the mother who bore them. My former spouse and children stayed in the house, and she provided the lion's share of care to them, taking a teaching job herself to supplement the household income that had been cut in half.

You may have had similar experiences. You've been through a divorce or have been terminated from your job or, perhaps, you have had a debilitating illness that has caused your income stream to dry up. Whatever it may be, you understand all too well how devastating something like this can be.

During the first year of that most difficult time, I quit giving. I had grown up giving not only a tenth of my income but, at times, giving beyond a tithe. That's how I had been raised, what I believed I should do, and it's what I did. But I now know that my giving was motivated by my position, not my passion. I was a pastor and felt giving was expected of me (a slightly different version of the "fair and equal giving" motivation for giving). My giving was obligatory and had little heart. Parenthetically, the law of abundance still worked for me. As I look back on those years, I realize that, while my giving might have been done from a more personally rewarding motivation, it enabled the law of abundance to operate, and I always had plenty. What I gave away would always return.

In spite of this, I found myself justifying the need for the money I was accustomed to giving away. So I quit giving. You may have done this too when circumstances have gotten financially tight. Against everything I said I believed, I used the money I would have given to charity to provide for my own needs and wants. This made sense. After all, I had to survive too. Besides, I reasoned that this would only be temporary suspension of my gifts to charity. As soon as I got back on my feet and got my income level back where it was at one time, I planned to start giving again.

Unfortunately, that's not how it turned out. The law of abundance is one of those laws that you can break yourself on. My decision to divert my charity did just that, and it was the worst decision I could have made. Instead of getting out of my financial crisis, which I had planned to do by year's end, I was in deeper debt and worse off financially than I had ever been. I owed credit card companies several thousand dollars, which was anathema to me. I knew better than to live on credit cards. I had counseled people for years about avoiding unnecessary debt and all credit card debt. But there I was, using credit cards to buy groceries and, ultimately, in a greater financial mess than even the year before.

But through all of this, six simple yet significant words kept haunting me: "If you give, you will receive." I hit rock bottom. Seeing no other way out, I cried and prayed and cried and prayed and cried some more, knowing the whole time that there was one way and only one way to rectify the mess I had made of things. I had to give up trying to save myself and, once again, give myself back to God and put my resources back into the service of the kingdom. After a lot of thought and a lot more prayer, I did that. At first, I took small steps simply because I was afraid, but then, as my faith and confidence in the laws of this universe grew, I took larger ones.

Within a year, almost to the day, I was financially free. You could call it a miracle, and I suppose that's what it is, given the gravity of the financial mess I had made of things. But it's the way God has designed his world. "If you give, you will receive." It's not rocket science. Within one year from the day I got the financial priorities of my life in order, I not only paid off those debts I had amassed, but I was earning an income greater than I had ever earned in my entire adult life.

It was during that year when what I used to say I believed about giving became what I know about giving and this law of abundance that's associated with it. At times, there can be a chasm as wide as the Grand Canyon between what you might say you believe and what you know. A belief is something you pick up along the way. What you know is what picks you up. Knowing becomes a significant part of you. What you know is not simply something you believe is true. You know it's true. What you know isn't necessarily a religious creed you might glibly say in unison with others while reciting the beliefs of your faith on Sunday. Rather, when you know something, as opposed to when you simply believe something, that knowing becomes one of the organizing principles around which you order your life.

Ask people today, for example, if they believe in Jesus Christ, and a whopping percentage of the American public will say, "Well, of course, I believe in Jesus Christ." Does that make them followers of Jesus Christ? Not on your life. Real followers of Jesus don't just call themselves "Christian" because they hold baptismal membership in some parish or because they say they've professed faith in him. Profession without practice is perfunctory at best. Real followers of Jesus Christ are those who are trying to be Christ-like. There's a huge difference. Christ-like people are committed to living their lives like unto Jesus himself, paying close attention to what he said and diligently seeking to pattern their lives after him.

So where does that leave a significant percentage of people who today fill church pews? I can't say for certain. What I can say is that Jesus clearly said to give. Yet, in virtually every church in America, approximately half the members who say they believe in Jesus give nothing of themselves or their resources either to his church or beyond his church. Draw your own conclusion. The church is full of people who say they believe in Jesus, but there may only be a few who really know Jesus Christ. While I'm hardly the judge of who does and who doesn't, for me anyway, the knowing of something— in this case, Someone—has become far more significant than simply believing something.

What do you "know" to be the truth as opposed to what you've been taught to "believe" is the truth? When you know what you believe, then what you believe takes on a whole new dimension.

• "A life that matters is_____." How would you fill in the blank? If you've never tried this exercise, go ahead. Fill it in. "I will know that my life has mattered—really mattered—when _____."

You may find it tougher to finish the statement than you might think at first. But if you'll spend time in meditation and contemplate what a life that really matters means to you, I think you'll discover that almost anything you conclude will in some way involve giving—the giving of yourself both materially and nonmaterially. Try it. There are vast numbers of worthwhile causes in this world. Start with the place where you receive your spiritual instruction, but don't be duped by some selfish minister who wants you to give to him the lion's share of your charity. Do your homework even if you feel everything is above board. Above all, talk to God about it. Whatever you decide, do it from your heart and do it with gratitude. And be as generous as you can be.

The founder of the Salt Lake City-based chemical manufacturing company Jon W. Huntsman recently contributed more than $200 million to establish and fund a cancer institute in Utah, more than $50 million to a school in Pennsylvania, another $50 million to help rebuild Armenia after a destructive earthquake rocked the country in 1988, and tens of millions to overcome poverty and build shelters for women and children who daily face domestic violence. Huntsman explained his motivation to give by saying, "It is essential to live a productive and meaningful life. Philanthropy provides an enormous sense of purpose. Too many wealthy people are under the mistaken impression that the true measure of financial success isn't what you make but what you keep. It's ultimately how gracious you are and what you can do to make the world a better place."[2]

Readers of a story like this are sometimes inclined to say, "Well, he should be giving money away. Just look how rich he is!"

But then I read about Thomas Cannon who was anything but a multimillionaire. In fact, he was known in Virginia as the "poor man's philanthropist." Though his story was told many years ago by Time magazine, his example is as contemporary as this morning's news.

Cannon was a postal worker in Richmond, Virginia. He earned less than $20,000 a year, yet managed to give away more than $30,000 of his own money in the previous five years. He would send most of it in $1,000 checks to complete strangers whose misfortunes and setbacks had been brought to his attention. A few of his beneficiaries? An orphan from Columbia who needed heart surgery and a couple who had parented more than forty foster children.[3]

When I found his remarkable story on the Internet (I honestly do not recall how I did so), I wondered if he might still be alive. I wanted to talk to him, if possible, since I would have only been twenty-one years old when his story first appeared in Time.

I Googled his name. Pages and pages of articles about him appeared on the screen of my computer. One, however, in the *Richmond Times-Dispatch*, reported that he died of colon cancer in 2005. The entire city of Richmond memorialized his life and his mission. In fact, when the newspaper asked the public about how the community should honor him, scores of e-mails, letters, and calls came from people wishing to preserve his spirit and emulate his life. I find it genuinely inspiring to read about the impact this modest, decent man had on thousands of people.

Cannon recorded a cassette tape of his "final instructions" for his family. Those who heard it called it "pure Cannon, firm and funny."[4] After he was gone, he said he wanted his name attached to "no building, no bridge, no street, no scholarship, no stream, no highway, no nothing. On second thought," he said that the only exception was if the U.S. Postal Service, where he had worked for many years, wanted to create a stamp in his honor. "That," he said, "is permissible."

I laughed when I read that, and I understand there are those who are, in fact, working toward having him so memorialized. But stamps honoring individuals can be made no sooner than ten years after a person's death, except in the case of U.S. presidents.

Wouldn't you love to have had the opportunity to meet Cannon? Don't you know this man must surely have had an infectious love of life and was living, if anyone ever has, the life he really wanted? A life that mattered?

How would you describe a life that really matters? Is it one that makes the world a better place? Giving yourself includes giving your money even if you're not wealthy enough to establish your own family foundation or give a gift large enough that the hospital board would name the new research wing after you.

Will Rogers used to say, "We can't all be heroes; someone has to sit on the curb and clap as they go by." The fact is, just being a cheerleader for others can be heroic. Jesus called it giving a cup of cold water in his name (Matt 10:42).

It might be something as seemingly insignificant as the giving of a larger gratuity than a waiter might expect along with a pleasant, forgiving smile or an understanding word to a person who's overworked, likely underpaid, and who has mistakenly brought you an entrée you did not order. There was a time when careless mistakes by a table server would have offended me. I would have taken it personally and voiced my displeasure to the server just as quickly, cutting him or her down to proper size for the needless offense.

Occasionally, I still wrestle against such demons, but I am happy to report that I am much better these days at catching myself before I say something unkind or demand that the manager reduce the cost of my meal. Instead, I am discovering today just how amazing it can be when an unexpected but kind word rescues a person's feelings of failure. By giving kindness, I find my own feelings of annoyance are diffused and replaced with positive inner feelings. It's that law again—what you give away comes back to you. Under unpleasant circumstances like these, I try to do the unexpected—in the situation above, I might leave the normal 20 percent gratuity, but then leave another 5 percent or 10 percent more simply as a gesture of unexpected kindness.

• What you can give away is limited only by your imagination. I am still amazed when I think about it, but when I made the decision to follow my heart and write this book, something significant occurred to me. I realized if I were to succeed, God would have to give me the words to write and the stories to tell. Not surprisingly, as I stated elsewhere, he has done just that. In fact, at every turn, when I have needed something to make a point or to illustrate an idea, what I have needed has suddenly appeared. It has been amazing.

You might dismiss that notion as purely coincidental. At one time, I would have joined you in wagging my head in disbelief. But I can't do that anymore. God has demonstrated to me in many different ways that he has designed this world so that everything is as it should be, and when I conduct my life in faith that it is, I am much

more at peace with myself and the world around me. I don't have to
strive, because what I need will arrive just when I need it. God wants
it to be this way so that I might be free to live in complete trust in
his promised provision and stay focused on my purpose in life—to
give myself away. The freedom in this approach to living is remarkable.

This is one of the mantras of my life: "I receive all things as
God's gift to me; I learn from all things as my gift to myself; and I
live what I learn as my gift to the world."

Time and time again, in an almost magical kind of way, God has
given me the perfect story, anecdote, or quote at just the time I
needed it. The following is a perfect example of what I mean.

When I reached this point in the writing of the book and began
thinking about what story I wanted to tell, I closed my computer at
the bidding of a flight attendant as our plane neared its destination.
We were landing in Dallas, and I had about an hour before my next
flight. I headed for the nearest Admirals Club of American Airlines.
I do this often when I have a few minutes between connections.

I walked over to the complimentary newspaper rack. I was in
search of *USA Today*, but the complimentary issues must have been
taken already. There were other titles but none familiar to me. So I
just grabbed one and it was not until later that I noticed the newspaper I had picked up was that day's issue of the Fort Worth
Star-Telegram. I had never heard of this newspaper or read one of its
issues. But that's what I held in my hand, and, though I was unaware
at the moment, God was preparing to give me what I needed for this
section of the book.

I'm at that place in my own life where I no longer believe there
are random events. Instead, everything that happens in my life,
whether good or bad, carries within its unfolding a gift from God.
This day would be no exception.

While there were several sections to the newspaper, I happened
to select section "B," and there on the front page was God's gift. Staff
writer Noor Elashi titled this story "Celebrating a truly life-giving
gift." In my work, I often tell people of the varied ways they might
give. There are, of course, the typical monetary gifts, but even these

can be expressed in many different forms. For example, there's a trust fund you might establish and make someone or something the beneficiary. There are paid-up insurance policies you might designate to a person or institution as the beneficiary when you die. This is just the tip of the iceberg.

Just as there are material and monetary gifts you might give, there are many other ways to give that are nonmaterial in nature— such as the unexpected word of kindness as I described earlier. But the kind of gift Elashi was writing about takes charity to a whole new dimension.

Jamie Cadiz of greater Fort Worth was suffering from a genetic illness that affects slightly more than a half-million Americans: polycystic kidney disease. Jamie had been living with the disease for several years, but at age forty-seven, her kidneys began failing and she was sure she would go the way of her father who, suffering from the same genetic disorder, died at the age of forty-seven himself.

Carolyn Morris, Jamie's mother, watched as her daughter rapidly deteriorated. She knew Jamie had to have a kidney transplant soon or she would be preparing for a second funeral. But Jamie had a problem; she was not a match with more than 90 percent of kidney donors.

One day, Carolyn Morris decided to hand out packets of information at her Southlake Boulevard Church about her daughter's desperate condition and urgent need for a matching donor. Scott Clarke got the "call." Inside that place where all of us hear the gentle promptings of God's Spirit of generosity, Scott Clarke said he heard the voice. He knew he was the one to help Jamie Cadiz. Later, in fact, he explained that he leaned over and whispered to his wife as they sat in church, "I'm the match. Something in my heart tells me I'm it."

But Judith, Scott's wife, was not so certain of Clarke's call. After all, she and Scott were the proud parents of three young children. "What if one of our children needs a kidney or I need a kidney?" Judith reasoned. "But then," she went on, "I thought this must be God's plan, and he will take care of us and our needs in the future. We must do our part today."

On the occasion of the Clarkes' fifteenth wedding anniversary, rather than spending the evening at a restaurant or going to the theater, Scott entered the operating room at the University of Maryland Center and donated one of his kidneys to Jamie Cadiz. Strangely, when Scott awakened from surgery, he still remembered their wedding and whispered a "happy anniversary" song that he made up while still lying on the hospital gurney and feeling the effects of anesthesia. Today, Jamie Cadiz is alive and well because of the "life-giving gift" that Scott Clarke gave to her in the form of a healthy kidney.[5]

When I read the story I was reminded of something Leo Tolstoy once said: "All people live, not by reason of any care they have for themselves, but by the love for them that is in other people." It may not be a kidney God prompts you to give away, but your world is filled with many Jamies who need love and kindness and too few Scotts who have both to give.

NOTES

[1] Hay House Books, 2005.

[2] Samuel Greengard, "Money for Nothing," *American Way* (1 September 2006): 44.

[3] *Time* Archives, "Setting a High Standard for Giving," http://www.time.com/time/magazine/article/0,9171,945798,00.html.

[4] Bill Lohmann, "Keeping Cannon's Memory Alive," *Richmond Times-Dispatch*, 3 August 2005, http://www.timesdispatch.com/servlet/Satellite?pagename=RTD/MGArticle/RTD_BasicArticle&c=MGArticle&cid=1031784215644.

[5] Noor Elashi, "Celebrating a Truly Life-Giving Gift," *Star-Telegram*, 23 October 2006, 1B, 10B.

8

Myth 4

"The Standard for Giving Is the Tithe"

*Nothing that you have not given away will ever be really
yours.*

—C. S. Lewis (1898–1963)

*Real generosity toward the future lies in giving all to the
present.*

—Albert Camus (1913–1960)

*To live a pure, unselfish life, one must count nothing as one's
own in the midst of abundance.*

—Buddha (563–483 bc)

This chapter is mostly for people of faith who are involved in a religious community. In many if not most of them, the tithe (giving 10
percent of household income) is held up as the scriptural standard
for giving.

Don't believe it. It might have been a good standard, given that it
appears to have served well the saints of old. Tithing is mentioned
dozens of times in the Old Testament alone. It might even be a good
goal to challenge people of faith to aspire to today, given the decline

in annual revenues in many churches the last few years. But to teach that tithing is the standard to follow today rests on a faulty reading of the New Testament.

Tithing is not taught in the New Testament. Not explicitly, anyway.

In the Old Testament, there's no question that the tithe was the standard. In fact, it was the law with many nuances and complications.

But, in the New Testament, it isn't so. If you hear anyone say it is, you can be sure they've not done their homework.

This is a bold assault on a commonly held belief. Many sincere people will not only disagree with this assertion but will be offended and go to great lengths to prove me wrong. But the New Testament simply does not hold up the tithe as the standard for giving. Besides, there's a much better way to teach people to give, and I'll demonstrate that to you later in this chapter. But first, a little background.

LEARNING TO TITHE

I grew up as a Baptist. I heard tithing taught in religious education classes and preached from the ambo all of my life. In fact, over the years, I've done my own share of preaching and teaching on tithing.

The earliest memory I have of tithing came at the age of fourteen. I got my first job. It was a paper delivery route. Early every morning, I delivered the community newspaper to slightly more than 100 households. In those days, we not only delivered the paper each morning, but we also had to make monthly rounds to collect the fees.

One morning after my first month as a paper delivery boy, I finished making my rounds, went to the basement of our house, and carefully spread the money on the hood of our washing machine like a jeweler displaying precious stones on a black velvet canvas. I counted and separated what portion was to be sent to the newspaper business office. What was left was my profit.

If my memory serves me correctly, I think I earned that first month a grand total of twenty-four dollars. Not much, to be sure.

But, to a fourteen-year-old in the late sixties, those were pretty stellar earnings.

I caressed those bills, waved them in the air as a winning athlete might wave a trophy above his head, and imagined all the places I would go and things I would buy.

Presently, I noticed my father standing at the door to the utility room where I was reveling in my riches.

"So, how'd you do?" he asked.

"Twenty-four dollars."

"Twenty-four big ones?" he echoed. "Great, son. I'm proud of you."

"Thanks, Dad."

"So, I guess you'll need an envelope for your tithe?" he asked as if he were expecting me to be thinking the same thing.

"Excuse me?"

"An offering envelope," he explained as if he didn't hear the shock and even sarcasm in my question. "I knew you'd be looking for one so I brought you a tithing envelope. This way, you can put your tithe in it and drop it in the offering plate in church on Sunday."

"You're not serious, are you, Dad?"

"Serious? Son, I'm very serious. A tithe of your earnings is 10 percent. That's $2.40, by my calculations. But I suppose you can figure that for yourself."

I took the envelope, counted out $2.40, and placed it in the envelope with about as much excitement as one might pay a traffic fine.

Years later, I learned what Saint Paul said to the Corinthians: "You must each make up your own mind as to how much you should give. Don't give reluctantly or in response to pressure. For God loves the person who gives cheerfully" (2 Cor 9:7).

One thing is for certain. Saint Paul wasn't describing me. I broke all the rules. And had I known that verse at age fourteen, I would have invited my father to a duel of serious debate. I had not decided what to give in my own heart. In fact, I had not planned to give anything at all. All twenty-four dollars were spent, as far as I was concerned. What I did give was given reluctantly and under compulsion, an obvious violation of Paul's instructions, and my father should have known better. That was my first lesson in tithing.

TITHING AMONG VARIOUS RELIGIOUS GROUPS

For more than thirty years, I've been a minister, and for the last ten of those a church and parish consultant. Having consulted now in virtually every denomination in America—Evangelical, Protestant, and Roman Catholic alike—it's been interesting to learn what these various religious traditions teach about tithing. What I've discovered is not only intriguing but varied.

Like the Baptists I grew up with, there are those that regularly teach tithing and spend a lot of time debating whether tithing should be on the gross or net of one's earnings. I know a minister who likes to say he's willing to debate this with any person who is tithing, either on the gross or net, but not with any person who is doing neither. He isn't doing much debating these days.

Most of the people across these varied religious traditions don't really practice tithing (most households that practice charitable giving actually give 3 percent or less of household income). But there is a tacit acceptance of the pretense that they are.

Not long ago, I was making a report to some clients. I noted that the average household gift to their church was slightly more than $2,100 annually. Yet when I surveyed the congregation and asked, among many other things, on what a member based her or his giving decisions, the overwhelming majority reported, "My giving decisions are based on a tithe of my income."

That response surprised me at first. It doesn't anymore for the simple reason that I get it so often—and not only from members in Baptist churches but from members in many Evangelical and Protestant churches.

Do the math. If $2,100 is a tithe of income, then the majority of people in the church where I was providing consultation were annually earning about $21,000. Most of them would qualify for government assistance. If I told you the name of this church and the sort of neighborhood in which it is located, you'd know that $2,100 was anything but a tithe of income.

How do you explain this disconnect? I suppose one explanation is that they're all lying. For obvious reasons, I would prefer another explanation. One might be that they really don't know what the word tithe means. I might be inclined to believe this explanation were it not for the fact that most of these Evangelical and Protestant traditions are, by and large, always talking about tithing. At least, they did until recently. Some have now adopted what they call a "seeker-sensitive approach" in their public worship services. In many of these churches, talk about giving is left out of the public arena and relegated to small-group Bible study classes.

But where it is regularly discussed, I wonder how people could not know that a tithe means 10 percent of one's income, irrespective of the gross or net issue. I expect this when I am consulting with Catholics. I find many Roman Catholics, if they use the word at all, let "tithe" refer to whatever it is that they might give. As a matter of fact, I recently heard one Catholic say, "I'm tithing 3 percent of my income."

"Did you say that you are tithing 3 percent of your income?" I quizzed, just to give him an opportunity to see if he would catch the contradiction. He didn't.

"That's right," he replied.

That's like someone saying to you, "Here's a carton of a dozen eggs," only to discover, when you open the carton, there are only four.

Probably the most plausible explanation is that there's a kind of reinvention by many of the meaning of tithing. People have heard about tithing for so long (and just as quickly dismissed it, I might add), that they don't really hear it anymore. In fact, I have the feeling that when you ask these people whether they tithe, it's as if they hear you asking not "Do you give 10 percent of your income?" but "Do you regularly give?" Tithing no longer refers to the amount of one's gift as much as it does to the regularity of one's giving. The amount could be anything.

WHERE THE TITHE BELONGS

The one thing I've discovered that is fairly consistent among all Evangelicals is that they believe the tithe is to be given to the church. By that, they mean the local church. That is, if their members wish to give to other causes, that may be okay. But such giving should be over and above the tithe because the tithe belongs to the local church.

Where do they get this idea? It comes from the prophet Malachi who instructed the Old Testament worshippers to "Bring all of the tithes into the storehouse . . ." (Mal 3:10). These people interpret "storehouse" to mean "church-house." I'm a bit suspicious of that interpretation and application. If God intended us to build the case that the tithe belongs exclusively to the local church, I'm inclined to think there would be some kind of instruction to this end in the New Testament—but, of course, there is not.

While a few traditions dismiss tithing altogether, the majority of Christians, regardless of their religious background, do not practice giving a tenth of income to anything. In fact, they're not even close. Furthermore, if researchers are correct, less than 3 percent of those who claim to be Christian actually tithe. If those who respond to these researchers' questions misunderstand the meaning of tithing the way hundreds I've questioned over the years seem to misunderstand it, that 3 percent is likely far less.

While some religious leaders and churches unapologetically dismiss tithing as an Old Testament concept having little application today, my experience has been that the majority of sincere religious people do not so quickly discount it. Some teach that the tithe refers to all of one's charitable giving, but they don't try to convince their constituents that the tithe belongs exclusively to the church. For example, if they personally believe in tithing, some Catholic leaders will teach the appropriateness of the tithe but they will suggest that it be divided equally, 5 percent to the local parish and 5 percent to the Diocese.

All of this raises an important question: Which tradition is right? They can't all be right. Which one has correctly interpreted the New Testament teaching?

In my opinion, they've all missed it. Even a cursory reading of Jesus' teaching will reveal how infrequently he spoke about tithing. In fact, in those few places where Jesus did speak about giving, what you see him instructing people to do is to give it all away. Good thing only a few people today have taken that suggestion seriously.

WHAT JESUS REALLY TAUGHT

Neither Jesus nor any of the New Testament writers teach us to tithe—at least not explicitly. I'm aware that some will dismiss me for saying this, but it's the truth. Others might feel such a suggestion will further erode the practice of tithing and fuel the financial crisis many churches are facing, but I don't think so.

The central theme of this book is that there is a better way. If the church would help people find a more wholesome motivation for giving, I believe churches and charities everywhere would abound with the resources they need to carry out their missions.

Many church leaders proudly tell me that they "expect" their members to tithe and outline those expectations to all new members. Yet, in almost all of these churches, only a minuscule percentage of people actually tithe. What's the problem? All the talk in the world about what a person "should" do won't cut it. I'm inclined to ask the leaders who tell me this, "If that's what you expect of your people, why are 97 percent of them ignoring you?"

I think a better way is by example, if you are in a leadership position. What are you learning about life's purpose in giving? How has giving changed your own life, outlook, and perspective on the world? What has generous giving done for the daily living of your life and that of other people in your church? Do you encourage your members to share what they are learning about giving and how their giving has changed their lives? What are the human stories of change and hope your church is bringing to the community and world? Is the telling of these stories encouraged as your members discover the joy of living by giving themselves away?

What I'm suggesting is, if there were less talk in the church about "what" Christians are supposed to do and more living testimonies about "why" and "how" giving has changed people's lives, the budgetary needs of your church would take care of themselves. In fact, the church would always have what is financially needed when this is the focus of ministry. When people begin finding the life they've always wanted by giving themselves and their resources away and are encouraged to share their experiences, the financial needs of the church would always be met. Furthermore, the church would find many Christians not only moving toward the tithe, but beyond it.

Giving will change how people live their lives. If you're a church leader, start with yourself. This is where it must begin if any change is to take place in your church. If your giving is perfunctory and you're doing it only because of your position, then you have nothing to share except the "shoulds" and "oughts" about giving. That is not a sustaining motivation, as history has demonstrated. Were you not in the position you are, you wouldn't be giving either. When you begin discovering life in the giving of yourself away, the rest will take care of itself.

What did Jesus say about tithing? There are only two places where he even mentions it, and actually these are the same words but recorded by two different writers. In reality, then, we have only one thing he said about the subject, and what he did say was hardly in a complimentary tone.

In Matthew 23:23 (and the parallel passage in Luke 11:42), Jesus says, "Woe to you, teachers of the law and Pharisees, you hypocrites! You give a tenth of your spices—mint, dill and cumin. But you have neglected the more important matters of the law—justice, mercy and faithfulness. You should have practiced the latter, without neglecting the former."

Whatever you may conclude from this, Jesus was hardly instructing his followers to tithe. In fact, if he's instructing them to do anything, it's to practice "justice, mercy, and faithfulness." That's clearly his greater concern.

There are those who will argue that, since Jesus appears at least to affirm tithing ("you should have practiced the latter, without neglecting the former"), then we can conclude he must expect his followers to tithe.

Not so fast. Admittedly, Jesus doesn't release the people of his day from the practice of tithing, but neither does he definitively instruct his followers, then or now, to practice it. I don't see how anyone can argue with integrity that this vague statement of Jesus means he expects his followers to tithe. If tithing was as big a deal to him as it seems to be with many clerics today, then why didn't he have more to say about it here or elsewhere? What we have here is a simple acknowledgment by Jesus that, while tithing may be appropriate, it is not nearly as appropriate as the demonstration of "justice, mercy, and faithfulness."

I can't tell you how many churches I've consulted with over the years that seem more interested in how they might increase their revenue than in speaking out against injustice—like the genocide currently taking place in Darfur where, just this morning, the news reported nearly a half-million people have been slaughtered. It's a good thing we've got news reports. Otherwise, I wouldn't get much from many of today's pulpits about injustices like this taking place in our world. Where is the justice and mercy in the church today? I think this is the sort of thing Jesus meant by his scathing rebuke against the religious community of his day.

Take it a step further. There is no indication anywhere in the New Testament that Jesus himself ever practiced tithing. What we have are four Gospels full of stories of Jesus practicing "justice, mercy, and faithfulness." In my own opinion, if the contemporary church pursued the virtues of justice and mercy with half the energy it seeks to defend the practice of tithing, the world would be a much better place and the church a much healthier place.

WHAT THE NEW TESTAMENT TEACHES ABOUT TITHING

"What about the New Testament?" you ask. "Is there anything in the rest of the New Testament that would help us defend tithing as the standard for practice today?" Not much, frankly. In fact, apart from what we've seen about tithing in the teachings of Jesus, there are only two other New Testament books where tithing is even mentioned: Luke 18:12 and Hebrews 7:5-9.

In Luke's Gospel, the rich young ruler is defending his religious life to Jesus by saying, among other things, that he has tithed all he possesses. When he acknowledges that to Jesus, you can almost hear the elders shout, "Amen!"

But Jesus wasn't impressed. If you're looking for a defense of tithing, you're not going to get much help from this story. In fact, in light of what Jesus instructed this fellow to do, you might want to steer clear of this story altogether. It is here that Jesus suggested that, to obtain eternal life, the rich young ruler would have to give away everything—not just tithe. This may be getting at the heart of Jesus' teaching about giving and what was likely the practice of his own life. It isn't an easy teaching to accept, much less to practice.

The references to tithing in chapter 7 of Hebrews illustrate the Old Testament practice of tithing by Abraham, the Levites, and Melchizedek. In all of it, the writer of Hebrews is obviously building a case for the priesthood of Jesus, not a case for the practice of tithing. To read anything else here is to misread the message. It's all about Jesus Christ and his supremacy as a High Priest capable of atoning for the sins of humanity. The writer is not developing a treatise to defend the Old Testament practice of tithing.

I think you can see where all of this is going.

Maybe you're wondering, "If tithing is taught in the Old Testament, shouldn't we at least practice it today even if we aren't clearly instructed to do so in the New Testament?"

Again, I think that's pushing it too far. Admittedly Jesus said, "I did not come to abolish the law but to fulfill it'" (Matt 5:17), but that does not mean he expects his followers to tithe. The law also taught an "eye for an eye, and tooth for tooth" (Exod 21:23-25). But, thankfully, we don't live by that method of justice anymore.

The way Jesus fulfilled the law was to change the way the law was interpreted by his contemporaries. For example, in response to the law pertaining to the equal distribution of justice and punishment (eye for an eye), Jesus said, "But I say, don't resist an evil person. If you are slapped on the right cheek, turn the other, too" (Matt 5:39). When I read this, I wonder how Jesus would expect his followers today to apply his reinterpretation of the law when it comes to the war in Iraq, for example. Nobody disagrees that America was slapped on 9/11—more like a severe beating. But when I read these words of Jesus, I can't help but doubt whether going to war with Iraq was the kind of response that's consistent with what is the clear teaching of Jesus here—to turn the other cheek. It was Gandhi who said, "An eye for an eye only ends up making the whole world blind." There's a curious oddity to me, and that is why Gandhi and other modern saints seem to have understood and lived by the teachings of Jesus more than many who claim to be Jesus' followers do today.

The law also taught that anybody guilty of adultery was to be stoned to death (Lev 20:9-11). Forgive my bluntness, but if we applied that law today, we'd have a lot of funerals to conduct even among those who frequent the pews on weekends. Don't try to use this "fulfillment of the law" argument to defend tithing. That'll get you nowhere.

SO WHAT DOES THE NEW TESTAMENT TEACH ABOUT GIVING?

Little instruction is given at all. No specific amount or percentage is outlined anywhere in the New Testament. What is taught is that we simply give in response to and in gratitude for the experience of God's grace and God's gifts to us.

Saint Paul said, "Each man should give what he has decided in his heart to give . . ." (2 Cor 9:7a). It is a decision of the heart. Nothing more, nothing less. And that makes it a personal, practical decision. No one is to dictate to any other what that amount should be. That keeps this whole matter squarely where it should be kept—between you, the receiver, and God, the giver.

MODELS OF GIVING

Interestingly, a search of the New Testament will reveal models of giving but little instruction about giving. With a few exceptions in the Epistles, there is little taught on the subject. Even in those few places where there is instruction, it is usually in the form of an example of those who have learned to give.

Here's a sampling.

Giving is demonstrated as deriving from the nature of God's character. Saint John opens his story of the life of Christ by saying, "For God so loved the world that he gave his only Son . . ." (John 3:16a). God gave his Son. The rest of the story of Jesus is an example of how he gave himself to his Father, to others, and, ultimately, to all of humanity in his death by crucifixion.

Giving is demonstrated in the New Testament as our direct response to God's grace. Since grace is God's unmerited gift to us, giving is our unmitigated gratitude to God.

Take Mary of Bethany (John 12:1-3). Having experienced the mercy and forgiveness of Jesus, her response was to give and to do so extravagantly. She broke open an expensive bottle of perfume and lavishly poured it over his feet. The disciples were bothered. I'm always amazed at how out of step the disciples were with Jesus' spirit and purpose in the world. "Why wasn't this costly perfume sold and given to the poor?" they asked (Matt 26:8-9). On the surface, their question seems reasonable enough.

I often consult with churches on raising resources to build, rebuild, or, in some instances, renew worn-out facilities. In virtually every place, I'll hear someone object, saying, "Why are we spending all this money when this money could be given to the poor?" The question is a reasonable one, and, frankly, there are times when I am inclined to ask the same question of some churches that seek my advice. But I seldom see these critics of the church's decision to spend money on facilities emptying their own pockets for the poor. Some are quick to tell the church how to spend its money even as they mismanage their own.

In the case of Mary of Bethany, my own experience has taught me that there is a time in the life of every serious follower of God when a sincere longing rises within the soul to do something extravagant as an expression of gratitude to God. I suggest that if you ever have that impulse, act on it! Do something extravagant. It can be the prelude to discovering the life you've been looking for.

Jesus responded, "Let her alone, for she has done a beautiful thing for me" (Matt 26:10). For those who have experienced the transforming miracle of divine grace at the deepest levels of human experience, there's an almost insatiable desire to give and give extravagantly. Extravagant giving is always the response to an extraordinary experience of grace.

If you follow this impulse, your giving might defy explanation. It might exceed what's reasonable. But of this I am certain: It will not require the law of the tithe for motivation. Neither will it need a list of expectations outlined in a new member's class about what's expected of newcomers to the faith. Instead, when your life has been divinely transformed by grace, you'll find your response is spontaneous, genuine, extravagant, and, at least in your mind, logical. You'll suddenly find yourself on the road of the life you've always wanted.

If there is anything the New Testament teaches about giving, it is this: the deeper your experience of the divine, the higher your generosity will reach. Under these circumstances, neither principles nor rules about giving will ever be necessary. This is the teaching we can infer from the example of Jesus and the writers of the New Testament.

As a matter of practical application to the church, when church leaders are as passionate about experiencing the divine themselves and guiding others to do the same as they are about filling the offering plates, the need for money to fund ministry will take care of itself. The church will always have more than enough to fulfill its mission if leaders lead more from experience motivated by grace and less from expectation motivated by law.

In a nutshell, it is not necessary either to make the New Testament say something it is not saying or to defend a practice that's clearly not taught in the New Testament. Instead, follow your heart. You wouldn't be reading this book were you not so inclined to find something that you have not yet found either in your life, your church, or in the examples around you. You are precisely where you're supposed to be at this time in your life. In fact, I'm convinced you are standing at the precipice of a new level of living and giving altogether. If you'll keeping moving in this direction and start giving as a response of gratitude to what you are feeling inside, you'll start experiencing the fullness of life that God desires for you. Ask him to show you how and where. He will and you'll know. The need will appear at just the right moment. Don't try to create it yourself. Wait on God. He'll bring the need right to you. This will be a little awkward at first, but with time and practice you'll become adept at knowing when and where God is prompting you to give. You don't need to concern yourself with what percentage of income you're giving away when you're living like this.

If you follow your heart, God may lead you beyond the tithe. Interestingly, I know people who are giving away what would be equal to 20 and 30 and even 50 percent of their income and having the time of their lives for it. They are compassionate people who are involved in making this world a far better place in which to live. They live worry free. They stress over nothing. They have an infectious joy for life and live in absolute surrender to and dependence upon God. They have found the life they once thought only Wall Street and Madison Avenue could give them. As they continue to respond to God's grace and gifts, their lives are limitless and their growth in giving is equally limitless.

There's Zacchaeus in Luke 19—a man whose transforming experience of grace motivated him to give a double portion to those whom he had cheated before his encounter with Christ. Doing what is right, and then some, is always a normal response to grace. Your giving never has to be cajoled or coerced when you've experienced grace.

There are the words of Saint Paul in his Second Letter to the Corinthians. The Apostle encouraged them to pursue excellence in the grace of giving just as passionately as they were pursuing other disciplines of their faith (2 Cor 8:7). To make his point, Paul told the Corinthians about his profound experience with the religious community in Macedonia. He wrote,

> *Now I want to tell you, dear brothers and sisters, what God in his kindness has done for the churches in Macedonia. Though they have been going through much trouble and hard times, their wonderful joy and deep poverty have overflowed in rich generosity. For I can testify that they gave not only what they could afford but far more. And they did it of their own free will. They begged us again and again for the gracious privilege of sharing in the gift for the Christians in Jerusalem. Best of all, they went beyond our highest hopes, for their first action was to dedicate themselves to the Lord and to us for whatever directions God might give them.* (2 Cor 8:1-5)

While we are uncertain as to the precise nature of their "much trouble and hard times," most scholars agree the Corinthians were either suffering from a natural calamity or being persecuted for their faith. Whatever the nature of their hardship, the result left them economically poor. Aware of their circumstances, Saint Paul edited his expectations and assumed whatever gift he received from them would be modest at best.

How surprised he was. Not only did they meet his modified expectations, but they far exceeded anything he could have imagined. Their generosity ignited a blaze of questions in Paul's mind. "What is this? From where did such generosity come? Under their economic conditions, how could they be so generous?"

Then, as if remembering his own encounter with the divine grace that transformed him into a passionate follower and the greatest theologian in the history of Christianity, he understood where their generosity came from. "They first gave themselves to God," he wrote, "then to us in keeping with God's will" (2 Cor 8:7). They gave themselves to God first.

That's where it begins for any of us. The secret to finding the life you've always wanted begins by the giving of yourself completely to

God. Don't assume that people who regularly attend religious services have done this. Many of them have not. Otherwise, their places
of worship would not be having the financial problems I see in many
of them. Some churches may be teeming with people, but that
hardly means those crowds of people have either experienced grace
or are living the life they've always wanted. The fact is, a discourag-
ingly high percentage of them are not.

Don't let that stand in your way of finding the life you really
want. The abundant life Jesus came to give you is yours for the
receiving. When you receive the gift of life, you will respond by
giving yourself. It's the way God has designed his world.

The financial crisis many religious communities face is a spiritual
crisis. Until religious leaders are willing to acknowledge this, the
church will continue to see declining revenues. When the experience
of God's grace becomes the centerpiece of Christian ministry, rather
than adherence to expectations and rules, people will naturally and
generously give. People learn from other people. Church leaders
must focus on letting these people bear witness to the realities of
their changing lives, lifestyles, and attitudes toward living. As others
hear and experience God in these ways, they will pursue the same
course, because everyone wants to be happy. Everyone wants a life
full of meaning. As people experience divine grace, they will look for
opportunities to give for the difference grace has made and is making
in their own lives and in the lives of others. Generosity will never
wane because the fulfillment they experience through giving will
make the pursuit of excellence in giving the centerpiece of their life.

The result? The church will be doing what the church is supposed to be doing—helping people find the life they're looking for.

GRACE EMBRACE

I once heard about sisters who were helping their father make pan-
cakes—their traditional Saturday morning breakfast. As it neared
completion, he said, "Girls, wake up Mom and tell her breakfast is
ready."

As siblings are prone to do, they turned their father's simple instruction into serious competition. Racing to get to the bedroom first, the older and faster of the two took the lead early in the race. Reaching the finish line first, she jumped into her mother's lap, threw her arms around her, and then, as if to add insult to injury, turned to her younger sister who had just appeared in the doorway, and snobbishly said, "I've got all there is of Mommy. Ha! Ha! Ha!" With that, she stuck out her tongue.

Not seeing the wicked tongue of her oldest daughter, but sensing the wounded spirit of her youngest, Mother offered the other knee. With outstretched arm, she invited her youngest to join them.

Slowly, the youngest daughter climbed onto her lap while mother nudged her closely to her heart. She accepted the invitation and nestled securely in her mother's arms, then looked at her older sister, and said, "You may have all there is of Mommy, but Mommy has all there is of me."

When you've experienced God's grace embrace, you'll feel a longing greater than anything else you've ever felt—a longing to give yourself to him thoroughly and completely. And, yes, even financially. In fact, the greatest proof that you've experienced God's grace embrace may be this: the life you get when you give your jar of costly perfume and the gratitude you feel as God continually repairs and refills your jar—or, your life. Thank Mary of Bethany for that.

SUGGESTIONS FOR GIVING, THEN GETTING THE LIFE YOU'VE ALWAYS WANTED

• What has your religious tradition taught you about giving? How have those teachings influenced your giving patterns today? Regardless of what you believe about tithing, what significance does giving have to you? Whatever you may give, do you give as a matter of obligation or because you would feel guilty if you didn't? Is most of your charity a mere tax break? Do you ever use your giving as a means of bartering with God for something that you perceive to be missing from your life or from the life of someone you love? Are these the motivations for giving that bring you the kind of joy you

desire and the life you really want? If not, why not go back to God
and ask him to help you give yourself completely to him and see
where that takes you?

• If you are a church leader, you might be wondering, "How can I
create the atmosphere in my church where God's grace embrace
might be experienced by people?"

It's simple, but it must begin in you. As you experience God's
transformative grace in your own life, you yourself will become more
generous and, as a result, an example of generosity. As you give more
of yourself to God and others, and as you learn to give away your
own resources, you will experience more of the life you've always
wanted. When that happens, your life will be magnetic and your
enthusiasm contagious. It will transform all you do—your lifestyle
will be simpler and your attitudes will be positive. If you are a pulpit
minister, your preaching will become more passionate and conversa-
tional. You will cease yelling to make your point. Your life will be the
point. You will start sharing, with ease and transparency, the sheer
amazement at what you're discovering on your own path with God.
Instead of always searching for stories or anecdotes to make your
homilies interesting, you'll discover a rich repository of ideas, stories,
thoughts, etc., born out of your own experience. You will no longer
have to preach someone else's sermons. You'll be the creator of your
own homilies because your study of Scripture will be richer and
more meaningful. This will both inform and transform your preaching. When you start living the life you've always wanted, you'll
discover that a transformed parson unleashes the possibility of a
transformed parish.

Second, I suggest you offer to your people the opportunity to
join you in a class of discovery that you yourself lead. A small class of
eight to ten people who agree to diligent study, mandatory attendance, and a willingness to be open to giving—to God, to each
other, and to others financially and otherwise (according to ability),
and in thoughtful and spontaneous fashions.

Meet weekly for fourteen weeks. Each week of study, focus on a
New Testament example of giving. While there are many others, here

are a few to help you get started.

1. *Seeing God as a Giver: **Psalm 24:1-10***
2. *My Security: **Matthew 6:19-33***
3. *The Seed: **Matthew 13:3-23***
4. *The Talents: **Matthew 25:14-30***
5. *The Two Debtors: **Luke 7:36-50***
6. *The Good Samaritan: **Luke 10:25-37***
7. *The Rich Fool: **Luke 12:13-21***
8. *The Ten Lepers: **Luke 17:11-19***
9. *The Rich Man and Lazarus: **Luke 16:19-31***
10. *The Rich Young Ruler: **Luke 18:18-30***
11. *The Widow's Mite: **Luke 21:1-4***
12. *Giving Out of Joy: **2 Corinthians 8:1-7***
13. *Expanding Gratitude: **2 Corinthians 9:1-5***
14. *Sowing and Reaping: **2 Corinthians 9:6-12***

Spend the first ten minutes in quiet mediation and prayer, leading all participants to focus on God and to relax in his presence. The next thirty minutes might be devoted to plumbing the depth of the divine message through the Scripture or story. A period of focused prayer and meditation on the Scripture should follow, while the final thirty minutes might be spent sharing experiences of giving each has encountered the previous week. If you'll practice a process similar to this, your own life and the lives of the participants will transform within the first few weeks. Everything about your life and that of theirs will take on a new dimension. Ego will be held at bay, and both God and giving will take front and center. Attitudes will be changed, lifestyles will become less materialistic, and generosity will be abundant. Your church life will never be the same again. Repeat this process at the close of the fourteen weeks. Train a lay leader to conduct a fourteen-week experience within your church and start an ongoing cycle of transformation.

I strongly encourage you to follow this or a similar path. It will produce more lasting change and have a more positive impact on the life and ministry of your parish than any other single thing you may do.

In recent years, there's been an upsurge across the country in the number of churches that sponsor and send their own short-term lay missionaries to do mission work in the U.S. and abroad. This has transformed the lives of many precisely because when you give yourself away, you find the life you've always wanted. The same sort of transformation will come as you teach people to give their money away as well. In fact, one of the premises of this book is that, if you will help people give their money, they will give other aspects of life—their time and their talents.

• The deeper the experience of grace, the higher the level of generosity. That generous spirit not only applies to your material resources, but to your internal attitudes as well as your lifestyle and relationship to others and to this world.

Take, for example, the spirit of forgiveness and the capacity to offer mercy to someone who has wronged you. The degree to which you are able to extend forgiveness is directly related to the extent to which you have received it. To offer forgiveness, you must have received forgiveness yourself. Remember, you can't give away what you don't have. You can apply this principle to any virtue—compassion, patience, kindness, self-control—any grace you may wish to examine. The depth of your expression of love, for example, always follows the height of your experience of love.

No story more aptly demonstrates this than the story of Mary who anointed Jesus with perfume in the home of Simon the Pharisee (Luke 7:36-50). Read and meditate on the story, and you'll discover that what I'm saying applies not only to the spirit of forgiveness but to other virtues as well, including the virtue of giving.

Standing behind Jesus, the woman wept and wiped his feet with her tears, pouring perfume over them. Disturbed by the fact that Jesus wasn't bothered but more likely blessed by her behavior, Simon mumbled in disgust to himself, "This proves that Jesus is no prophet. If God had really sent him, he would know what kind of woman is touching him. She's a sinner!" (Luke 7:39).

But aren't we all, Simon? This one inescapable fact seemed to elude him.

Knowing what he was saying, Jesus turned to Simon and told him a parable. A man loaned two other men some money. The first had borrowed a much larger sum than the other, but both were in debt and both were unable to repay the debt. Knowing this, the generous man canceled their debts.

What was Jesus saying by this story? All of us are represented by one of the two debtors. Some have huge debts. You might say that these have made a thorough mess of things—credit card debts so high there's no chance of ever paying them off, creditors threatening to press charges, and so on.

Others, though, have much smaller debts but are debtors nonetheless. In either case, there are no resources to repay those debts because even the capacity to repay the debt is a gift from God. This was the point Jesus was making.

In the spiritual realm, we are all sinners in need of grace and mercy. Sin means to "miss the mark." Some may miss the target only slightly while others are nowhere near. But in reference to the bull's-eye, and this is the point, everyone misses the mark. Both the woman of the street, who anointed Jesus' feet, and Simon, the respected religious Pharisee, needed the gift of grace. The difference is that the woman recognized the gift and received it. Simon did not and missed it.

Again, the deeper your experience of God, the higher your level of generosity. If you're having a hard time finding a spirit of generosity in your heart, you might take an honest look at what you've received, or not received, from God above.

It is no mistake that Jesus illustrated the receiving and giving of forgiveness with money and debts. Much of life can be likened to a monetary transaction. We receive. We give. But it always starts with our reception. We receive everything before we have anything. Church leaders, you can't ask people to give away what they don't have. Have your people experienced grace? Genuinely? I didn't ask, "How many baptisms did you report to the association last year?" Have you experienced grace yourself? Grace precedes giving and giving will always result from the experience of grace.

• Earlier, I pointed out that there's a part of your personality you could call your ego that ascends to the throne of your life when you're a young person and begins asserting its control and independence. Some theologians might call this the birth of sin-consciousness. But before this, you are completely on the receiving end of life. In your mother's womb, for example, there was nothing you did but receive. After your birth, you were given everything you needed if, of course, you were fortunate to be birthed by caring and loving parents. The point is, you were a receiver, not a producer. In fact, you were not in a position to produce anything, much less earn, or acquire, or give.

But when your ego started asserting itself and demanding its independence, everything got turned around. You began to define your own importance by your performance—what you managed to create, the things that you produced, the stuff you collected, the titles you earned. You soon developed this notion that you are the giver. Not God. Not your parents. After all, it's your stuff to give away. You created it. You earned it. You are now the producer and the protagonist in the drama of your own life. Nobody can tell you what to do, where you must go, or how to live your life. You are, in the words of William Jennings Bryant, the "captain of your soul."

Ego thrives on this sort of stuff—the gratification that comes from the illusion of independence and self-advancement. But the problem is that this pathway is a dead end. While ego development is a normal experience of growing up and becoming independent is part of the maturation process, there's a sense in which you must become like a dependent child again if you are to experience the life you've always wanted. Ego would rather you remain independent, believing your happiness depends on you—what you can do, accomplish, and acquire. But the day will come when the producing, amassing, and recognition no longer gives you want you want.

That may be why you are reading this book. You don't feel as gratified as you once did. At this year's award banquet, it no longer meant anything to be recognized again as "Salesperson of the Year." All you know is that, while you "have it all," you really have nothing at all, and you feel more bankrupt of spirit than ever before. You struggle just to find the motivation to get out of bed in the morning. You thought you would find the life you always wanted by making a god of yourself and by lining the trophy case of your life with material accomplishments. But you're discovering you really have no life at all. You have lots of stuff but little or no significance.

You may even be one who's practiced tithing to your church most of your adult life, but you don't enjoy doing it. When you're honest with yourself, you know your giving is motivated more by habit than happiness. Your giving may even cause you to feel smug or proud at times—an attitude that makes you wonder how the church would operate without your generosity. Lately, you've been expecting the church more and more to conform to your way of thinking. In fact, you've even used your giving at times to hold the church hostage to your way of thinking. You give, but, frankly, you don't really know why. Maybe your giving is really for ego-gratification.

Transformation, or what the Bible refers to as salvation, simply means that the ego that seized control of your life many years before and appointed itself commander-in-chief must be deposed. You will become a transformed person when you realize, or more accurately, receive the gift of recognition—the recognition that God has provided a way to reverse your situation and return you to that place where you are, once again, the receiver. Salvation is simply the recognition (a gift in and of itself) and reception (a capacity that's a gift, too, you see) of God's grace and forgiveness. When this happens, what the Eastern mystics describe as "the awakened life" becomes your life. Your eyes are suddenly wide open to see and know that both the capacity to receive and give are themselves gifts from God. It dawns on you that all is gift. This awakened awareness is the inauguration to the life you've been looking for.

Jesus said, "Unless you become as a little child, you cannot enter the kingdom of heaven." Children are receivers. Their hands are always open because they have nothing to give—no judgment of others, as in the case of Simon toward the woman, or self-justification, as in the case of Simon toward Jesus. Children just receive, enjoy the simple things, and simply have fun. To experience the awakened life is like becoming a child all over again. The kingdom belongs to children. Want to be a child again? Open your hands and your heart to the Father. He's been waiting for you to grow tired of the world of your ego.

• There's something else. Simon could not extend forgiveness to the woman because he had not experienced it himself. The only thing he could do was judge her because judgment was the only thing he had to give—that and the flip side of judgment, which is self-justification. You can give only what you possess. If you are filled with prejudice and judgment, then that's what gifts you have to give to the world. No grace and no mercy but plenty of criticism, racism, judgment.

The world is filled with critical, judgmental people who apparently don't understand that what you give away comes back to you. If you feel you're bombarded by criticism and judgment from others, you might take an honest look at what you are giving to your world. It's true that what "goes around, comes around," which may explain why you're frequently comparing yourself to others and trying to lift up your own importance by putting others down.

And what about God? Does he seem distant and remote to you these days? Unapproachable? Harsh? Rather than feeling accepted by him, do you feel judged? Sure, you go to church every week, but you really don't feel his nearness anymore, do you? Be honest with yourself. You think he doesn't like you, which might explain why you feel so distant from him. As you think, so you are. What your mind ponders, you own hand delivers. If you're handing out judgments and criticisms to others, should you be surprised at the criticism you feel from others? Or the judgment and displeasure you feel from God? Those who judge are judged. It's the way God has designed his world. What you give to others, you receive from others. If you want your relationships to those closest to you to be better than they presently are, stop looking at what you wish you could change in them. Instead, look at what needs changing in you. You receive what you give. You give what you have.

• Apply this principle to your capacity (or lack of it) to forgive the person who has wronged you—even in unimaginable ways. If you're finding it impossible to forgive because of the wrong you've suffered, there's only one reason why you cannot—you don't have it to give. The word "forgive" comes from two words meaning "to give away." If you have not received forgiveness, you have none to give away. If you'll accept this gift from God, your own reservoir will always have a supply to give to others.

Do you often find yourself being offended? If so, that's usually a telltale sign you're still living under the tyranny of your own ego. The ego-dominated person is an easily offended person. If this describes you, then you're likely to find yourself measuring your own acceptance to God by comparing yourself to others and judging them as inferior to you.

This was Simon's problem in the story described above. While you might be the first to admit you're anything but perfect, you are also the first to look at others and conclude that you're at least better than they. Until your ego is brought under control, you'll have a hard time receiving anything from God and you'll go through life being easily offended. This is why, if you faithfully support your church, you sort of look down on others who don't. It offends you that so many don't do what you, if the truth were known, are not really sure why you do yourself. Want to rediscover joy in giving and living? You'll have to come as a child again. No pride. No ego. No offense.

Since what you think about grows, if you dwell on those things around you that offend you, feelings of offense will only grow within you. Before long, you will look for things to offend you, and, when that happens, your life will become loathsome even to you.

Are you tired of living this way? If you are, may I suggest that you receive from God the capacity to relegate your ego to its rightful place and become as a little child once again—that is, to receive his grace, love, and mercy? Don't complicate it. It's really quite simple. He's made you ready for this moment—this could be your breakthrough to the life you really want.

• These are such important principles to learn, and they can positively change your life. For example, there is nothing that will ever happen in your life—indeed, no harm anyone might bring upon you but what you have the capacity to respond to with grace and forgiveness. If all you have within you is grace, then when someone thrusts a spear of harm into your side (whether by their words or through their actions), as they did Jesus centuries before, all that can come out of you is "Father, forgive them . . . ."

By capacity to forgive, I'm not suggesting that you'll stoically pretend there's no pain and suffering or act as if the injury you suffered from someone or something is an illusion of your mind. Nor am I suggesting that you'll have the capacity to enjoy in some masochistic fashion the harm others have brought upon you, intentionally or unintentionally. To the contrary, what I'm saying is that you will feel the pain and know the emotional and physical anguish that comes with it, but you'll have the inner resources to give something good in response to something evil.

Here's the secret in all of this: when you receive what God gives (grace, compassion, forgiveness), you'll never be without what you need for every situation you might face. It could be the need to rise above the injury, or simply to give thanks to God for all you have learned and will learn through the suffering, or the need to forgive and extend mercy to that person who has deeply wounded you. In any event, you'll have the capacity to live the life you've always wanted—a life filled with inner peace, permanent happiness, and authentic love.

Saint Paul put it this way: "I can do everything with the help of Christ who gives me the strength I need" (Phil 4:13). The Apostle said that Christ gave him the strength to face everything. Do you suppose the Apostle really meant "everything"? If he didn't mean "everything," then tell me what he intended to exclude. "I can do everything but forgive." "I can do everything but be happy." "I can do everything but find the life I really want." I don't think that's what Paul meant. Do you?

• Ask yourself what impact this approach to life might have on your views, and that of our society, regarding the issue of capital punishment? Or war, for that matter? Was Jesus kidding when he said, "Don't resist an evil person! If you are slapped on the right cheek, turn the other, too" (Matt 5:39)? And, elsewhere, wasn't it Jesus who said, "Love your enemies! Pray for those who persecute you! In that way, you will be acting as true children of your Father in heaven" (Matt 5:44-45)?

I find it difficult to believe how anyone can read these words from the Sermon on the Mount and justify capital punishment or going to war. Isn't it an oddity to you how the church is more inclined to turn to Augustine's Just War theory to defend a nation going to war than it is to live by these clear teachings of Jesus? Who is the church following these days, anyway? Apart from the principles he espoused during his short life on this earth, you would think we'd be smart enough these days to figure out that waging war makes losers of everyone. The Greeks used to say, "War is bad in that it begets more evil than it kills."

• Jesus closed the conversation with Simon with an interesting observation: "A person who is forgiven little shows only little love" (Luke 7:47). That statement alone aptly sums up what I'm saying. A person who is forgiven little forgives little. A person who is forgiven little is only a little forgiving. Get it? The problem in the pew today is that far too many have experienced far too little of God's forgiveness— real forgiveness.

Here is the secret you must learn if you are to find the life you've always wanted. If you have been given little, you will give little. That's the ultimate irony in all of this, because everything you are and all that you have is a gift to you—even the capacity to acknowledge that everything is a gift may be life's greatest gift.

I love the way Frederick Buechner describes God's grace:

> The grace of God means something like: Here is your life.
> You might never have been, but you are because the party
> wouldn't have been complete without you . . . . Nothing can

ever separate us. It's for you I created the universe. I love
you. There's only one catch. Like any other gift, the gift of
grace can be yours only if you'll reach out and take it.
Maybe being able to reach out and take it is a gift, too.

It is.

A closing thought. Remember that giving is not the way to the life
you've always wanted. Giving is the life you've always wanted. When
you get this, you've got it. And when you've got it, you'll know it.

Receive everything as God's gift to you.
Learn from everything as your gift to yourself.
Live what you learn as your gift to the world.

9

MYTH 5

"GET THEM INVOLVED AND
THEY WILL GIVE"

*What you are is God's gift to you; what you do with yourself
is your gift to God.*

—Danish proverb

*Life is not lost by dying; life is lost minute by minute, day
by dragging day, in all the thousand small uncaring ways.*

—Stephen Vincent Benet (1898–1943)

*Look lovingly upon the present, for it holds the only things
that are forever true.*

—Dr. Helen Schucman, A Course in Miracles

I recently spoke at meeting of the National Association of Church
Business Administrators before church and parish administrators as
well as pastors and denominational leaders from a variety of faiths.
Afterward, a man approached me and observed, "I suppose you
know your views about giving are vastly different from what most
believe in any of the religious traditions represented here today." As I

drove back to the airport, I was thinking about how accurate he was. Many of my ideas are out of the mainstream.

I had not flown in or out of the local airport before, so I wandered around with a look of intimidation much like a freshman on his first day in high school. I entered the most familiar-looking room in the airport—the men's restroom. The entrance was large and wide with two smaller entrances inside its alcove. I stepped through one of the entrances and set my bags in the middle of the floor.

Men's restrooms don't vary much. But, oddly, when I walked into this one, I suddenly felt as if I were really somewhere I had never been before. As I glanced around the room, I discovered there were no urinals. Instead, this restroom was equipped with individual stalls, each with a swinging door that could be latched from the inside. I thought, "This is strange. I don't think I've ever seen a men's restroom without urinals."

That fleeting mental observation of the oddness of this restroom gave way to a feeling of acute embarrassment that hit me like the proverbial ton of bricks. This restroom had no wall fixtures because it was not the men's room at all. I was standing in the middle of the women's room. A wave of panic swelled over me. I grabbed my bags and dashed for the entrance door while audibly defending myself just in case somebody was listening, "But the sign clearly said 'Men's Restroom,'" I argued.

Fortunately, I think I escaped notice. But when I returned to the entryway off the airport corridor, I realized that the entrance was larger than normal to accommodate the traffic both in and out of the women's restroom to the left and the men's restroom to the right. Coincidentally, the restrooms were clearly marked, but instinctively I had turned to the left.

I smiled at myself because the embarrassing incident reminded me of my typical reaction to religious and cultural expectations, maxims, and dictates. If someone tells me I must believe a certain way, I will automatically question that and, in some instances, I'll immediately go left or right of that expectation. That reaction succeeds in purchasing a little time to think it through for myself. Incidentally, the fact that I react this way hardly puts me in a class alone. Many churches, for example, have been telling their members for decades that they are supposed to tithe. Many of you reading this have grown up or are currently members of the church where tithing is regularly taught and with passion.

Do you tithe? Not likely. There's about a 95 percent chance you don't. You see, just telling a person to do something because your tradition says they're supposed to do it is hardly the way to motivate a person to adhere to particular behavior patterns.

What You Believe and What You Know

It is important to find truth for yourself, and not because someone insists you must accept a belief or because church history and tradition have dictated a particular viewpoint. I am not discounting what either of these has taught us. Nor am I diminishing the truths they have revealed. I simply do not believe any person should accept something just because the majority of people may believe it. "All a majority may mean," someone once observed, "is that all the fools are on the same side."

One of the reasons I appreciate my home church is because it genuinely encourages you to think for yourself. I'm in more churches in one year than most people will be in a lifetime. This church is surely one of the only churches in America that identifies itself as "a thinking, feeling, and healing community of faith." Since the "feeling" side of my faith needs no encouragement, I appreciate the fact that the church expects my brain to come with me to worship rather than being parked in the church lot. Bertrand Russell, British mathematician and philosopher, said, "In all affairs, it's a healthy thing now and then to hang a question mark on the things you have long taken for granted." When it comes to question marks, I could be convicted for hanging many in my lifetime.

With all their differences, one thing most religious traditions share is their desire successfully to pass their beliefs and traditions to the next generation. After all, religious traditions are always only one generation away from extinction. So pastors preach and teach what they feel people should believe about God, the Bible, church traditions, and many other things, including the subject of giving. Because the church is a teaching community, transferring the religious beliefs from one generation to the next is not only normal but expected. Yet many of these faith communities seem to want people to accept their traditions and beliefs tacitly without ever questioning or examining them. That is clearly not the way to ensure the longevity of important religious traditions and teachings. In fact, just the opposite is the case: the perpetuation of faith requires both the teaching and testing of that faith by individuals within each new generation.

What belief or tradition grounded in truth has ever been threatened by the questioning or doubting mind? None that I'm aware of. If faith is to be authentic and precious religious and cultural traditions are to be preserved, every person must be encouraged to examine, even question, those beliefs. As they do, they will discover truth. Jesus said, "And you will know the truth, and the truth will set you free" (John 8:32).

Rather than being a liberating force, an unexamined belief can imprison your soul. Paradoxically, what you know by questioning and self-examination is liberating. You may believe a truth, but that will do little for you. When you know a truth, you hold the keys to personal freedom, growth, and genuine individuality.

What does this have to do with giving? Everything.

The premise of this book is that life in all its fullness is found in giving. I know that to be true, but I did not come to that conviction because my faith tradition said I must believe it. I have forged that conviction on the anvil of my own experience. If it were little more than a belief, as it once was, I would not have gone to such lengths to put my convictions in writing or searched for months to find a publisher. Nor would I have decided to give to charity whatever profit this book might produce.

My intention is to live the life I've always wanted, and that means to receive every divine opportunity to give myself away generously as the fulfillment of my life's purpose. That intention has changed my life. Consequently, I have come to believe that giving yourself away is the central purpose of every person's life. Also, I believe not only that generously giving yourself away will positively change your life, but also that as your life and those of others are changed, the world also will be changed.

I not only believe this; I know this.

But you must discover this truth for yourself. I know that, too. Throughout this book, I want you to question everything you read. Do more than simply question it because, if that's all you do, your ego may deceive you into dismissing what I'm saying altogether. Remember, ego is the part of you that would edge God and giving out of your life and hold you to a path of self-centered living. It does this to keep you from experiencing a life that would be truly fulfilling. Why? The reason is simple: ego can survive only in an inner environment of self-absorption. As long as it has you fooled into believing that your fulfillment in life is found in self-seeking, self-serving ambitions, ego has you in its grasp. That's why the vast majority of people are still looking for fulfillment in all the wrong places—money and material stuff, personal recognition and accomplishments, titles and promotions, and so forth. Ego has them thinking that happiness is found outside of themselves. But when you know that happiness is within you and is readily experienced as you give yourself to your real purpose in life, that knowledge will lead you to pursue the kind of generous lifestyle I'm describing in this book. That pursuit is a death sentence to your ego.

So test my suggestions. Don't test God. That's unacceptable, although many Christians seem to think that putting God to the test as it pertains to giving is allowed, even encouraged. That's a misreading of Scripture. Testing God in any way is clearly forbidden by Jesus. I'll discuss this in detail in chapter 11.

But there's no reason not to test what I'm suggesting. To do so, you'll have to start giving yourself away. You cannot test the premise of this book in a purely academic fashion. Instead, you'll have to practice it—but, if you will, even for a short time, I am confident where it will lead you. You'll soon find yourself on a path, albeit narrow and challenging and sparsely traveled by others, that leads to life abundant and life eternal. Once you start down this path, you'll not turn back. I know this.

THE MYTH OF INVOLVEMENT AND GIVING

For as long as I can remember, church members and church leaders have felt that, if people get actively involved in church, the level of their financial support will increase. This is a myth.

Many churches in America have an orientation process for new members or persons expressing interest in the church; this is where the myth is most often perpetuated. As part of the orientation process, there's usually a crash course in the core values and beliefs of the church followed by some type of spiritual gifts or personal interest inventory. By doing this, churches and church leaders are attempting to orient new members or interested seekers. (Surprisingly, I have found many churches that have no orientation process in place at all. But that must be the subject of another book.)

The spiritual gifts inventory church leaders frequently administer to new members helps these leaders know not only new members' interests but what gifts for service and ministry these members might bring to the church. In churches where there's a concerted effort to incorporate new people into the life and fellowship of the church, you will often find this myth at work. Sometimes, another myth altogether is at work, too. It's the myth that all you should have to do is tell new members that they are expected to give—because giving is not an option in the Bible—and that will be enough to motivate them to give. The earlier discussion should be enough to dispel this myth. If you've ever been a parent, you've probably learned there are better ways to motivate the right behavior in your children than by barking out demands.

Getting a person involved in church or giving a person a position of leadership in a church will not necessarily lead her or him to give financially. Jesus himself made this clear, and we'll have a look at his words soon. But first, a recent experience from my own life will serve to illustrate what I'm saying.

THE SAXOPHONIST AT CHRISTMAS

Christmas was rapidly approaching as I was completing this chapter. One evening, Pam and I went to a toy store to find a something for the little guys in our extended family. The sounds of Christmas filled the parking lot but not the expected bells of the Salvation Army. Instead, a fellow was standing in front of the toy store and playing Christmas carols on an old, rusty-looking saxophone. He was not an accomplished musician, to put it politely. More often than you could tolerate for long, he would hit one of those notes that reminded you of the days when your younger sister was learning to play the clarinet in the bedroom down the hall.

Pam went into the store while I walked over to drop a few dollars in the bucket the saxophonist had attached to a music stand. In between notes, he paused long enough to grab a breath and mutter in a heavy Latin American accent, "Thank you and Merry Christmas." I responded in similar fashion and then went into the store.

Though the ads in the morning newspaper contained the toys for which we were searching, we discovered they had sold out several days before. As we were leaving, the musician was still playing carols and hitting as many wrong notes as right ones.

"How much did you give him?" Pam whispered as we walked toward the car. She just assumed I had. She knows me pretty well.

"Just five hundred dollars," I responded with a smirk I tried to disguise. But because she knows me so well, Pam is not easily fooled. She played along, nonetheless, and replied as if she had fallen for the joke, "You better not have or . . . ." She left the conclusion of her response to my imagination. Of course I had not. I smiled, she smiled, and the two of us went on with our shopping expedition.

But I could not get the saxophonist off my mind. I had approached him as I entered the store and dropped five dollars into his makeshift offering plate. It was no big deal, as I'll spend nearly that much on a cup of gourmet coffee on almost any given day of the week. "Instead of five dollars," I silently wondered, "suppose I had given him five hundred dollars. Would that have made any difference, not only to him but to me, too?"

I concluded it would have. I could not have given him $500 and be done with him as easily as I was with the $5 donation. In fact, had I been serious enough to give him the larger amount, I would have wanted to stop, talk to him, and get to know more about him. That is, I would have wanted to know more than the obvious fact he was an inexperienced saxophonist playing carols while standing on a toy store sidewalk. I would have asked, "Sir, do you have a wife? Children? If so, how are they doing? Will you be celebrating Christmas this year? What about food? Do you have anything to eat? Clothes to wear? Where are you from, anyway? Can I help you in some way other than just paying you a few dollars for playing Christmas carols on your saxophone?"

In other words, a larger, more serious gift would have created in me the desire for a deeper and more significant conversation—perhaps even some kind of relationship, some point of involvement in his life.

GIVING AND LAY LEADERSHIP IN THE CHURCH

Token giving, the kind customarily practiced in the church these days, requires little or no personal involvement from the donor. You can give a few dollars, as most do, make yourself feel better, and go your merry way. But serious, generous giving significantly changes the landscape of your personal involvement. You will always be motivated to make a greater investment of time and energy when you go beyond token giving. Giving your money is like putting money in the bank. The more you do, the more your interest grows.

For many years now, I have been working closely with clergy and lay leaders in virtually every denomination in America. In almost every place I've worked, I've found people in positions of leadership and authority in the church with little or no record of financial commitment. That is to say, as far as the church's ministry is concerned, they give either minimal financial support or none at all. Yet they hold positions of church leadership. How does that happen?

One explanation might be that ordained church leaders often do not know there are laypeople in positions of leadership within the church who do not financially support it. They do not know this because they have chosen not to know what their donors may give to the church. I'll have more to say about this, for there is yet another myth that's behind the decision by ordained persons to remain in the dark as to individual contributions.

Even if they don't know, I usually know there are people in positions of leadership who do not give because, in many of the places where I provide consultation, I am permitted access to the contribution records of donors. Where I am not permitted, it is usually because a few people believe they are the divinely appointed guardians mandated to protect that information from me and anyone else other than, ironically, from themselves. But when that information is withheld from me, it's frequently because these guardians don't want me to know what they're giving or, more accurately, what they're not giving.

I am professionally bound to protect the confidentiality of the information entrusted to me. And I do. But there are times I will reveal this much information to church leadership: "Individual contributions are confidential, but you should know that you have people in positions of church leadership who have little or no record of financial support." That statement is almost always met with great surprise from ordained leaders—unless, of course, the ordained are among those who don't give either. That reality I have encountered more frequently than I'd like to admit, and it presents an entirely different and sometimes complex set of challenges.

Assuming the clergy are not among the majority who give little or nothing at all, I believe they should know when the church's organizational structure has enabled lay leaders with minimal or no financial support to end up in leadership positions. Why? Because that awareness almost always leads them to question, first, whether it matters (and, obviously, it matters to me or I wouldn't be writing this) and, second, if it does matter, what may need changing in their organizational structures to keep that sort of thing from happening in the future.

I am not suggesting that there is any ulterior motive on the part of these people who give little or nothing yet hold leadership positions in the church. The overwhelming majority I believe are sincere people. The problem as I see it is with the process, not the people. The issue is, "Should a person hold a position of spiritual leadership, often making decisions as to the ministry direction of the church, when his or her own financial commitment to those ministries is minimal at best?" I would say no.

The other explanation is the myth itself, which asserts that, if you can get a person involved in regular attendance and in activities within the church, growth in giving will occur naturally.

Unfortunately, this is not so. Getting a person more involved, or placing a person in a position of church leadership, will not necessarily lead that person to start giving or to give more. It might happen, but the idea it will happen is fundamentally flawed, as the words of Jesus clearly demonstrate.

JESUS SAID, "WHERE YOUR TREASURE IS . . ."

Recorded by Saint Matthew, these words of Jesus may rank among some of the most familiar yet most misunderstood words he ever spoke. In Matthew 5:19-21, Jesus says, "Don't store up treasures here on earth, where moths eat them and rust destroys them, and where thieves break in and steal. Store your treasures in heaven, where moths and rust cannot destroy, and thieves do not break in and steal. Wherever your treasure is, there the desires of your heart will also be."

What he does not say is noteworthy. Jesus did not say, "Wherever your heart is, there your treasure will also be." But that is precisely how we have read and interpreted his words. That also explains how people get into positions of church leadership without ever being asked, "Is your present level of financial support commensurate with your financial capability?" And then, the equally important question, "What does the level of your charity say not just about your capability but about your readiness to assume a position of spiritual leadership?" While these may be difficult questions to ask, should they not be asked of all lay leaders and, for that matter, perhaps all professional leaders as well?

I believe so. How can a person provide spiritual direction and leadership to a church in such an important position as the

Stewardship Team or Finance Committee while giving negligible personal support to that church?

What Jesus did say provides a perspective that is clearly outside both the paradigm and practice of most churches. Jesus said, "Wherever your treasure is, there the desires of your heart will also be." That is to say, heart follows treasure, not the other way around. Or, to put it a slightly different way, both your interest and your intentions follow your investment. While you may financially invest in that which you value most, it is far more accurate that you value most that in which you have invested financially. Passion follows pocketbook. It's a simple but sure concept.

A New Paradigm

I frequently suggest to church leaders the following: Since it is their heartfelt desire to see people experience significant and sustained spiritual growth, perhaps the most helpful thing they could do is to offer a growth-in-giving seminar and a financial planning seminar. Both are needed, just as every church or parish must have an annual pledge campaign and an occasional capital campaign. Contrary to popular opinion, churches that frequently and unapologetically teach giving don't find people leaving in protest. That's a popular myth in and of itself. Some of the largest and fastest-growing churches in America frequently talk about money issues, how to handle money and materialism, and the importance of giving. Churches that are viable in the future will have leaders who understand that Christian giving reaches into three different pockets:

1. The annual giving pocket—This is the ongoing, annual giving that makes the church's ministries possible. This kind of giving enables the church or parish to employ and pay professional leaders, provide ministry locally and abroad, maintain facilities, and keep the lights on.

2. The capital giving pocket—Every church will eventually need to build, expand, renovate, or buy property. Occasionally, churches and

parishes will need to encourage special giving through a capital fundraising effort. This kind of giving is normally over a three- to five-year period and is always "over and above" annual giving. That means churches must encourage members to make a special sacrifice of some sort to give this gift above their annual support.

3. The legacy pocket—This pocket may be the deepest but most neglected pocket by churches and church leaders today. Even after all these years, I'm still amazed when people in the church, even those who are among the few who provide the lion's share of financial support, give me the proverbial deer-in-the-headlights response when I ask them, "Will you consider including the church or parish in your will and estate planning?" Surprisingly, the majority of people say to me, "It's never occurred to me." Just as I believe I am divinely encouraged to generously give from my annual earnings, I believe I must also consider how I might make a gift from my accumulated assets.

People are seeking reliable guidance in financial planning. In fact, most people are lost when it comes to organizing their financial lives. The next time you're in the supermarket or bookstore, for example, take a look at the magazine rack, and you'll get some idea as to the need. In between the glamour magazines with bikini-clad, anorexic-looking females on one side and those with freakish looking, bulked-up muscular males on the other, you'll find plenty of popular reading on how to make, earn, spend, and save money. Money magazine, for example, is the largest business and personal financial management publication in the world with a paid circulation of nearly 2 million and a monthly readership of more than 8 million.

Why? Because people not only need help in financial matters, but they're looking for it. Church leaders who are transparent and share from their own experience how they've learned, or are learning, to handle financial matters—and, most importantly, how their own generous giving and living is transforming their lives—give others a most needed and desired service.

CASE STUDY IN GIVING AND GETTING INVOLVED —RICK AND KAY WARREN

He would not likely agree with me, but I suspect that, when the church historians write about the most influential church leaders of the twenty-first century, Rick Warren will rank among the top five. And maybe higher. Whatever you may think of him or his theology, no other person in this century has had a more significant impact on churches across every denomination than Rick Warren. Billy Graham and Pope John Paul may also rank among the top five, but in terms of the impact on the institutional identity and the corporate structure of churches and parishes, Warren stands alone. I'm in churches of virtually every denomination in America, as well as those that claim no denominational affiliation, and, without exception, churches and church leaders everywhere have not only read Warren's book, *The Purpose Driven Church*, but have attempted to apply some or all of its principles of leadership, structure, and church or parish mission identity. Warren's books have sold millions of copies and have been translated into multiple languages. *The Purpose Driven Life*, for example, holds the distinction of being the best-selling hardback book in American history.

One reason Rick Warren has become so popular is because Rick and his wife Kay are transparent and honest themselves. They not only give, but they are involved in the causes to which they've made significant financial investments. They know the joy of giving and are themselves role models of generous philanthropy and activism in kingdom causes. Rick Warren believes strongly in what he calls the "stewardship of affluence" and the "stewardship of influence." These two ideas were life-altering concepts to him. To varying degrees, all of us have a little of both—affluence and influence. But few have much of both. Among those ranks are people like the Warrens, who believe because God has given them both affluence and influence, they are to be responsible managers of both.

With the enormous wealth that began flowing to the Warrens, Rick and Kay started praying about how God might lead them to be good stewards or role models of both their affluence and influence.

As a result, today the Warrens practice what is known as "reverse tithing." That is, Rick and Kay live on 10 percent and donate 90 percent of their income to three foundations: Acts of Mercy, which serves those infected and affected by AIDS; Equipping the Church, which trains church leaders in developing countries; and The Global PEACE Fund, which fights poverty, disease, and illiteracy around the world. Furthermore, Rick and Kay no longer take a salary from the church Rick serves, and, in addition, the two have repaid the church all of his salary from the last twenty-five years.

I can hear the cynic who reads this reacting, "If you make the amount of money he's made, you could afford to live on the 10 percent and still have more than most." That may be true, but there are far more important observations to make and questions to ask, such as, "What inspires them to do this? What's the motivating factor to give away 90 percent of their income? Has their religious tradition dictated they must? Are they driven by ego and its desire for recognition? Or could it be something else entirely?"

It cannot be ego that motivates the Warrens. His bestselling books, appearances on national television, and invitations to consult with presidents and with religious and political leaders worldwide bring him more recognition in a single day than many celebrities would receive in a lifetime. The desire to give away the lion's share of their wealth is hardly explained because of recognition deprivation.

No religious tradition has dictated to the Warrens that they must live on the 10 percent and give away the 90 either. While I don't know him personally, I've heard Warren speak often enough to know that he is an independent thinker and will not be told by anyone what he must believe or do.

There is no other explanation as to what motivates Rick and Kay Warren other than their personal gratitude to God, the joy they get from giving, and the sheer bliss they must feel at being involved in many worthwhile causes into which they have generously invested.

Today, there are more than 7.5 million millionaires in America alone. That compares to 100,000 or fewer millionaires just 50 years ago. There are nearly 9 million affluent households in America— households with a net worth of at least $1 million excluding primary residences. And the number of "emerging affluent" is growing at an incredible pace.

Maybe you're one of these millionaires. If not, you likely know one of the infamous millionaires next door, as Thomas Stanley and William Danko referred to them in their book by a similar title. But how many of them do you think have made a similar decision to give away the bulk of their income? I don't know about the millionaires you know, but among the ones I know, it would never even occur to them to do anything remotely similar to that of Rick and Kay Warren. Don't let ego use cynicism to keep you from a life of generosity. You deserve better than that.

AND OTHERS LIKE THE WARRENS . . .

Until recently, most of the media images that filled our television screens seemed noxiously absorbed with the grotesque greed and the brazen extravagance of celebrities (and celebrity wannabes), with their huge and ornately furnished houses (or "cribs," as they call them), and the prodigal lifestyles that frequently surround much of their egocentric love of attention, money, and material madness. But lately (and none too soon, I might add), we're seeing more of the Rick Warren types featured on television and in news outlets. At least, I think so.

Consider, for example, the recent media frenzy over the largest charitable gift in modern history (and perhaps all of history) made by Warren Buffett to the Gates Foundation. And, speaking of the Gateses, I frequently see Bill and Melinda in the news as well, not only because of Bill Gates's leadership at Microsoft, but because of their philanthropic activities—disease, poverty, and illiteracy elimination—through their foundation, which is now the largest of its kind in all of history.

There are others who seem to be getting a lot of media attention, too. What about Mutombo the Medicine Man? Have you heard of him? Normally, someone like Dikembe Mutombo, at 7 feet tall with shoe size 22, would be known only for his size and salary as NBA player for the Houston Rockets. In Mutombo's case, however, he's most widely known for his philanthropy. He's raised $20 million through his foundation, including $15 million of his own money, to build the Biamba Marie Mutombo Hospital in the capital city of Kinshasa in the Democratic Republic of the Congo. The 10-acre, 300-bed facility boasts state-of-the-art medical equipment and will serve as a teaching hospital to help the few overworked doctors who serve a city of 6.5 million people. Mutombo hopes his hospital, named after his mother, will draw doctors from around the globe to work pro bono.

Mutombo came to the United States in 1987 to attend Georgetown University in Washington D.C. with hopes of becoming a medical doctor and eventually returning to his homeland. At the request of the school's coach, however, Mutombo joined the Georgetown basketball team, and the rest is history. He plans to retire from NBA soon so he can give himself full time to the real passion of his life—giving.[1]

Mutombo's philanthropy is getting a lot of press. But not nearly as much press as that of Oprah Winfrey. The media regularly reports on her personal involvement in charitable causes associated with her Angel Network and other foundations. More recently, she created a media firestorm when she opened her $40 million, 50-acre Oprah Winfrey Leadership Academy in South Africa in January 2007. Ultimately, it will provide its 450 students with textbooks, uniforms, and meals, as well as teaching girls "to be the best human beings they can ever be."

Is all of this media attention signaling a shift in emphasis? Or am I just more in tune with the activities of philanthropists because I'm writing this book? Time will tell. Meanwhile, I'm encouraged that a few of those who seem to draw an inordinate amount of the public's attention are taking a positive stand in favor of philanthropy and generosity as a lifestyle. Aren't you?

Take Bono. Bono may be the most widely recognized name in the world today not because he's a rock star, but because of his financial generosity and personal activism. Bono is not just a media spokesperson for AIDS and debt relief in Africa. He is the chief activist in the campaign to eradicate AIDS. Because of his personal philanthropy, Oprah calls Bono the world's "reigning king of hope."

He didn't earn that title because of his vocal achievements, though he is a talented singer. Nor did he draw the accolade because of his financial charity, though he gives away vast sums of money. He earned that distinction for one reason: Bono gives himself. He gets personally involved and seems to draw his greatest fulfillment not from entertaining people on a stage but by serving people who are helpless and voiceless. His financial generosity is the launching pad for his personal involvement. Heart has followed his treasure.

GIVING IS MEDICINE FOR THE SOUL

The National Institute of Neurological Disorders and Stroke at Bethesda, Maryland, recently studied the brain activity of 19 men and women, each of whom was given $128 and asked to make choices about whether to keep it themselves or give some or all of it to charity. The researchers discovered that giving, even when it didn't personally cost the donor any of the money provided, activated two areas of the brain. One area was the mesolimbic network—that part of the brain where dopamine is released, giving rise to pleasurable and euphoric sensations during activities such as eating and sex. The other area of the brain was the subgenual area, which plays a significant role in helping people form meaningful relationships and attachments to others.[2]

In other words, the study concluded, when you give, you not only feel better, but you are better. Your outlook and attitudes are more positive. Your capacity for being more relational and involved is enhanced.

I'm no scientific researcher, but I've done a lot of observing over the last decade. What I've observed is that, when people give generously, they are not only personally enriched, but they are also more actively involved. They are healthier and happier. And the world around them is better off because, rather than being part of its problems, they're actively involved in producing solutions.

The converse is also true. Inactivity or a lack of involvement is directly related to the degree of one's financial investment. There are scores of celebrities, for example, who give charities permission to borrow their celebrity for fundraising purposes. These celebrities may themselves make token gifts to those charities that borrow their influence, but they never get very involved beyond that.

Why? Because token giving is most often ego-driven. It's giving done either to soothe one's guilt or to draw attention from others. But when these celebrities make significant financial gifts to these charities, you'll always see them do more than just loan their influence. They get actively involved in the charity and passionate about it.

The same is true in the church. The primary reason most church attendees are only marginally involved in the church is because their giving is minimal. It is here that church leaders must change the focus of their energy and message. I believe church leaders must challenge people not only to increase their giving but to grow in the grace of giving and do both without hesitation or apology. The end result will be greater involvement.

But don't make the mistake of assuming that, by greater involvement, I mean the frequency of church attendance or the number of committees and jobs these persons become willing to assume in the church. Some may and perhaps should. But I believe a broader understanding of involvement in kingdom-building causes will be seen and must be embraced by the church. As people learn to give their financial resources away more freely, they'll look for ways to be involved not only in the church but, more importantly, in the world. Both places of involvement must be embraced and advocated by the church.

While selfish, ego-dominated church members must continually be begged, cajoled, or shamed into involvement and often praised and thanked just to keep them there, it is never so with ego-free, financially generous people. They look for ways to be involved, some in the church but all of them in the world. And, it's the world that really needs these selfless, Christ-like people.

It was Jesus himself who gave his followers the metaphor of "salt." If the church is like a saltshaker and Jesus' followers are like salt themselves, then for that salt to have any worthwhile impact on its environment, it must be released from the shaker. The goal of the church should not be to see how full the shaker can get, but how much salt the shaker can disperse into the social, economic, and political structures of this world.

In an article about how pastors measure spiritual health, researcher George Barna observed, "Stewardship is rarely deemed a meaningful measure of church vitality." I am suggesting that church leaders must make giving a significant measure of spiritual maturity. I believe that the chief barometer of one's spiritual health is stewardship, not how often a person attends church or how many committees he or she serves on. What many religious leaders seem to forget is that the paltry 2 to 3 percent of annual household income members typically give to their church plays an unmistakable role not only in the church's vitality but in the donor's personal involvement in the church's ministry in the world. Barna concluded many leaders obviously don't realize low percentage giving is "an indicator of lukewarm commitment."[3]

When I was young, I often heard church people say, "Give until it hurts." I never liked the phrase because I think I intuitively felt what the medical researchers have substantiated. Rather than hurting, the more you give, the better you feel. And "more" doesn't refer to the size of your gift but to the personal sacrifice involved.

I understand, nevertheless, what those who used the phrase were trying to say. If you are giving financially but not involved personally, your giving is nominal at best. When giving is great enough, however, to "hurt" so to speak, then your involvement will be automatic. "Where your treasure is, there your heart and mind will also be," said Jesus. Apparently, he knew something the rest of us need to know.

But don't let me tell you what to believe. Try it for yourself. Give and you'll get involved.

SUGGESTIONS FOR GIVING, THEN GETTING THE LIFE YOU'VE ALWAYS WANTED

• Want to feel better? Start giving. Want to feel a lot better? Give, not until it hurts, but until it starts to feel good. It will. And the more generous you are, the better you'll feel. If you give in this way, you'll get involved, and involvement is where real living is experienced.

If you're a church leader and you wish to see people more involved in ministry, then I suggest you give your attention to developing a leadership strategy that regularly encourages growth in giving. People will become more involved in ministry when growth in giving becomes a greater priority. But I do not recommend that you either insist people "tithe" or make the giving of 10 percent of income the goal of Christian giving. Nor would I recommend that you tell people the tithe belongs exclusively to the church. None of these positions is scripturally defensible. Besides, dictating to people what they must believe is clearly a failed strategy. Instead, make growth in giving a priority in your own life. Then, teach people by your own example and that of others what happens when you become generous in giving. Be specific. Be transparent. People respond to real-life examples, not to edicts.

As people grow in giving and experience a richer and more meaningful life, they will give much more than they currently give to the church and to other charities. It isn't helpful to make people feel they are under some Old Testament obligation to give any particular percentage or amount either to the church or any other charity. Wherever they receive their spiritual inspiration, they will give generous support. God may direct people to give to other places too—and with that giving, their life and time will follow, as it should. This is how ministry should be defined—not by how many parish committees are served by a member or by keeping score on how many worship services or Masses are attended each year. The church will always have the leadership it needs when the emphasis in ministry is properly directed.

This isn't rocket science. Generous people are the happiest, the most active, and the most involved people in any culture. It's the way

God has wired us. Generous people are the most successful, too. That is, they are the most successful at getting beyond ego with its infatuation with self. You cannot be generous and self-centered simultaneously. But you can be stingy and self-centered at the same time. Just look around and you'll see a culture filled with such people. At times, you and I can be such people. But generosity is the fastest way to overcome the self-gratifying ego. The church's ministry should be designed so as to help people understand these realities and overcome them.

If you want to be less self-centered, permit the spirit of generosity to guide you. You don't need to beg God to do this. He's more than ready to free you to be generous and to find your life by giving it away. God is generous, and those who are generous are most like God. The word "generosity" comes from a Latin word meaning "of noble birth." When you are generous, you are most closely connected in lineage to divine nobility. You are closest to the heart of God and to genuine love himself. The most well-known verse of Scripture, John 3:16, says, "For God loved the world so much that he gave . . . ." Loving and giving, giving and loving—they go hand in hand.

• Most of the examples of philanthropy I've referred to in this chapter are of high-profile people capable of giving huge sums of money and who, because of their wealth, probably have more time to devote to philanthropic causes. Where does that leave average folks like you and me who have to work every day just to make a living and survive? In comparison, what difference could you and I possibly make in a world where our gifts are smaller and our time more limited?

First, stop the invidious comparisons. That's ego stuff. Remember, five-talent people are expected to produce five-talent returns. Instead, celebrate who you are, what you have, and be grateful for where you are in your life. Until you can celebrate these basic things, you're not ready to move on.

Be generous with what you have. Join a "Circle of Giving" group. They're springing up everywhere. These are groups of ordinary people, getting together regularly for social interaction and to pool together their financial resources so that they might multiply the impact of their charitable giving.

That's the message in the story of the little boy who gave Jesus his five loaves of bread and two small fish. Thousands had come to hear Jesus speak. As the day drew late, Jesus wondered how they might find something for the masses of people to eat. Philip and Andrew, overwhelmed at the daunting challenge of finding food for such a crowd, despaired. But a nameless little boy offered his lunch. "I have two bologna sandwiches and a can of anchovies." He started with what he had and offered it. That's all God asks of any of us.

Andrew the Apostle looked at the boy's paltry gift and asked, "But what good is that with this huge crowd?" (John 6:9).

Who are you more like? Andrew or the boy? Do you spend most of your time looking at your life situation and feeling jealous toward others? Do you look at your meager resources and wonder what difference your gifts could make? Do you focus on what's missing in your life and on your limitations? Or do you instead offer what you have and surrender the results to God?

God has never asked anyone to do anything he has not provided the means to do. It is true God has asked people to do some rather remarkable things. The Bible is replete with such examples. Your own life may be, too. But in every instance, I know of no person God has ever "hung out to dry." All God asks is that you start where you are. Then, in time, as you demonstrate your willingness to make good use of what he's given and to trust him for the results, you'll have more and greater opportunities to be generous. This is how his universe works. Keep your eyes wide open and observe him at work. He will multiply your generosity, your capacity, and your opportunities to be generous. In the process, he will fill your life with incredible meaning as you become more involved in making a difference in your world. As your personal worldview changes, so does the world around you. No one should look around and ask, "What's wrong with the world?" without first looking within and asking, "What's wrong with me?"

What you give away will return to you, too. If you're like me, it will take several reminders for that truth to sink in. In my judgment, it is the most important law of life among seven important laws to which the medical doctor and spiritual advisor Deepak Chopra refers in his book *The Seven Spiritual Laws of Success.*[4] What you give, you receive. Christians who are learning to give generously and to give themselves away refer to this universal law when they say, "You can't out-give God." You really can't. I know this. But you'll have to discover this truth for yourself.

Do you remember the 2000 movie *Pay It Forward* that starred Kevin Spacey and Helen Hunt? It was a profoundly moving motion picture. But what you may not know is that the movie was inspirational in triggering a worldwide movement known as Kingdom Assignment. You can read the entire story at the website www.kingdomassignment.com.

Denny Bellesi, founding pastor of a nondenominational community church in Southern California, drew inspiration from the parable of the talents and the movie Pay It Forward, which promoted the idea that someone who is shown a favor should show kindness to three other people.

Remembering the story Jesus told of the master who gave talents to three workers with instructions that they trade and multiply them, Bellesi decided to borrow $10,000 from the church's coffers, distribute it in increments of $100 to 100 members of his congregation, and give them similar instructions.

It all started at a Sunday service. Bellesi asked volunteers to come to up front without first explaining what he wanted them to do. Volunteers gathered at the front where he began distributing new, crisp $100 bills with the following three instructions: (1) This is God's money, not yours. (2) You are to take this money and do something for the kingdom. But whatever you do must be outside the church. Finally, (3) you are to report back in ninety days and tell what you've accomplished with the money.

Can you imagine being one of these unsuspecting volunteers on that Sunday morning? Bellesi later admitted he had absolutely no idea how the people would respond or what the results would be.

What happened next, nobody would have ever predicted. When all was said and done, Bellesi's experiment made the nightly news, the Oprah Winfrey show, People magazine, Woman's Day, Reader's Digest, scores of local newspapers around the country, and countless national radio talk shows. Most importantly, though, the original $10,000 had multiplied into a windfall of more than $1 million for hundreds of good causes—such as support for a Boy Scout troop in an impoverished inner city and the building of a homeless shelter and a transitional shelter for battered women.[5]

Are you ready to begin with what God has given you? Do you see the opportunities to be generous that abound around you? When you see them, do you seize them? When you are ready to live the life you've always wanted and are willing to risk being generous with your financial resources, even when your gifts pale in comparison to others, you'll discover a joy like you've never known before. Instead of making excuses about not having time to be involved, you'll not only find the time, you'll have the motivation.

It begins with the recognition that all you have is gift to you from God, undeserved and unearned—just like the parishioners who received the $100 gift from Pastor Bellesi. When you know this, not because I say it's the truth, but because you've discovered this truth for yourself, you will no longer feel as if you own anything. Instead, a great sense of indebtedness will sweep over you, and, from that moment on you'll feel as if everything you have is on loan to you from God. Instantly, any feelings of insignificance will disappear from your life. You'll no longer excuse yourself or feel you have neither the influence nor the affluence of a Rick Warren or a Mutombo to make a difference in the world. You'll be that difference yourself.

Our local paper recently reported the story of two Central Kentucky women who attended the Oprah Winfrey Show in Chicago when they and other unsuspecting persons were given, during the taping of the show, $2,000 with instructions to give it away and document their experiences.

On their drive home, cousins Tammy Kossatz and Samantha Frederick began making plans as to what they would do with the money they were given. Here's a sampling of the plethora of projects that sprang from their efforts: the cousins arranged for four women to receive makeovers at Posh Salon, including skin care, hair and dental care, makeup, new clothes, and a post-makeover photo shoot. But that's not all. There was a flight from another continent to Lexington, Kentucky, for a grandmother who couldn't afford to the cost of the trip to see her grandchild; landscaping for the family of a victim of Comair Flight 5191 that had recently crashed in Lexington, killing all but the co-pilot; a hot breakfast for some public workers; and a break from cleaning bathrooms for some custodians.[6] Do you suppose the gifts that were given to them from someone else made any difference in the lives of others? If you can see the parallels to your own life, you are on the verge of a great discovery.

If you cannot, you'll likely find yourself saying things like, "Well, if somebody gave me $2,000, I could be generous, too."

But Somebody has given you something. In fact, everything you have, no matter how insignificant your ego has made you feel it is (which, incidentally, is how ego holds you in the clutches of jealousy and comparison), is gift from God. When you're tired of your ego making you feel resentful and you become generous with what you have, life in all of its abundance and joy will start coming together for you and coming to you in ways that will exceed your imagination.

Contemporary author Eckhart Tolle once said, somewhat counterintuitively, "Abundance comes only to those who already have it." You may not think what you have is all that abundant. And you may feel you can't part with anything you have because you've worked hard for it.

But it all depends on your perception, your perspective, and your readiness to pursue the life you've always wanted. When you're ready to accept gratefully where you are in life, generously invest some of the resources you have, and, as a result, creatively involve yourself in the world around you, you'll begin to experience inner freedom, joy—and, paradoxically, abundance. As your generosity grows, so will your abundance and your opportunities to be generous. If it is true, as Tolle has suggested, that "abundance comes only to those who already have it," it's also true that the perception of scarcity will persist for those who always feel they have too little.

• "The purpose of life," said Robert Byrne, "is a life of purpose." Interesting play on words. Have you decided what life's purpose is for you? You should know by now that I believe life's purpose for everyone is inextricably bound up in giving yourself away. Giving yourself away is the investment of your life in the lives of others and in this world. The fastest way to get on this path of purpose is to start being generous with your financial resources. What Jesus said I have found to be true not only in my own life but in the lives of countless people I've met in the last decade. "Where your treasure is, there your heart will also be." When you give your resources, it is much more natural to give yourself. In fact, you'll discover as you give yourself away that you are freer to accept yourself, creatively express yourself, and be content in all circumstances.

Lately, when I think of self-acceptance, creativity, and contented-ness, I think about Marvin Francis, an inmate at a maximum-security prison in Kentucky. In 1986, Marvin Francis was sentenced to life for the brutal murder of a Hopkinsville grocery store owner. While his intentions may have been robbery only, as antisocial as that is itself, the circumstances surrounding the robbery quickly spiraled downward toward the unimaginable.

Francis had not anticipated that his robbery victim would him-self be armed, but for quite some time, Seldon Dixon Sr. had been carrying a small handgun for protection. When Francis pointed a .44-caliber in Seldon's face and demanded the day's earnings, Seldon drew his own pistol. The two exchanged gunfire and, when it was all over, the fifty-six-year-old grocer suffered four fatal gunshot wounds.

Marvin Francis was quickly convicted and sent to prison; few expect that he will ever be paroled. And perhaps he should not be. In fact, some might argue he sacrificed his right to live when he chose to take the life of another and, therefore, Francis should have received the death penalty himself. I'll leave those judgments to others. What I find amazing is the manner in which Francis has chosen to manage his life situation. He has made the decision to give and to give himself to something useful and creative.

Over the years, I've known many people in far less challenging circumstances who complain about their lack, what's missing in their lives, and resent others they deem luckier and more successful.

Until his incarceration, Francis had never picked up a paintbrush. In fact, he had never visited an art museum. But today, art is his whole life. As a matter of fact, his artistic genius and creative expression have made him an internationally acclaimed artist. Using as tools a toenail clipper, the end of a headphone jack, and a paintbrush handle he has carved into a sculpting stick, Francis turns toilet paper papier-mâché, coated with paste and painted with acrylics, into sculpted works of art that leave viewers speechless. Recently, his work won first place in one of Europe's most famed competitions for sculptors.

His disturbing art graphically depicts how incarceration stunts the human soul. Yet the thought-provoking sculptures are commanding prices as high as $3,000 each. If you're like me, at first I found myself wondering, "What would an inmate do who is not likely ever to be free with money in amounts like this?" But I learned later that, with this money, Francis regularly gives to charity, including a children's fund run by prisoners.

Rather than celebrating, here's what ego will do to you when it comes to a story like this. Ego will make you might feel that, if you had nothing more to do than sit around all day long at somebody else's expense, you could be creative, too. But, of course, you cannot because, as a responsible person, you have to work and make a living. Or ego will make you feel that prisoners should be prevented from making money while incarcerated, or, if they do make money, everything they earn should go to a victim's family or be given back to taxpayers for the costs associated with their imprisonment.

Maybe a prisoner should never be allowed to make any money. I don't know. What I do know is that ego, with all its subtlety, will slip in and make you not only think such thoughts but become obsessed with them so that you don't see what's good about this story and exemplary in Francis's life. Ego will create this and other mental diversions to take your thoughts away from one salient fact. Here is a man who will spend most if not all of his adult life in prison.

Rather than becoming obsessed with envy toward others who are free or self-absorbed and defensive, insisting on his own innocence, Morris is giving to charity and is giving his life away in artistic self-expression. The world is filled with people in far better circumstances doing far less—and acting resentfully in the process. The example of Francis should give pause to all of us.

Francis knows that neither his gifts to charity nor his art will ever make up for his crime. He also knows how unlikely it is that he'll ever be released. Yet no matter where he spends the rest of his life, Francis remains focused—giving himself away in artistic self-expression and giving to charity from the resources he generates with his art. "This is what I do," he said. "It is what I am."[7]

Carlos Castaneda used to say, "Things don't change, only the way you look at them." How do you look at the circumstances of your life? You may not be incarcerated, but your soul may be caged in a prison of self-pity and jealousy because your opportunities haven't been as lucrative as they appear to have been for others. When you decide to see things differently, then what you both see and experience will be different. Norman Vincent Peale would often put it this way: "Change your thoughts and you change your world."

What would help you see things differently? What would help this world be a different place? By now, I'm sure you know. Give and you'll get the life you want. Giving will not only make your world better, but the world around you will be better, too.

> *Accept yourself as God's gift to you; celebrate yourself as your gift to yourself; and give yourself away as your gift to the world.*

NOTES

[1] C. C. Williams, "Mutombo the Medicine Man," *Sky* (December 2006): 76-79.

[2] Holly Hall, "Sex, Drugs and . . . Charity? Brain Study Finds New Links," *The Chronicle of Philanthropy* (7 December 2006).

[3] George Barna, "Surveys Show Pastors Claim Congregants Are Deeply Committed to God but Congregants Deny It," *The Barna Update*, 10 January 2006.

[4] Deepak Chopra, *The Seven Spiritual Laws of Success* (San Raphael CA: Amber-Allen Publishing, 1994).

[5] Lynn O'Shaughnessy, "Paying It Forward," *The Chronicle of Philanthropy* (31 August 2006).

[6] "Pair gets others to join Oprah's generosity," *The Courier-Journal,* 6 November 2006.

[7] Andrew Wolfson, "Captivity breeds creativity," *The Courier-Journal,* 19 November 2006, A1-A3.

10

Myth 6

"Your Charity Is a Private Matter"

In the same way, let your good deeds shine out for all to see, so that everyone will praise your heavenly Father.

—Jesus (Matt 5:16)

Don't do your good deeds publicly . . . . Give your gifts in private, and your Father, who sees everything, will reward you.

—Jesus (Matt 6:1-4)

Charity is never so lovely as when one has lost consciousness that one is practicing charity.

—Anthony DeMello (1931–1987)

Two of the quotes that open this chapter are from Jesus himself. Standing alone, each quotation is unambiguous. But together, they present yet another paradox. The two statements introduce the sixth myth that, across the philanthropic landscape, may be the most universally shared myth.

Is your charity supposed to be private, even anonymous? Or should your good deeds be open and transparent for others to see?

On one hand, Jesus said,

> *"No one lights a lamp and then puts it under a basket.*
> *Instead, a lamp is placed on a stand, where it gives light to*
> *everyone in the house. In the same way, let your good deeds*
> *shine out for all to see . . ." (Matt 5:15-16).*

But just a chapter and a few verses later, Jesus said,

> *Watch out! Don't do your good deeds publicly, to be admired*
> *by others, for you will lose the reward from your Father in*
> *heaven. When you give to someone in need, don't do as the*
> *hypocrites do—blowing trumpets in the synagogues and*
> *streets to call attention to their acts of charity . . . . Give*
> *your gifts in private, and your Father, who sees everything,*
> *will reward you. (Matt 6:1-2)*

Which is it? "Let your good deeds shine"? Or "Don't do your good deeds publicly"? If I have learned anything in the last decade, it is that few of the myths about giving discussed in this book draw more emotion than this one. Ask almost anyone whether his charity should be open to the public or a private matter and you can be sure to get an opinion—from the church house all the way to the White House.

He may hold strong convictions about many things, but whenever I've watched Vice President Dick Cheney in public interviews, he has always appeared stoic and emotionless. Except perhaps once, when the press reported that Cheney's charitable contributions for the year would amount to approximately 1 percent of his total income. Here's what I observed.

A reporter approached Cheney with the question, "What do you think is the proper level of giving for a person who has millions of dollars, in terms of percentage, that is?"

Not a bad question in my opinion and, quite frankly, one that any public official should anticipate. But Cheney's reaction was more emotional than at any other time I've ever seen. In fact, his reaction suggests he must have been ticked off by the question, feeling an area of his private life had been broached. Cheney tersely responded, "That's a choice that individuals have to make. It's not a policy question, but a private matter, a matter of private choice."

Cheney isn't alone in his opinion. As a matter of fact, there was a time in my own life when I would have agreed with him. While I no longer feel this way, I did not come to my present position quickly or easily.

CHARITY IN SECRET—THE EARLY DAYS

I grew up in a religious tradition that both taught and practiced privacy regarding one's charitable contributions. It wasn't a written doctrine or dogma, but in practice, few things were more sacred than the secrecy of your gifts to charity. For someone to talk publicly about her or his giving was tantamount to boasting, or trumpet-blowing in the streets, and regarded as violating Jesus' instruction on modesty in giving.

By the time I became a professional minister, I was proud to be able to tell my church members that I had no idea what any of them gave. I held the view that, if I knew, it might affect how I felt toward people. Even worse, it might influence the way I treated some persons within the church. I wanted to believe that I treated all people equally.

The truth is, though I wanted to believe I didn't, I really did treat people unequally. There were always people in the churches I served whom I regarded as carrying more influence with me than others. It's hard to admit this now, but it's true. Any one of those persons could have called me with a need, even at 3:00 am, and I would have responded without hesitation. But there were others who, if they even had the nerve to call at such an hour, I would have questioned within myself whether it was necessary to respond immediately or put them off until morning.

But regarding financial contribution records, I was most consistent. I treated everyone the same and looked at no one's history of giving to the church. In fact, I considered it a violation of their privacy. That would all change, however, when I became a church consultant.

DISCOVERY OF GIVING IN THE SCRIPTURES

It was not until after I left the pastoral ministry that I began asking, "What does the Bible really teach about giving?" What I discovered startled me. In fact, knowing what I do today, I'm perplexed as to how I went through my entire post-graduate theological study and half my life in the professional ministry where the study of Scripture was a regular practice and never saw how frequently or directly the Bible speaks to the subject of giving. Not only is Scripture replete with examples of giving, but the issue of privacy regarding one's charity is not found in any of these examples.

Does that surprise you? It surprised me, because one of the first things I confronted was the fact that, if it was important to God that your charity be cloaked in secrecy, there must be examples of charitable privacy in either the Old or New Testament. But there is not. In fact, I found the opposite. There's nothing private at all in the examples of charitable giving. Here's a sampling of what I found.

DAVID'S GIFTS FOR BUILDING THE TEMPLE

The best Old Testament example of this is the story of David and his fundraising enterprise for the construction of the temple as recorded in 1 Chronicles 29. You might recall that David wanted to build the temple himself. But God denied him that privilege because of his propensity to wage war. Instead, God would direct David's son, Solomon, to build the temple. Intent on having his part in the construction nevertheless, David launched the fundraising enterprise to make it possible. He called the congregation together and detailed, with amazing precision and openness, what his personal contribution to the project would be. Here's what he said:

> And now, because of my devotion to the temple of my God,
> I am giving all of my own private treasures of gold and
> silver to help in the construction. This is in addition to the
> building materials I have already collected for his holy

> *temple. I am donating more than 112 tons of gold from*
> *Ophir and 262 tons of refined silver to be used for overlay-*
> *ing the walls of the buildings, and for the other gold and*
> *silver work to be done by the craftsmen. Now then, who*
> *will follow my example and give offerings to the Lord today?*
> *(1 Chr 29:3-5)*

Nothing private about his giving, is there? It doesn't end there, either. In response to David's question, the leaders recited what they would themselves give for the construction of the temple. Again, there's amazing openness on the part of the leaders. You cannot help noticing that the details associated with their gifts are astonishingly specific.

If you're looking for Old Testament proof that charity should be a private matter, you'll have to gloss over this story. Of course, you might explain, "That's because it's in the Old Testament. You can find a lot of stuff in the Old Testament that's clearly forbidden in the New. But it's clear in the New Testament that your charity is to be done in secret."

Really? Have you looked closely at the New Testament to confirm this impression?

THE WIDOW'S MITE

One day, Jesus was in the temple watching people place their contributions in the collection plate. A widow made a small, private donation, after which Jesus made a startling, public declaration.

"I tell you the truth," Jesus said, "this poor widow has given more than all the rest of them. For they have given a tiny part of their surplus, but she, poor as she is, has given everything she has" (Luke 21:3-4).

Not only is there nothing secret about the widow's gift, it is Jesus himself sharing her gift and its amount to the entire assembly. How's that for privacy?

THE GENEROSITY OF BARNABAS VERSUS
THE INSINCERITY OF ANANIAS

Take another example—that of Barnabas and the contrasting story
of Ananias and Sapphira. As you might know, chapter divisions and
verse assignments were added long after the original writers penned
what is now regarded as the canon of Scripture. While those divisions help in the public and private reading of Scripture, they have
resulted in the loss of interconnectedness that often exists between
stories. The twin stories of Barnabas in latter part of Acts 4 and
Ananias and Sapphira at the beginning of chapter 5 is a good example. It is unfortunate that these two stories are rarely read in concert,
because Luke, who authored the Acts of the Apostles, clearly
intended the example of Ananias and Sapphira to stand in juxtaposi-
tion to that of Barnabas.

Read the entire story together. It quickly becomes apparent what
Luke was saying to the early church.

> *All the believers were united in heart and mind. And they felt that*
> *what they owned was not their own, so they shared everything they*
> *had. The apostles testified powerfully to the resurrection of the Lord*
> *Jesus, and God's great blessing was upon them all. There were no*
> *needy people among them, because those who owned land or houses*
> *would sell them and bring the money to the apostles to give to those*
> *in need.*
>
> *For instance, there was Joseph, the one the apostles nicknamed*
> *Barnabas (which means "Son of Encouragement"). He was from the*
> *tribe of Levi and came from the island of Cyprus. He sold a field he*
> *owned and brought the money to the apostles.*
>
> *But there was a certain man named Ananias who, with his wife,*
> *Sapphira, sold some property. He brought part of the money to the*
> *apostles, claiming it was the full amount. With his wife's consent, he*
> *kept the rest. Then Peter said, "Ananias, why have you let Satan fill*
> *your heart? You lied to the Holy Spirit, and you kept some of the*
> *money for yourself. The property was yours to sell or not sell, as you*
> *wished. And after selling it, the money was also yours to give away.*
> *How could you do a thing like this? You weren't lying to us but to*
> *God!"*

> *As soon as Ananias heard these words, he fell to the floor and*
> *died. Everyone who heard about it was terrified. Then some young*
> *men got up, wrapped him in a sheet, and took him out and buried*
> *him. About three hours later, his wife came in, not knowing what*
> *had happened. Peter asked her, "Was this the price you and your hus-*
> *band received for your land?"*
>
> *"Yes," she replied, "that was the price."*
>
> *And Peter said, "How could the two of you even think of con-*
> *spiring to test the Spirit of the Lord like this? The young men who*
> *buried your husband are just outside the door, and they will carry*
> *you out, too."*
>
> *Instantly, she fell to the floor and died. When the young men*
> *came in and saw that she was dead, they carried her out and buried*
> *her beside her husband. Great fear gripped the entire church and*
> *everyone else who heard what had happened. (Acts 4:32–5:11)*

I won't try to explain the mysterious deaths of Ananias and Sapphira. I'll attempt something simpler—an explanation as to what might have motivated them to do something so insincere, even deceptive.

When read together, these two stories are obviously meant to stand in stark contrast to each other. You have, on one hand, the transparent and generous Barnabas who donated the profits he received from the sale of property to the apostles. They took the money and distributed it to those in need. Note that there's no secrecy surrounding his donation. Everyone not only knew about his gift but, presumably, celebrated his generosity. Luke made sure all later generations would know what Barnabas gave by recording it.

By contrast, you have the dishonest, selfish Ananias and Sapphira. What motivated them to make a donation similar to that of Barnabas but with such different and disturbing consequences?

The answer is simple: ego. It was their egos that lifted their selfish, envious heads in reaction to the community's praise of Barnabas. Driven by the egocentric need for others' approval and adulation, Ananias and Sapphira went out, sold a piece of property, and donated a portion of the proceeds under the pretense of donating it all. That is, unlike Barnabas, they withheld a portion of the profits but let the community of faith believe they were donating all of the profits.

That was their evil and that was Luke's warning to his readers. Luke did not record these stories as a lesson on secrecy regarding charitable contributions. To the contrary, Luke wanted the community to know about the generosity of its members. He also wanted to warn the community to guard against the subtle deception of the ego. Of course, he didn't call it ego, but the behavior of Ananias and Sapphira is certainly consistent with what we know about the sinister nature of the ego.

Ego is always jealous when another gets more attention. At such times, it can lead you into all sorts of pretense and hypocrisy, just as it did Ananias and Sapphira when it watched with envy as the community applauded Barnabas.

Want to know the telltale sign that ego is at work in you? If you've ever had feelings of envy or jealousy when someone has been recognized and publicly applauded for their generosity, you can be sure that ego is at work in your heart. But the recognition of ego can be a good thing. It generally means that you are beginning to move beyond its control over your thoughts and feelings. So don't condemn yourself for the envious feelings ego generates in you. Instead, simply recognize ego's presence; in that recognition, you'll feel God's power to step up and renounce those feelings. This is the beginning of your liberation and the discovery of the life you've always wanted.

Ego will sometimes manifest itself as fear and defensiveness when someone suggests you share the details pertaining to it. Or a feeling of dread will overtake you when the details of your charitable giving are about to be revealed to others. I think this is what caused Cheney to react as he did when the reporter asked him about the extent of his contributions. Giving 1 or 2 percent of income to charity is hardly cause for applause, especially from someone whose personal wealth and political position permits him to sit with those in the upper echelons of wealth and power.

I'm not judging Cheney—just making an observation. I recognize the reason for his reaction, because I have witnessed the same in some of my own actions and reactions. It's the reaction of an ego under threat. Everyone battles the ego. I certainly do. And since the charity of most Americans is anything but exemplary, the ego would rather that reality remain hidden. In fact, it's one the strongest reasons why the myth of privacy about charity has survived for so long. It's much safer to the ego to surround one's charity—or, in most instances, the lack of it—with secrecy.

Luke's final observation is revealing: "Great fear gripped the entire church and everyone else who heard what had happened" (v. 11).

What fear gripped the church?

Given the grim details of Ananias's and Sapphira's sudden demise, it might have been the fear of death that gripped them. Certainly, the mysterious manner in which they died would have made the front page of the morning news, complete with pictures of the couple as they were carried from the sanctuary draped in sheets.

As foreboding as death may be, howeer, it was not the fear of death that gripped them. Rather, it was the fear of exposure—the fear of being found out. Apparently, Ananias and Sapphira were not the only ones guilty of pretense regarding charity. There were others, probably many others, just as there are today. Pretense about giving is the evil work of the ego.

Luke recorded these stories as a warning to the early church (and to the rest of us as well) that to give for the wrong reasons is dangerous. To pretend to be giving when you are not may be even more dangerous.

This is why I believe it has become so important to people that their giving be a secret matter. That way, they can talk about being generous without ever being so. They can pretend to be giving when really they are not. They can encourage others to give without ever giving themselves. Luke was, therefore, warning the early church that pretense over giving is precarious—even a dangerous thing to allow the ego to perpetuate in the human heart.

Much of the silence about giving in both the public arena and in the church is not because people are afraid someone might learn what they give; rather, it's because someone might discover they're not giving. Or that what they're actually giving is far less than what they want others to think they're giving. This is the sinister, selfish, and subtle work of the ego. It's also how the ego preserves itself.

When you allow charity to go public and permit people to openly and humbly share the joy they experience through generosity, ego is threatened. Ego would rather hold us imprisoned in manic and materialistic pursuits of power, possessions, and prestige. That way, it ensures its own survival and prevents you from becoming a generous person who experiences life as God intended.

JESUS ON CHARITY

You might concur with everything I've written thus far but still object, "Everything you are pointing out might be right, but didn't Jesus himself clearly say that charity should be done in secret?"

Let's go back now and read again what Jesus said—only this time, look beyond his words and listen for the concern beneath them. What you'll discover is this: Jesus' concern is not the public mention of your charity but the private motive behind it. Understood this way, his warning is not so different from that of Luke himself.

There are two important observations to remember: First, if Jesus meant for us to interpret his words to mean that our charity must be done in secret, then I am certain his words about prayer should be interpreted similarly. His instructions about prayer appear in the next section.

> When you pray, don't be like the hypocrites who love to pray publicly on street corners and in the synagogues where everyone can see them. I tell you the truth, that is all the reward they will ever get. But when you pray, go away by yourself, shut the door behind you, and pray to your Father in private. Then your Father, who sees everything, will reward you. (Matt 6:5-6)

Don't people pray in public all the time? Sure they do. So to insist that Jesus' principal concern in the previous passage is that charity be exercised in secret, you will also have to conclude his principal concern here is that prayer be expressed from a closet—that is, in secret and not in public as well. It's inconsistent to insist on the former but not the latter.

Second, in order correctly to interpret Jesus' words either about the practice of charity or the place of prayer, you must look beyond his words for his warning. What you discover is that the subtle work of the ego is what you must guard against in charity and in public prayer. Ego is obsessed with the status you hold in the eyes of the world, what you've attained, how much you have, and, in this case, the recognition ego craves from others for your charity and public prayers. If it can, ego will corrupt your best motives. This is Jesus' concern and warning. Piety can become a performance practiced purely for the praise of people.

The Master Teacher was not instructing people to keep the details of their charity a secret but the motives for their piety in check. On one hand, he would not counsel to "let your good deeds shine out for all to see . . ." and then turn around and contradict himself by saying, "Don't do your good deeds publicly . . . ."

There's nothing wrong with the philanthropic actions or the generous gifts of benevolent people being known by others or shared with others. In fact, doing so will lead everyone, as Jesus said, to "praise your heavenly Father" (Matt 5:16). But guard against the craftiness of the ego. It will corrupt your motives, if possible, and lead you to exult more in the compliments of others than in your charity to others. Ego feeds off the praise of people to remain alive and motivated. This is how sinister it is. Though normally obsessed with getting stuff as a means of sustaining its identity, ego will gladly let you give stuff away if, in the giving, it can lead you to enjoy more the feelings of separateness from others it creates and, worse, the feeling of superiority over others.

A BALANCED APPROACH

I am not saying that every act of benevolence or gift to your church or favorite charity should be made plain for others to see or even shared publicly. That's not my point. It is balance I'm encouraging.

I've changed my views over the years regarding the public or private nature of charity (including my own). But I'm still uncomfortable talking about my giving, and I'm equally uncomfortable when others know the details of my charity. In fact, I find it much more satisfying to give to others and to those causes I believe in, whether planned or spontaneous, without the recipient or anyone else ever knowing anything about it.

But within the charitable arena—and that includes the church—the myth of secrecy regarding charity has been the practice for much too long. So long, in fact, that it has taken on a life of its own. Privacy has become sacred to many folks, and there's nothing sacred about privacy at all. In fact, privacy itself can be a place of pride. What's needed today, instead, is balance. There's a time and place for everything, and sometimes sharing the details of your benevolence can motivate others and even be a blessing to others and to God, as Jesus suggested.

Every truly generous person I've ever known has learned to be so from someone else. I've never met anyone who awakened one day and said, "I think I'll start to be generous with my material wealth." I suppose that a few people, feeling a deep sense of appreciation for the opportunities that have rewarded them with much wealth, have become generous without the benefit of any human examples. Motivated by a deep feeling of obligation to give something back for all they've been given, these people become philanthropists entirely on their own. They feel so lucky to have so much that they are driven to do something for someone else. When they follow these impulses, they soon discover that being generous not only is fun but also gives them far more than all the wealth they've accumulated has ever given them. These people become some of the most generous philanthropists in our society and role models for everyone else.

But for most people, generosity is learned. Ask them where or how they learned to give, and they will always tell you. That's part of the reason I've written this book. If just a few folks who read this find motivation through one of the examples of generosity I include and begin to experiment with giving, not only will they discover the real purpose of living, but in that discovery they will experience joy and fulfillment exceeding anything they've known before.

When you think about it this way, it's a good thing that your "giving mentors" didn't insist on secrecy regarding their charity. They may have kept their benevolence from others, believing themselves in charitable privacy, but thankfully they let you in on their charity. Had they hidden their benevolence from you, you might never have learned to give.

Let me tell you about a woman named Beverly, whom I met a few years ago in New York. She is a role model of generosity. Yet until recently, only a few people knew her story. I hope to change that.

I had invited Beverly to an interview at the parish where she is a member and where I was conducting a feasibility study in preparation for a major capital campaign. Her church had outgrown its facilities and, for more than a year, had been hosting meetings, identifying options, and consulting with architects, all under the capable guidance of a liturgical consultant. Finally, a master plan was developed that lay and professional leaders embraced. I was invited to test the parish at large for support of the plan and determine whether they had the financial capability to build the larger church they obviously needed.

Just a few minutes into conversation with her, I knew I was interviewing not only a most generous person but one who was truly living the life she had always wanted. That's not to say Beverly's life has been easy. To the contrary, her life has been hard and filled with severe trials.

Beverly and her husband were the parents of seven children. In the mid-nineties, things were not going well for them financially. Her husband was working sixty- to eighty-hour workweeks just to provide for their needs. But with one daughter planning a wedding, another in college, mortgage and car payments, and the other typical expenses associated with raising a family, they were not making it. In fact, they were getting deeper and deeper into debt. Like the friends they socialized with regularly, Beverly and her husband gave little to their church and even less to other charities. It wasn't that they were opposed to doing so. They simply did not feel as if they could afford to give when their family's financial needs were so great.

But at a Bible study social for women, Beverly began discovering the teachings of Jesus regarding generosity in giving. One day, she approached her husband with the suggestion that they take seriously those teachings, downsize their lifestyles, and start giving 10 percent of their earnings to their church. His response was "You can't be serious!"

Beverly was very serious. Though they had a tight monthly budget for household expenses, she told her husband she was going to start giving a tenth of that money to their church. He reluctantly agreed, but only on the condition that she did not come back to him before the end of the month saying she needed more money for household expenses. The whole thing was terribly frightening to her. She had no idea what would happen. But she followed her heart and pursued her plan.

There's an old English proverb: "The hand that gives, gathers." That's exactly what happened to Beverly. That next month, the first check Beverly wrote out of the household expense checkbook was to her church. She then wrote all the other checks for the other household bills. Cynical and suspicious she would be short and need more money, Beverly's husband asked, "So, how much more do you need?"

"None at all," responded Beverly, trying to hide her own astonishment and excitement. "In fact," she further explained, "I've written all the bills for the month and, for the first time, we don't have a deficit this month but a surplus of fifteen dollars."

That initial experience in giving started Beverly and her family on a journey of charitable giving that has resulted in one of the most remarkable examples of generosity I've ever heard of. When I came to this chapter, I contacted Beverly and said, "Do you remember when I asked you to share your story to the parish during the capital campaign?"

"Yes," she replied. "That was one of the most difficult things I ever did."

"I'm sure it was, but publicly telling your story affected hundreds of parishioners in an overwhelmingly positive manner."

"I hope so," she responded.

"Now, Beverly, I have another request. Would you give me permission to share your story with a larger and broader audience?"

"What do you mean?" she asked. I could hear the perplexity in her voice.

I told her that I was writing a book about giving, then getting the life you've always wanted and that I knew of no one who was a better role model of the kind of life I was trying to describe.

"You are one of those rare humans, Beverly, who has learned the difference that generosity can make in your life, and I think your story should be told. It would inspire others to pursue a similar path."

Beverly agreed, saying that her own children had been encouraging her to write a book and tell of their experiences. So she wrote it out sent it to me by e-mail. For obvious reasons, I've edited many of the details and changed the names and personal matters to protect her family. But her name really is Beverly.

Those early experiments in charitable giving propelled Beverly on a path that over time would strengthen her faith so much so that today generosity is the central purpose of her life. For those who know her, it's no longer surprising to see her give anything away (including, very recently, her car!) to a family who needs it. But even that degree of generosity pales into insignificance compared to some of the things Beverly believes God has directed her over the years to donate to those in need. On one occasion, for example, she gave a house she owned to a family in her community who had been evicted from theirs.

How does Beverly manage to do these remarkable, even unimaginable things? Beverly has learned the principles of generosity I have set out in this book. She knows firsthand that to give is to receive. She never minces her words, but will gladly tell anyone that everything she's ever felt God lead her to give away he has returned to her in some way. If he didn't, it was stuff she didn't need and has been better off without. This reality has given Beverly freedom from the materialism that enslaves most everyone else. Each day of her life is filled with spontaneity as she eagerly watches for the opportunities to give herself away to family, friends, and those whom God brings across the path of her life. I have learned that there is nothing Beverly won't give away. But I also know there's nothing Beverly ever needs. She knows that God will supply everything she and her family needs. As well as anyone I've ever known, Beverly embodies complete confidence in the principle of the divinely designed world: "Give and you will receive" (Luke 6:38).

For some people, Beverly's generosity is absurd. For me, Beverly is a modern example of Mary Magdalene, who broke open her jar of costly perfume and lavishly poured it over Jesus' head (Matt 26:6-10). If you recall the story, you know it was the disciples of Jesus who were most bothered by her unthinkable extravagance. Beverly has experienced similar suspicion and judgment, ironically from people whom you would expect to appreciate her example of generous giving. Fortunately, she has never let their egocentric judgments dampen her spirit. She continues to be a blessing to others and lives a most blessed life.

If you think I'm telling Beverly's story to suggest that if you learn to give, your life will be a storybook fantasy of happily-ever-after living, you are mistaken. Life will be more meaningful, to be sure. But that doesn't mean your life will be easier. In fact, in many ways, it might be more challenging.

It wasn't easy for Beverly. Shortly after her family and she began learning the joys of giving, there were struggles, setbacks, even tragedies that awaited them. For Beverly, these became tests of faith. Perhaps the most tragic difficulty she faced was the day her husband was involved in a car accident that resulted in his death a few days later. Left with seven children to raise and a part-time job, Beverly remembers standing in her kitchen and crying out to God, "Now what am I going to do? How will I ever provide for these children?" She distinctly recalls God saying, "I will take care of you and provide . . . trust Me."

She did. God provided. And God continues to provide—abundantly. After she surrendered that day in the kitchen to God's providential care, Beverly has never succumbed to the impulse to keep for herself what she believes God prompts her to give away— even through the dark moments of life.

You can see why I asked Beverly to share her story publicly with the parish at large and sought permission to retell a portion of her story in this book. Her life, faith, and willingness to live in surrender to the promised care of God frees her from attachment to the material stuff of this world and makes each new day a discovery just waiting to happen.

Was it easy for her to share publicly how she has learned to be generous? No easier for her than for any conscientious person who is motivated by the purpose to give themselves away rather than live for the praise and applause of others. Catholic mystic Anthony de Mello once put it, "Charity is never so lovely as when one has lost consciousness that one is practicing charity." This is the life purpose of every genuinely charitable person.

Were people blessed by hearing her story? I can think of at least one person who was. Since most of what we learn is not through exhortation but observation, I'm thankful there are some people who are willing to let their "good deeds shine out for all to see" (Matt 5:16). Praise of the heavenly Father waits for this illumination.

SUGGESTIONS FOR GIVING, THEN GETTING THE LIFE YOU'VE ALWAYS WANTED

• If you're learning to be generous, you have a story that should be told. (If you're not genuinely generous, you probably have a lot to hide.) Contrary to our cultural conditioning, it isn't necessarily more spiritual to be silent about your giving. Admittedly, no one should go around flaunting their charity for all to see. That's the work of the ego. But don't be unnecessarily private about your charity, either. Sometimes good deeds should be done surreptitiously, as when giving something directly to someone less fortunate (Jesus called it "giving alms to the poor"). But sometimes, your charity should be open for all to see. Only you can decide when it is appropriate, but no one approach is more spiritual than the other.

• Do you want to develop the capacity to share your stories of generosity without feeling as if you're blowing your own horn? The conditioning that suggests it's egotistical to talk about your charitable contributions to the church or other charities or to share the spontaneous acts of kindness you might engage in during the course of a day will not be easy to overcome. It should be, however, and it can. But it won't happen overnight.

Here's what I would suggest: Start talking more openly to those closest to you about your charitable actions. Most relationships could benefit from more conversation, anyway. In fact, sharing your giving history might be one of the most benevolent gifts of charity you could ever give to the person you love most.

Tell your spouse, children, or closest friend of your experiences that day—how, for example, you caught yourself as you were about to shake your fist in disgust at the guy who cut you off on the freeway that morning, but instead you gave him the benefit of doubt and, therefore, a friendly wave and smile. At the moment you felt the impulse to react with your raised and angry fist, it occurred to you that his day might have gotten off to a bad start, so you gave him the benefit of the doubt and changed your response.

It's the ego that gets offended and interprets everyone else's behavior as personal, rude, and offensive. Granted, sometimes other folks are just plain rude. But then, isn't your behavior sometimes rude too? In either instance, the offender might be completely innocent of intentional malice. He or she might be burdened or preoccupied. Jesus said, "Do to others whatever you would like them to do to you" (Matt 7:12). Practicing the Golden Rule, as it's known, will hold ego at bay.

Be mindful of how you feel inside when telling your stories. You'll learn to notice when ego slips in and you start enjoying the compliments others give you for your acts of benevolence as much as you do the benevolent acts themselves. Recognize the presence of ego. You don't need to declare war against it or feel sinful for its presence. It's part of who you are. Just acknowledge its presence. In the acknowledgment, it begins to lose its grip over you. In the recognition alone, your higher self will become stronger even as the ego grows weaker.

It also helps to talk openly with each other about missed charitable opportunities. This is another way to keep the ego in check. I can give you a fresh, personal example of what I mean.

Just today, I blew it. Only hours before I sat down to finish this chapter, I was standing in line to place a to-go order at a popular soup and sandwich shop. I tried to beat the lunch crowd by getting there at 11:30. Apparently, everyone else had the same intent, because the restaurant was completely full.

I was about the sixth person in line to place my order. Of four choices, I got in line three because it looked as if it might be the one moving the fastest. I was in a hurry. I had to get back to this book, you know. Unlike others, I thought to myself, I have deadlines to meet and responsibilities to fulfill.

I knew better, but the ego is so subtle. Whenever I rush about and rob myself of the gift of this moment in some illusory pursuit of a nonexistent future moment, God has a gentle way of reminding me it is this moment that's his gift to me. So, I believe God inspired my choice of the slowest line.

After several long minutes of waiting, I was finally separated from my cashier by one more pair of customers—a mother and daughter. I was visibly agitated by that point. But as luck might have it, the mother and her daughter were ordering not only for themselves, but for several others. It looked as if the mother had scribbled these orders on an advertisement for diapers she had torn from a magazine for new mothers. To make matters worse, in between each order, she chitchatted with the cashier about everything from the frigid cold temperatures we had been having to the high school basketball game the Friday night before.

I finally let out a frustrated sigh. I didn't mean to. It wasn't all that loud and I thought I had managed to keep it to myself. But, apparently, it was loud enough to be heard by the daughter. She looked around and glared at me as if I was being some kind of impatient nincompoop. You know what? I was. Not only had I blown it by letting my offended ego take over my thoughts, but, worse, I let my ego express itself. I didn't do the very thing I'm urging here—offer patience and kindness as a charitable gift in any and all circumstances.

You might be thinking, "With all the 'real' problems we face in this world, why do you make an incident so trivial into such a big deal?" Correction: for one thing, I don't want to make this into a big deal. I'm showing you how the principles I discuss in this book work out in your daily life. You can take any one of my examples as a microcosm of what goes on in this world at the macro level. The world's bigger problems will never be solved until the little ego issues inside of each of us get resolved.

As soon as the daughter glared at me and I recognized my impatient behavior, I offered a prayer of blessing for the mother and her daughter and I asked God to replace my impatient thoughts with more pleasant, understanding ones. He did. Instantaneously.

If, as Emerson said, "The ancestor of every action is a thought," then the thoughts you think affect both the way you feel and behave. Replace negative thoughts with more positive ones and you'll not only feel better, but you'll behave better.

For all I knew, they were placing orders for family and friends gathered at the hospital next door and taking something good to eat—maybe even as a celebration. Since she was reading orders from the torn page of a magazine for new mothers, it might have been that her older daughter had just brought a newborn into this world. That would make her a grandmother and the daughter an aunt, and both perhaps for the very first time. That would explain her willingness to chitchat with a stranger. She was obviously happy. I was the one who was making myself miserable and unhappy. It wasn't their fault. It was faulty, egocentric thinking on my part.

None of the new and replaced thoughts may have been accurate, but the real question is, what does it matter? The answer is, it matters greatly, if a life of peace is what you really want. The recognition and replacement of my impatient thoughts with pleasant ones instantly made me feel more at peace within and more understanding of others around me. It brought me squarely into the present moment, which is the only place any of us can truly live freely.

When you're constantly thinking about something else you must do or some other place you must be, it is little wonder ego slips into your thinking with thoughts that engender feelings of offense when others aren't cooperating to help you get to some future moment. Instead of enjoying this moment as God's charitable gift to you, you make yourself anxious and full of stress, longing for something else. Finding the life you really want starts with little changes in everyday thinking and living.

The one thing I regret about all of this is that I owed them an apology, and I didn't give it. I watched them leave with their order without saying anything to them. I missed an opportunity to give an important gift—to myself, but more importantly, to the mother and her daughter. The gift of saying, "I'm sorry."

Learn to talk to those closest to you about the charity you have given to others. But don't forget also to share when you fail to give something good. It'll help you be more at peace inside, more successful the next time you're in a similar situation, and more comfortable talking about your charity to others.

• There's something else: If you want to be patient in all circumstances, then you must practice patience with yourself. If you want to be forgiving, then you must learn to forgive yourself. When you blow it like I did, for example, don't kick yourself. Your ego would enjoy that. It doesn't care where it finds life to survive, even if it finds it in your guilty feelings over blunders you make. It'll use self-incrimination as a means of jacking itself up if it has to. It doesn't matter to ego. It's out for survival by any method possible. Just acknowledge your failure and move on. Remember, when you first received God's forgiveness through Jesus Christ, his forgiveness was for all your past failures and future ones as well. But to know the power and freedom of that forgiveness, you must stay in the present moment. Therefore, in the mere acknowledgment and acceptance of your failures, you are not only staying in this moment but you are empowering yourself to prevail the next time you're standing in a long line. Though I no longer remember where, here's something I have never forgotten psychologist Wayne Dyer once saying. "Once you no longer need the lessons that unpleasant experiences give you, you will no longer have the unpleasant experiences." Now that's an interesting thought.

• Overcoming the cultural myth of silence about your charity starts with learning to share the details of your charity with those closest to you, including those times you fail to be charitable. But it also helps to share in small-group settings. I do this frequently when I conduct financial campaigns in the local church. For example, when a campaign leadership team at a church has gathered for a training session with me, I will have previously enlisted and coached respected laypeople in that church and had them share how they learned to give, why the present campaign is important to them, what they believe God is leading them to give, and how they arrived at that level of commitment. Critics usually refer to the "preferred" procedure of Jesus to keep one's charitable giving a secret. Or they argue that I'm interested in having only persons who are planning to give the "big" gifts share with others. I trust this chapter has exposed the former argument for the myth it is. The latter argument is only partially accurate. It's not that I want "big" givers to speak. Instead, I want those with a big heart to share—those whose love for God and his church have led them to make significant financial sacrifices. Though not always, those are persons who are usually making significant financial gifts. In those instances where they are not making the larger financial gifts, the level of personal sacrifice they reach to make whatever their gift may be far overshadows the amount, anyway. In my experience, when listeners know that a person's gift, whatever its size, is given out of personal sacrifice, they are most often deeply moved and inspired to examine themselves. The result is almost always transforming. Only those persons so thoroughly obsessed with their ego are offended by these shared stories. And it is usually because what those persons are planning to give, if anything, is far less than their capability. But ego has motivated them to hide behind indefensible myths about charitable secrecy or a phony humility that only people full of pride would publicly mention their gift. In reality, they are the ones full of pride and ego and prefer pretense over genuineness. When I meet these critics, I usually have the feeling someone just carried Ananias and Sapphira back into the room. Better to admit you're not giving than to pretend you are.

• Proof again that this book is God's gift to me arrived moments ago. That's correct. I was finishing this chapter when an e-mail arrived from a couple in a church near New York City where lately I have been doing some consulting. I had asked them a few days ago to consider sharing their story in an upcoming leadership meeting of how the two of them had learned to give. They consented, and I offered to help them edit their story for both brevity and clarity. Here's a slightly edited version of what I received from them:

> Hi, Steve. A little history first: Beth and I came from different back-grounds. Her parents went to church every week. They were givers. Generous, too. Though they didn't talk much about it to the children, Beth learned to be generous by observing her parents. They gave regularly not just to their church, but also to people in need. It wasn't uncommon for her parents to load up the back of their station wagon with fresh vegetables from their garden and take them to a needy family. When giving to their church, her parents used the envelope system. [Some churches provide a year's supply of envelopes to members for their weekly or monthly contributions. It can provide valuable teaching moments as children learn generosity from their parents by example.]
>
> My parents, on the other hand, were not as disciplined in their churchgoing, much less their charity. Needless to say, my brother and I weren't faithful churchgoers. Never gave much either. When we did go, we might give a few dollars. We were among those you recently described as the "pocket-change givers" in church. That was us. We were among those persons who give, but give little and with little thought.
>
> But when I met Beth and we fell in love, I started going to church with her because I knew if I wanted to date her, I had to go where she was. And that was in church. Once we got married, I became a regular churchgoer. Again, it was one of those things I had to do if I wanted to see my wife, because with or without me, she was going to church. While we attended church regularly, this whole business of giving was a foreign concept to me. Beth and I would give a few dollars every week.

She always wanted to give more, but I insisted we keep it at the level of pocket change. After all, we had a mortgage to pay, college tuition to save for, and, of course, our own retirement to plan for.

Soon after we moved to New York, we joined a parish in our neighborhood. In some ways, it's hard to believe that that was fifteen years ago. For the first few years here, we came to church almost weekly, enjoyed it very much, but we were anything but generous in our giving. But one day, some friends at church invited us to a Bible study. We loved it. The friendships we made we'll carry for a lifetime. The things we've learned will go with us for an eternity. During the first few weeks of Bible study, it dawned on Beth and me that real living is found in giving. One evening when Beth and I returned home from the study, we made a commitment to each other and to God to make giving a greater priority in our lives. We started out at $50 a week and tried to increase it every six months depending on what we were bringing in.

Today, our giving is not a commitment or obligation or something we do because we feel guilty if we don't. We do it for the sheer joy it brings us. Our relationship to God is stronger when we give. Our lives are full of joy when we give. You are so right that the purpose of every life is to give. Last year, we finally got up to $175 per week. This year, we raised it to $200 per week. Have we missed this money? Not at all. Do we have enough for retirement? Not quite, but we're happy to report the mortgage has been paid off early and the kids have all graduated from college and we're debt-free. We get such joy out of giving and, like Father Jim, above-and-beyond the $200 per week we give to our church, we have some favorite charities we like to support such as Food for the Poor, Feed the Children, and some socially active organizations here locally.

Like most married couples, Beth and I don't have a perfect marriage, but when it comes to giving, that's one place I can honestly say we're always on the same page. We never argue or disagree when it comes to giving. We are blessed people and we're the happiest when we can be a blessing to others. This is our story. Hope it's OK to share. Thanks, Beth and Ben.

Hope it's okay to share? How could the public telling of a story like that be offensive to anyone? Oh, I can think of a few who would find it offensive.

11

Myth 7

"Test God through Your Giving"

Put me to the test.

—Malachi 3:10

You must not test the Lord your God . . . .

—Deuteronomy 6:16

What could you not accept, if you but knew that everything that happens, all events, past, present, and to come, are gently planned by One Whose only purpose is your good?

—from *A Course in Miracles* by
Helen Schucman and William Thetford

There are tests everywhere: standardized tests, IQ tests, personality and compatibility tests, job fitness tests, polygraph, medical, and nuclear weapons tests, breathalyzer, DNA, and stress tests.

We seem to test everything. There is even a "Death Clock" website where you can test fate: enter your birthday, your gender, your basic attitude—optimistic, pessimistic, or sadistic—and whether you're a smoker or nonsmoker, and the Death Clock will calculate how much longer you have to live, down to the second! If that were not weird enough, the seconds are counting downward. As I write this sentence, for example, the Death Clock says I have 1,368,492,355 seconds left to live.

If you're inclined to believe such nonsense and discover you have but a short time left, you might find some solace in the fact there are several links on this website to places that will help you hurriedly put your house in order before the bell tolls for you—by writing a will and obituary, picking the music and planning your funeral service, even choosing a casket that fits your budget.

I don't know about you, but when I run across websites like this one, I'm convinced that there are too many people with too much time on their hands and too much access to the Internet.

TESTING GOD
—WHY NOT?

Since we test everything, why not test God too? The Bible gives permission to test him, doesn't it? In Malachi 3:10, God says, "Put me to the test."

But much earlier in the Old Testament, Deuteronomy 6:16 says, "You must not test the Lord your God." Which is it?

I recently pointed out this apparent contradiction to a seminar group I was addressing, when a participant spoke up and said, "Well, you have to read the context of both passages to properly understand this. People should not test God except in one place—in their giving. That's what it says in Malachi 3."

I both agreed and disagreed with her. I agreed that context is essential to understanding Scripture. But I challenged her conclusion—that the prophet Malachi is giving permission to test God through giving. In fact, I suggested that her explanation of Malachi is based on a myth that, though widely held, stems from a misreading of Malachi. Furthermore, I suggested that the myth itself is exposed when the context of Exodus and Deuteronomy is rightly understood.

THE TEST AT MASSAH

"You must not test the Lord your God as you did when you complained at Massah" (Deut 6:16). This raises two interesting questions: "What happened at Massah?" and "What, if anything, does complaining against God have to do with testing God?"

Exodus 17:1-17 describes what happened at Massah:

> *At the Lord's command, the whole community of Israel left the wilderness of Sin [a place, not a state of disobedience] and moved from place to place. Eventually they camped at Rephidim, but there was no water there for the people to drink. So once more the people complained against Moses. "Give us water to drink!" they demanded.*
>
> *"Quiet!" Moses replied. "Why are you complaining against me? And why are you testing the Lord?" But tormented by thirst, they continued to argue with Moses. "Why did you bring us out of Egypt? Are you trying to kill us, our children, and our livestock with thirst?" Then Moses cried out to the Lord, "What should I do with these people? They are ready to stone me!"*
>
> *The Lord said to Moses, "Walk out in front of the people. Take your staff, the one you used when you struck the water of the Nile, and call some of the elders of Israel to join you. I will stand before you on the rock at Mount Sinai. Strike the rock, and water will come gushing out. Then the people will be able to drink." So Moses struck the rock as he was told, and water gushed out as the elders looked on.*
>
> *Moses named the place Massah (which means "test") and Meribah (which means "arguing") because the people of Israel argued with Moses and tested the Lord by saying, "Is the Lord here with us or not?"*

Under Moses' leadership, the people of Israel left Egypt. On their journey to the land of promise, they encountered one trial after another. One of these trials was a shortage of fresh water. They came to their leader with their concerns. But what was a natural concern devolved into nagging complaints. Like any good leader, Moses listened to their concerns but, unfortunately, took their complaints personally. In fact, he was offended by them.

As he had done at the Red Sea, God provided a solution. He instructed Moses to strike a rock and fresh water would be provided. He did, the need was met, and Moses named the place Massah, which is a transliteration of Hebrew word meaning to "test" or "to put on trial."

Without the editorial comment in Deuteronomy, it would be difficult to find anything negative in what transpired at Massah. The people needed water and were concerned when the supply ran dry. As humans are prone to do, they complained to their leader, especially when they remembered what life was like in Egypt. Though they had been slaves under harsh conditions, compared to the perils they faced traveling as nomads in the desert, slavery no longer seemed like such a bad option.

It's amazing how memory gets edited—how different the past will appear when the present becomes difficult. For example, I often hear people talk about the "good old days." When I do, I'm inclined to ask, "Exactly when did those good old days take place?" For most everyone reading this, life today is vastly superior and certainly easier than even a generation ago.

The story in Exodus reads much like the morning news. No editorial commentary, just the facts are reported as they happened. But when you turn to Deuteronomy, the incident at Massah is judged as inappropriate. What happened in between the incident as it's reported in Exodus and recorded in Deuteronomy? It must have been significant, because the writer of Deuteronomy minces no words. He insists that Israel must never again test God as they had done at Massah.

MASSAH, THE COVENANT, AND FORTY YEARS OF WANDERING

Between the episode at Massah and its reference in Deuteronomy, forty years had passed. A covenant had been established between God and Israel and sealed in the giving of the Ten Commandments. Furthermore, by the time Deuteronomy was written, the covenant had been in operation for a generation. These realities are the clues to understanding and interpreting the problem at Massah and the admonition in Deuteronomy.

When Israel first left Egypt, they were just learning how to believe—how to trust God for daily protection and provision. But doubt and even disbelief must have dominated much of their thinking in those early days and manifested themselves in their incessant complaints. Nevertheless, God patiently permitted their tests and tolerated their complaints. For an entire generation, they wandered in the wilderness—a needless wandering precipitated by their fearful refusal to cross the Jordan and take possession of the promised land. That portion of their sad history is recorded in Numbers 13 and 14.

Throughout their forty years of wandering, God generously provided protection and provision. This explains why the writer of Deuteronomy, after a generation of divine care, considered it ludicrous that they would continue to test God for reassurance as they had tested him at Massah. In fact, after all God had done, to continue to test him was tantamount to a slap across his benevolent face.

GIDEON AND THE FLEECE

When you're first learning to believe, God permits you to test him. This was true for Gideon, as recorded in verses 11-16 of Judges 6:

> *Then the angel of the Lord came and sat beneath the great tree at Ophrah, which belonged to Joash of the clan of Abiezer. Gideon son of Joash was threshing wheat at the bottom of a winepress to hide the grain from the Midianites. The angel of the Lord appeared to him and said, "Mighty hero, the Lord is with you!"*
>
> *"Sir," Gideon replied, "if the Lord is with us, why has all this happened to us? And where are all the miracles our ancestors told us about? Didn't they say, 'The Lord brought us up out of Egypt'? But now the Lord has abandoned us and handed us over to the Midianites."*
>
> *Then the Lord turned to him and said, "Go with the strength you have, and rescue Israel from the Midianites. I am sending you!"*
>
> *"But Lord," Gideon replied, "how can I rescue Israel? My clan is the weakest in the whole tribe of Manasseh, and I am the least in my entire family!"*

> *The Lord said to him, "I will be with you. And you will destroy the Midianites as if you were fighting against one man."*

Gideon was threshing wheat in a winepress. I'm neither a winemaker nor a farmer, but I know that threshing wheat in a winepress is not normal. So why was Gideon doing this?

He was afraid for his own safety and trying to hide his labors from the Midianites, the fierce enemies of Israel. God instructed Gideon to be Israel's deliverer, but Gideon had little confidence in himself and even less confidence in God. So he asked for confirmation through a sign. Gideon tested God in an effort to know whether God would indeed be with him and guarantee both his safety and Israel's success. God obliged him, as recounted in verses 36-40:

> *Then Gideon said to God, "If you are truly going to use me to rescue Israel as you promised, prove it to me in this way. I will put a wool fleece on the threshing floor tonight. If the fleece is wet with dew in the morning but the ground is dry, then I will know that you are going to help me rescue Israel as you promised." And that is just what happened. When Gideon got up early the next morning, he squeezed the fleece and wrung out a whole bowlful of water.*
>
> *Then Gideon said to God, "Please don't be angry with me, but let me make one more request. Let me use the fleece for one more test. This time let the fleece remain dry while the ground around it is wet with dew." So that night God did as Gideon asked. The fleece was dry in the morning, but the ground was covered with dew.*

God agreed to Gideon's test not once, but twice. Why would Gideon have to test God more than once and over the same issue and question? Wasn't the first sign enough to convince him of God's presence (that is, the fleece wet with dew while the ground around was dry)? Why the need for a second sign (the surrounding ground wet with dew and the fleece dry)?

That's the problem with tests and signs. Not only are they easily misinterpreted, but they are also an unreliable method for discerning

God's voice and his direction in life. Furthermore, the feeling of reassurance that a sign will give can be short-lived.

If you're facing an important decision—such as whether to accept the premise of this book and risk living a generous life, or just seeking divine guidance in knowing what to do or which direction to take in life—the most trusted method I know of discerning what to do is to trust the divine intuition you learn to recognize deep inside your soul.

How can you develop such a capacity?

The word intuition is made up of two words: "in" and "tuition." Tuition means "to watch over." When you add the prefix "in," the meaning changes to "watch within." If you will learn to sit silently and watch your inner world, without judgment and without struggle, you will begin to recognize God's voice in that stillness. There is a depth to your inner world as vast as the visible universe around you.

God always speaks softly within the soul. But he does speak, and the only way to develop the inner awareness of his voice is through silent mediation and daily prayer. This is one of the most important gifts you could ever give yourself—the gift of time to meditate, to pray, and to nurture this inner world with its remarkable capacity to give you knowledge, guidance, and wisdom.

Without this awareness, you'll go through your life uncertain and apprehensive. You'll be dogged by feelings of insecurity, especially at those times when you face big decisions like a career choice or a partner with whom to share your life. Mother Teresa said, "We need to find God, but he cannot be found in noise and restlessness. God is the friend of silence."

If you'll train yourself to listen for God's voice through the silence of solitude, you will move beyond the need for signs or tests to give you reassurance and self-confidence. In the pursuit of silence and stillness, you'll discover serenity is the garden of productivity. Your productivity in the outer world is directly related to how you develop your inner world. It is in this inner world that you'll learn both to recognize and respond to God's Spirit. Here, you will find joy in living and spontaneity in giving.

I've been practicing prayer and meditation regularly for nearly two years. It is the single most important part of my daily routine. At first, learning to silence my mind and enter a space of stillness seemed impossible. Few of my thoughts were connected, and my mind would randomly race in one direction and then another. I wondered if I would ever learn to be still and dwell in a universe of silence. In time and with practice, I slowly began to quiet my mind. Today, I can step into the endless corridors of the inner world almost anywhere, regardless of how noisy it might be around me. While at first, I may have spent ten to fifteen minutes in meditation and prayer, I now occasionally find that an hour or two has passed before I emerge from this wonderful place of peace and tranquility.

Shouldn't I busy myself with more productive matters? If you have not learned the secret of stillness, this may sound like a silly waste of time. Previously, though I always said I believed in prayer and meditation, I never really practiced it. In fact, I would have felt it a thorough misuse of time to enter silence and solitude for longer than a few minutes. Not anymore. I know the value of meditation, prayer, and, most importantly, silence. It is in this inner world that I feel God's presence and have learned to hear his voice. When I emerge from the place of stillness and into the noisy world of commerce and busyness, I now do so with calmness and peace, an incredibly profound sense of joy, and a capacity to face whatever the day may bring with confidence, even anticipation. I have inner strength, little stress, and vastly superior productivity. In fact, I get more done these days than ever before, without the accompanying pressure. Most significantly, I no longer need outward signs to give me inner guidance about what to do in any given situation. I am learning to know God and listen as he speaks in and through my inner world of quiet stillness.

God seldom shouts. He doesn't need to for those who are listening. In fact, in our religious culture, those who shout the loudest are usually those with the shallowest inner life.

Until what you say you believe has been confirmed through silence and reflection, your faith will be a borrowed one at best— something you pick up from others and to which the little ego will desperately cling to preserve in you an illusion of self. But your beliefs may be disconnected from reality, and a borrowed faith will do even less for you when it comes to the daily living of your life. What's worse, you'll go through life with little confidence in God or yourself. You'll need signs and visible reassurance before you can advance in the direction of your dreams.

The more you learn through silence to recognize the voice of God's Spirit, the less you'll need signs or tests to provide reassurance or direction. This is true of a test regarding giving as well. Giving to test whether the windows of heaven will open and the blessings of God will pour out upon you, as Malachi described it (Mal 3:10), will no longer be necessary. You'll know this to be true. Your life will be one of inner tranquility and outward generosity. While God permits tests and signs by those with an immature and undeveloped faith, your faith will no longer need such props to help you face life, believe what God says, live and give generously, or confidently pursue your dreams. When you get to this place, you'll know you are living the life you've always wanted.

The alternative to this is to live a life dominated by fear and uncertainty. Instead of knowing the joy of generous giving, for example, you'll busy yourself with how much you can save and keep for yourself. You won't recognize this as self-centeredness and greed. Nor will you recognize that the mad pursuit of all that stuff is really motivated by your ego and your fears. Both are its source, however. Like so many, you'll seek and find every reason why you cannot give yourself or your resources away. The life you really want will continue to elude you. You won't find the peace and happiness you deserve. Instead, you'll continue to struggle just to survive, you'll never feel you have enough, and insecurity will daily plague you. I've even seen folks become addicted to legal and illegal drugs as they try to cope with so much self-inflicted depression.

TESTING GOD THROUGH YOUR GIVING
—MALACHI 3

The explanation above is necessary to our interpretation of Malachi's words about testing God through giving. Malachi lived hundreds of years after the establishment of God's covenant with Israel. For Israel to pocket the charity, the tithes, and offerings that belonged to God was a clear sign to Malachi that they were dominated and driven by fears of deprivation, feelings of insecurity, and an undeveloped faith in God. They withheld their charitable contributions and found plenty of reasons why they could not and would not give.

So Malachi mocked them for their little faith. With words drenched in sarcasm, he suggested they return to former days when their faith was immature and needed divine signs and wonders for reassurance. Sure, he encouraged them to test God through their giving, but he was not proud to do so. When Malachi is read not as front-page news but as an inside editorial commentary, you can hear the shame in his words. As far as he was concerned, Israel should have been far more advanced in their faith at this point in their journey with God.

Jesus' Word on Testing God

With this as background, Jesus' word on testing God is clearer. Just before Jesus launched his public ministry, he spent forty days in the wilderness. Though for different reasons, his forty days in the wilderness were reminiscent of Israel's forty years of wilderness wanderings. In the wilderness, Jesus was tested.

Notice the turn in direction. Whereas the Old Testament emphasis is on Israel testing God, the New Testament emphasis is on tests that come to you and me. In other words, not only do people test God, but God permits us to be tested, too. People test God for confirmation and reassurance. God permits people to be tested to help them move beyond the need to test him. The fact that you're reading this book, for example, may be a test—to see whether you'll believe its premise that giving yourself away is the divine purpose of your life and to put that and other principles in the book into actual practice.

One of Jesus' tests was to leap from the highest point of the temple. The act of leaping would have been to test to see if God would indeed send his angels to exempt him from the law of gravity and protect him from harm.

What was the significance of this test?

Jesus may have been wrestling with doubts about his public ministry. His humanness was never more evident than here. Perhaps he had questions about whether God would indeed take care of him. In this vulnerable state of uncertainty, the devil seized the opportunity to magnify his doubts. Here's what happened and how Jesus responded (Matt 4:5-7):

> Then the devil took him to the holy city, Jerusalem, to the highest point of the temple, and said, "If you are the Son of God, jump off! For the Scriptures say, 'He will order his angels to protect you. And they will hold you up with their hands so you won't even hurt your foot on a stone.'"
> Jesus responded, "The Scriptures also say, 'You must not test the Lord your God.'"

Though tempted to do so, Jesus refused to test God in this way.

Why? Because he was the Son of God?

Well, yes. But so am I. And there have been many times in my life when I've felt uncertain and have sought reassurance by testing God. I don't think that's why Jesus refused to test God. I expect that Jesus' tests in the wilderness are recorded (and we wouldn't know about them unless he told his disciples about them) to demonstrate not only how common they are to the human experience but how close he came to succumbing to them. That's the Jesus to whom I can relate.

It's safe to assume Jesus knew of the prohibition against testing the Father in Deuteronomy. Jesus was mature enough in both his life and faith relationship to God that to test him for reassurance was not necessary.

Getting to a similar place in one's relationship to God should be the goal of every serious Christian. When you do, you're free of anxiety, fear, distrust, and disbelief. You are truly at peace.

Maybe you still need signs to give you confidence to advance toward your dreams. Perhaps you're still at that place where you need to test God and see whether what he says about giving is really true.

If so, then put God to the test in your giving. Accept where you are without judgment. This is a normal part of the spiritual maturation process for everyone.

But don't be content to stay at this juvenile level of spiritual development. You'll miss the life you really want if you do. Instead, decide to move toward that place where you no longer need to test God in order to believe God's words. Recognize that you are being tested, too. Life's tests are designed not to make life miserable but to help you move beyond a life of fear and distrust to a life filled with faith and discovery. Recognize, for example, that the day you picked up this book was not some random, disconnected event. Since you are divinely destined to make choices, the decision to read this book may be a test to help move you toward the life God desires you to live—a life of absolute self-abandonment and trust in him.

Real life waits for this point in your spiritual development. You may not be ready yet to move in this direction; you'll know, however, when it's right for you. Having read this book, you'll remember just what you need to remember when that time comes. Of this much you can be certain: that day will come. More and more, you'll learn to surrender to God. But you could accelerate the process if you decided today to spend time training yourself through silence and solitude to recognize his voice. As you do, you will begin to know, not just believe, but deeply and significantly know what Saint Paul wrote to the Romans long ago:

> *I am convinced that nothing can ever separate us from God's love. Neither death nor life, neither angels nor demons, neither our fears for today nor our worries about tomorrow—not even the powers of hell can separate us from God's love. No power in the sky above or in the earth below—indeed, nothing in all creation will ever be able to separate us from the love of God that is revealed in Christ Jesus our Lord. (Rom 8:38-39)*

It is one thing to say these words are true. It's something else entirely to know they are true. You might wish to believe, for example, when the Bible says the most blessed life is found in giving, that it really is. But when you're honest with yourself, you're just not sure. The thought of giving frightens you. The idea of giving generously borders on absurd to your logical mind. You're simply not convinced any of this is true.

If this describes you, then why not test this? You might do as Gideon did and lay out a "giving fleece" of your own. While the prophet ridiculed the children of Israel for their lack of faith in God after centuries of being in covenant with him, maybe you haven't been a follower for long. Or maybe you've recently felt the need to go deeper in your faith journey with God, but right now you feel insecure and uncertain. Then, read Malachi's words as permission to test God with your own giving. In short, test the premise of this book. See if it is true that your giving will open heaven's windows.

Test and see whether

- you begin to experience freedom from the tyranny of your own ego;
- your bondage to materialism gives way to contentment with simpler living and maybe even a preference for a simpler lifestyle;
- you feel happiness and inner peace like you've never known before;
- you're empowered to live daily after having spent time in quiet meditation, silence, and prayer; and
- you begin to experience the life you've really always wanted.

What have you got to lose? Ernest Hemingway once said, "Every man's life ends the same way. It's only the details of how he lived and how he died that distinguish one man from another." What will distinguish your life? Could your distinction be that you were one of the few who truly believed God? Walked with him? Trusted his words? Lived by them?

Just as I am discovering (and as some of the folks I've described in this book are discovering), you, too, will discover the truth. When it happens, your faith will be stronger. You'll no longer need tests or signs. Instead, you'll trust what God says for you. You will know God intimately and personally. Your faith will be more than a catalog of inherited beliefs. It will become a deep and satisfying knowing that rises like a mountain from the depths of your soul. You'll have peace, contentment, and joy others spend their lives looking to find in all the wrong places. You'll be one of those rare persons about whom Jesus spoke when he said, "the gateway to life is very narrow and . . . only a few ever find it" (Matt 7:14).

You will have found it. And when the journey comes to an end, you'll not wonder, as did Willy Loman in Arthur Miller's Death of a Salesman. Of his life, Willy despaired, "Maybe I did not live as I ought . . . ." You'll know that you lived right and that the life you lived mattered. You'll be able to say, "I believed . . . I gave . . . I got the life I've always wanted."

SUGGESTIONS FOR GIVING, THEN GETTING THE LIFE YOU'VE ALWAYS WANTED

• Learn the art of living in this moment. God will always give you what you need to face any test that life may bring to you, but that capacity is given by God in the present moment only, not in some future moment or past memory. Learning to live in the present moment is itself one of life's most important—and challenging—tests. So catch yourself when your mind is obsessed with memories about the way life used to be or cluttered with thoughts about the way you wish your life was. If you fail the test of learning to live in this present moment, you'll miss the life you really want. That's a fact.

This was a large part of Israel's problem during those years they wandered in the wilderness. On one hand, they were constantly looking back with rose-colored glasses at the way life used to be in Egypt.

On the other hand, they spent an inordinate amount of time thinking about some future land they hoped to possess. But even their thoughts of this promised land were distorted, which is why they refused to enter it when the day to do so finally arrived. They misperceived their enemies who inhabited the land of promise as giants and themselves as grasshoppers by comparison. This is precisely the point Daniel Gilbert makes in his most recent book, *Stumbling on Happiness*. The research he and his colleagues conducted confirmed that, while human beings can imagine the future, they rarely imagine it accurately. That was never truer than in the story of Israel spying on the land promised to them and deciding it was too risky to pursue. Their failure at that test is recorded in Numbers 13–14.

While everyone needs a healthy appreciation for the past and hopeful anticipation of the future, present-moment living should never be sacrificed by either. This moment is all God gives you, which is what makes complaining detrimental to your spiritual journey.

It was for Israel.

Complaining about anything starts you on a downward spiral. When you complain, you dismiss this moment in preference for some other moment. But when you dismiss this moment, you are dismissing God's gift to you. Furthermore, when you dismiss God's gift to you, there's a real sense in which you also dismiss God. You may not intend to do this, but if it is true that this moment is God's gift to you, then to dismiss the gift is to dismiss the Giver. Because the present moment is God's gift to you, if you complain, you only succeed in dismissing him from your consciousness.

Does complaining in any way change the unpleasant moment? Of course not! A complaint is nothing more than a rejection of the present moment—a mental escape mechanism that can put you at a disadvantage.

How? If complaining dismisses the gift of this moment and the Giver from your consciousness, that leaves you to face the moment alone. That's no big deal as long as all of your present moments are filled with pleasurable, ego-gratifying experiences. But who complains about that sort of stuff? Complaints arise when the present moment is accompanied by something unwanted or unpleasant. Do you want to face the unpleasant moments without the benefit of divine consciousness? I don't.

Ultimately, if you complain, you're more likely to miss what you're meant to learn through the encounter or experience that accompanies the present moment. Here's how: Each experience in each moment carries with it a test. That means everything and everyone who enters your present moment does so as a test. Don't let your mind make some kind of conspiracy out of this. Just allow this notion to guide how you think about each moment of your life God gives you. You'll be much more capable of dealing with whatever the moment may bring you. And you'll maintain a teachable attitude. You'll learn and then live. Not the typical way, which is to live and learn.

It could be a simple test, like whether you're going to remain alert and truly present to each moment. Have you ever been in conversation with your spouse, for example, and he or she stopped and asked, "Are you listening to me?" Why would your spouse have to ask the question if you were truly present in the conversation instead of being somewhere else in your mind? Successfully passing simple tests like this will help prepare you to face life's bigger and more complex tests.

With appreciation, receive this moment as God's gift to you;
With anticipation, live this moment as your gift to yourself; and,
With participation, give this moment as your gift to others.

• What about the person who comes to you complaining about something or someone else? Or even complaining about you? Can this be a test? Sure. The way to pass it is to separate the complainer from the complaint. That is, when people complain about something, whether accurate or inaccurate, recognize that the complaint is theirs, not yours. If you take the complaint personally, you become its new owner. It's now your complaint. You also fail the test.

Don't beat yourself up. Just become aware. As your awareness increases, your grades will improve. Moses failed, at least at first. He took Israel's complaints personally. Too personally, in fact. When he did, it set up an impossible situation of hostility between the people and him. Whenever that happens, relationships will quickly deteriorate. Communication will be interrupted, and conflict will become inevitable. Someone rightly said, "No one can upset you without your permission."

The next time someone comes to you with a "gift" you don't want, such as a complaint, pay attention to your inner world. Before responding to the complainer, train yourself to take pause and look within. You don't need to be in a hurry to respond to the complainer. In fact, your momentary silence will give him or her occasion to pause as well. Notice how you feel inside. Watch your ego as it scrambles about to erect defenses quickly. Your blood pressure may rise. You may feel your face flush with anger. By paying close attention to what is happening inside, you'll stay in control of your ego and be better able to handle the situation. Just pay attention to what's going on inside of you. In time, you'll gain control of both your reactions and your responses. You'll begin to notice your blood pressure stays the same. Your face no longer flushes. Give yourself the gift of practicing these principles, and I assure you the day will quickly come when you find yourself giving healthy, wholesome responses in return for the unwanted gifts of complaint that come your way.

Most arguments in a marital relationship occur, for example, because one spouse complains, the other takes it personally, and the battle lines get drawn. If you'll practice separating your spouse from his or her sometimes hurtful words, you'll stay in control and not add insult to injury. You'll be able to receive your spouse for the divine gift he or she really is. Everyone deserves to be divinely received, even if what they have to give is anything but divine.

• My father had a stroke several years ago that put him on life-support equipment for his final few days. Signs are like the equipment used in life support. The need for signs is the need for life support, or you might say "faith support." To ask for a sign is to seek support for an immature faith. If your faith needs either, that's fine. I believe God permits the request for signs. But what's sad to me is to meet a person who should be sufficiently advanced and spiritually mature enough to no longer need signs as props for his or her faith. It's like meeting an adult who's still sucking on a bottle. The day should come when laying a fleece before God in an effort to discern his will is no longer necessary. The life you really want depends on this growth in maturity. Otherwise, you'll never get to that place where you can genuinely say with Saint Paul, "We walk by faith, not by sight" (2 Cor 5:7 [KJV]).

Take this as an example: If you need to test the premise of this book, do so. If it isn't enough for you that Jesus said, "Give and you will receive" (Luke 6:38), then dare to believe Malachi and test God through your own giving. See if God will open the windows of heaven and bless your life beyond measure.

If you don't test and see, what's the alternative? You'll be just another person of weak faith who dismisses the message of this book and chooses instead to live like most everyone else—under the domination of ego with all of its self-centered pursuits. You'll likely surround yourself with a lot of stuff and maybe even a lot of like-minded people. But you'll still feel alone, at times even lost, and almost always frustrated and discontented because the life you know you're living is not the satisfying life you really want.

Clearly, the preferred way is Jesus' way—to live and give your life away. But our popular culture—even our religious culture—often suggests that life is found only through getting, achieving, and aspiring to something other than who you are. But if you've made it this far without putting the book aside, either you agree with its basic premise or you would like to agree. If so, I'm suggesting you test it and see. You'll know soon enough.

The display quote that opened this chapter is from A Course in Miracles. Here it is again: "What could you not accept, if you but knew that everything that happens, all events, past, present, and to come, are gently planned by One Whose only purpose is your good?" In light of this chapter, I would alter it slightly to read, "What sign would you need, if you but knew that everything that happens is planned by God whose purpose is your good?" The answer is obvious.

12

CONCLUSION
A BRIEF SKETCH OF THE LIFE
YOU'VE ALWAYS WANTED

Giving yourself away is the prelude to the life you've always wanted. I've chosen to close this book by drawing a sketch of the person who has made this discovery and is living this life. This is by no means a finished description. Think of it more as a Van Gogh sketch before any colors have been applied. To most, Van Gogh's art is known for its brilliant, dazzling colors. What many may not know is that most of his artistic masterpieces were first sketched with a pencil. If you've ever seen one, you'll know that the images he sketched, though easily discernable and with an engaging complexity all their own, clamored for color, for something more. The sketches were unfinished.

The person I describe in this book is a work in progress. I am a work in progress. Though I am living the life I've always wanted, painting my own life and destiny is as yet unfinished. Take the following sketch, add your own artistic strokes and colors, and make your life the beautiful masterpiece that it is.

For me, it's not so complicated. The purpose of my life, your life as well, is summed up in two things Jesus said. The first is that the meaning of the law (and, I might add, the meaning of life) is summed up in the words from the Old Testament to which Jesus referred, "And you must love the Lord your God with all of your heart, all of your soul, and all of your strength" (Deut 6:5). The person who's learning to give himself or herself away first to God, then to himself, and last but not least to others is truly enlightened. No need to complicate this simple but deeply profound truth.

The other thing Jesus said was, "The kingdom of God is near" (Matt 3:2). But what is the kingdom and just how near is it? For all the good it does, the church is not the kingdom. Nor is it a place in some distant galaxy that waits for a future time to appear on planet earth. The kingdom of God is within you. It's as close as your heartbeat, nearer than the air you breathe. God's kingdom is found in the stillness of your inner world. That's God's address. If you are one of those rare persons living the life you've always wanted, you are an enlightened person who has not only awakened to the divine presence within, but you pursue that presence with both passion and devotion. But your pursuit is not a human striving that leads you on a prolonged and arduous quest to a superior but illusory level of spiritual living. That's the stuff of ego. It's just the opposite of this, in fact. The pursuit is its own reward. In other words, once you commence the journey to pursue God's kingdom, you are there. Instantaneously. It isn't the journey that leads you to this destination. To the contrary, this destination is the journey.

1. The people who are living the life they've always wanted don't look much different than anyone else. They are not like those who go through daily life pretending they have no cares in the world. Instead, they care deeply. They are passionate people, aware and alert to the world around them. Though not always understood, they are understanding. Their lives are characterized by tranquility, peace, contentment, and an abiding joy that enables them sometimes to laugh, but always to smile at life, at themselves, and at the world. Few of these people leave the world around them, shave their heads, and join a monastery. Rather, they live ordinary lives. But the difference is that they are learning to live and experience their temporal appearance on earth in expansive and extraordinary ways. During

the decade of my travels across this country, I've met these people in every conceivable walk of life. Some are insurance salespeople and clerks in department stores. Others are cab drivers and waitresses. Some are small-business owners; others own large businesses. They are flight attendants and human resource persons. Some are in management. Some are executives in major corporations, and some are assistants to the executives. They are sometime professional ministers. And many are among the multitudes of laypeople who attend a panorama of worship houses across America. These people don't find their identity, significance, and purpose in the careers they've chosen. Instead, their careers are given significance through their greater purpose, which is to give and to serve. That much of life they've figured out. For them, that much is all that really matters. Their lives are devoted to loving God, themselves, and everyone whom God may bring across the path of daily life. This understanding brings meaning to them personally and to the careers they've chosen. Their careers may change during their short stay on planet earth—often more than once. To these enlightened souls, a career is merely a stage upon which a grander drama of living and giving is played out.

2. The people who are living the life they've always wanted are at peace. There's no internal war going on—no discontent or self-contempt. They love themselves. They love the world too. But mostly they love God. They're at peace with him and that makes them at peace with themselves. They've surrendered to what is and because of this they know little suffering, though some of them subsist in forms wracked by suffering. They don't view God as if he were some kind of unpredictable, autocratic despot whose anger might be unleashed at any moment on anyone who may screw up in life. These people are friends of God. They not only know him, but feel his utter acceptance and are keenly aware of his presence in the world. Fear of God is foreign to them, although they have a profound reverence for him and observe with awe his glorious face in all of creation and in all his creatures, from the lowest to the highest. To them, God's face is seen in a majestic mountain, a rolling hill, a freshwater stream. The waves that crash upon the shore, the flower that silently buds at

springtime. Even a blade of grass on a summer lawn and a snowflake that gently falls in winter wears the face of God for these people. They hear him in the lion's roar in the jungle. But they also hear God's voice in the songs of a cricket at dusk. For these people, God's face is the face of every human being. Labels don't exist for the awakened, enlightened people who live the life they've always wanted. These people feel a deep connection with the entire human family. Political, social, cultural, or racial separations do not exist for these people. Because of this, they are often misunderstood, labeled, sometimes even hated. Though sometimes viewed as an enemy, they themselves have no enemies. They pray for those who despise them and extend love to those who take advantage of them. They can do no other. Since love is what fills them, no matter what another may do, neither retaliation nor revenge is possible. Such words are just not in their vocabulary. Neither are such desires.

3. Those who are living the life they've always wanted view themselves as complete. They accept themselves. They're not striving to be something else or somewhere else. While they are always expanding and becoming, they do so without feelings of discontent or disgust for where they are or who they are. They are hardly perfect or flawless. Not by a long shot. They have many imperfections. At times, they fail too. But they never see themselves as failures or victims. Instead, they take full responsibility for everything in their lives and everything to do. When they do fail, they're the first to admit it. But they don't stress over the failure or its admission. Just as quickly as they accept successes, they accept their failures. Since both are part of the human experience, they don't go through life punishing themselves for screw-ups or rewarding themselves for successes. They are independent of the applause of others. They are unmoved by the criticisms of others. Having no time for either, they're busy living out their purpose and giving themselves away. They learn from their mistakes, for they know life's most valuable lessons have been learned through them. They are the first to say, "I'm sorry, I was wrong, forgive me" and quick to make restitution for their wrongs. They know that the capacity to forgive others is directly related to the capacity to

forgive themselves. Full of self-forgiveness, they have plenty to offer those who need some.

4. Nothing ever goes wrong in the world of these enlightened people who live the life everyone wants. How could anything go wrong in a world they view as perfect, flawless? They believe everything is as it should be and can therefore accept everything as it is. They live in the present moment as if it were a gift from that inner Eternal Friend. As such, they welcome everything the moment may bring as a precious gift. They carefully unwrap it and celebrate its content. Sometimes they just observe it for the teachable moment it becomes. Whatever happens, they don't fret, fight, or flee. They don't need to because they know they never face the moment alone. They don't worry about having enough. They celebrate everything they have and whatever they need shows up when they need it. They have a calm, inner assurance because they know their Eternal Friend has resources inexhaustible and will provide them at just the right time. Whether the moment bears a blessing, setback, or temporary road-block, to these awakened persons, life is a discovery waiting birth. That's why they're called awakened or enlightened persons. Their eyes are wide open to the present. They don't have much to do with the past. They guard their minds against journeys into some illusory future. They don't waste the moment wishing life were as it used to be. Nor do they spend the moment hoping life might be different than it is. For these, life is what it is. They don't know how to be vic-tims of life's circumstances. They only know how to be victors over life itself. Because of this, they view everything that happens as a divine opportunity to enter more deeply into life.

5. Those persons living the life they've always wanted do so detached from this world. What Jesus said about being "in" the world but not "of" the world, these people get. They've given up attachment to things. Apart from the opportunities to serve and to give that these successes may provide them, they could not care less about titles they earn, promotions and recognitions they receive, trophies they're awarded, or stuff they might accumulate. They could walk away

from any of it because, emotionally, they already have—the day ego died and the life they've always wanted began. Today, their joy is serving—both God and the human family. They may have material things, but material things don't have them. They are free of the little ego that grasps for significance through status symbols and material possessions. For these, service is significance enough. Giving is immeasurably gratifying to these special people.

6. The people who are living the life they've always wanted are joyful people—genuinely joyful. They no longer search for happiness as if it were a pot of gold at the end of an imaginary rainbow. They inhabit the happiness they once sought. They greet each new day with enthusiasm and anticipation. Their world is bright and filled with joy. The "half-lived" life never describes these people, for they cram a lifetime of living into each day. They may say little, but people are drawn to them nonetheless. It's as if people instinctively know these rare souls have figured life out. That stirs a longing in all who meet the enlightened to know what they know. They are thoroughly spiritual and detached from the material. Unconcerned by an earthly form that's growing old and passing away, their attention is on the spiritual that's eternal. Intimate with an eternal God, they know themselves to be eternal. Knowing this, they fear neither aging nor death. In fact, they meet death the way they greet life—with confidence, peace, even laughter. They know death is not the end. In fact, for these, death is an entrance into that eternal world—one with which they've grown familiar. Entering the world empty-handed, these people know they'll leave the same way. They live, therefore, to give their lives away—who they are and what they have. The irony? The life these give, they get.

Jesus said, "The gateway to life is very narrow . . . and only a few ever find it" (Matt 7:14). These people have found it. Will you?